Yum!
Yes, It's a Piece of Cake!
Food-related Idioms and Expressions
for English Learners

MAY PARE

SAO
THAI
BOOKS

Tujunga, CA

D1010037

First Edition November 2011

Editors:	Arthur Jean Cox
	Roger Nelson
	James R. Oliver
Proofreaders:	Amber Eberlein
	Melissa Milburn
	George Ohanian
Cover & Interior Design:	Theresa Chayasirisobhon

Publisher's Cataloging-in-Publication

Pare, May
Yum! yes, it's a piece of cake: food-related idioms and expressions for English learners/ May Pare
p. cm.
Includes bibliographical references and index.
LCCN 2010913069
ISBN-13: 9780977392810
ISBN10: 0977392813

1. English language – Idioms. 2 English language – Study and teaching – Foreign speakers. 3. Food.
I. Title.

PE1460.P37 2010

Printed in the United States of America

To my husband, Larry Pare

Contents

About This Book

I used to ponder the idea behind the cliché *as American as apple pie*. Why apple pie? And although I knew the story about Marie Antoinette and the famous quote attributed to her, "*If the people don't have bread, let them eat cake*," it took me a while before I clearly understood its underlying meaning when used in modern-day context.

I learned of the sayings *there are plenty of fish in the sea; there's a lid for every pot* and *why buy the cow when you can get the milk for free?* from a coworker while we were discussing marriage. I also picked up such expressions as *(it) hits the spot; one for the road; good to the last drop; (to be) coffeed out; with all the trimmings/(with all) the works* and a lot more from my work as a waitress.

My husband would say things like *egg on his/her face, a fish out of water* and *rub salt in the wound*.

And so on.

Then I found that many of my foreign-born friends never knew most of such phrases.

This is why I wrote this book, to help other English learners like myself get a better grasp of food-related expressions that abound in the English language.

Over 1000 terms in the book are arranged into thirteen topics, covering the main kinds of food groups as well as expressions related to eating, drinking and cooking. The fourteenth chapter deals with terms and sayings that don't fit under any of the previous headings.

Each chapter is divided into two parts.

Part one, the main part, lists the most commonly used terms and expressions related to the topic/food group under discussion. Since this book is geared towards English learners, examples are provided to illustrate how each term is used. When applicable, a small section called "especially for English learners" is included to deal with such problems as terminology or certain slang terms.

Part two, titled "Other Terms and Expressions of Interest," deals with a few different things: terms with special meanings; expressions that may be no longer common but interesting nevertheless; easily confused phrases; spellings and pronunciation preferences.

The idioms, expressions and food-related terms discussed are American English, unless otherwise noted.

The origins of certain expressions, usage notes and personal language observations are also included.

Generally, the chapter contents are arranged alphabetically. Readers looking for any particular term should consult the index at the back of the book.

Cross-references are indicated in small capital letters, for example, see COOK ONE'S GOOSE on page 175. Linguistic terms used in the book (such as a catch phrase or a metaphor) are explained in the following page.

Although writing this book was not exactly *a piece of cake* for me, I have tried to make reading it *a piece of cake* for you.

And I hope you will find it useful.

May Pare

Terms Used Here

Allude To make an indirect reference

Catch phrase A phrase or slogan that is often repeated; it is usually associated with a character on a TV program or movie, a commercial, an entertainer or a political figure

Cliché An overused and trite expression or idea

What is "overused" or "trite" is often a judgment call; many phrases that are regarded as clichés by some people are considered idioms by others.

Cockney rhyming slang A mode of speaking wherein a common word can be replaced by the whole or abbreviated form of a well-known phrase which rhymes with that word, for example, *bread and honey* for *money*, or *trouble and strife* for *wife*

Derogatory An expression that disparages (insults) someone or something

Euphemism Substitution of a milder or socially acceptable term for one considered offensively explicit

Expression A set pattern of words that native speakers conventionally use to convey a certain concept.

It is used loosely as a general term in this book to cover idioms, clichés, hyperboles, metaphors, sayings, etc.

Hyperbole Deliberate and obvious exaggeration for effect or emphasis

Idiom A phrase in a fixed order with a special meaning that might not be understood by looking at the meanings of the words that comprise it

Irony A remark or remarks meaning the opposite of what is apparently said

Literally Something that is true or occurs exactly according to the words used; the opposite is *figuratively*, where the words are used metaphorically or symbolically

Metaphor A figure of speech in which a phrase that ordinarily designates one thing is used to designate another, thus making an implicit comparison. If you know all the words that make up a metaphor, you have a good chance of getting the intended image.

Onomatopoeia Words that imitate the sounds associated with the objects or the actions they refer to: such as *soda pop* (the bursting of gaseous bubbles when the bottle is opened) or *sizzle* (the sound of meat being fried)

Rhetorical question A question to which you don't expect an answer; usually because the answer would not provide any information that you do not already have and the other person knows this

Sarcasm Mocking or ironical remarks intended to wound

Saying A short sentence that expresses a general truth or contains advice or wisdom. It sometimes tends to merge with *proverb*. A saying is often called a proverb if it is of unknown and ancient origin.

Simile Words that describe by comparison using "like" or "as"

1
· · · · ·
About Fruits and Nuts

Fruit is the most palatable of the basic food groups. It satisfies our desire for sweetness.

ESPECIALLY FOR ENGLISH LEARNERS

TERMINOLOGY

Fruit vs. Vegetable

Generally, people categorize <u>vegetables</u> as foods that are eaten as part of a meal's main course and <u>fruits</u> as foods that are eaten for dessert or as a snack.

<u>Notable exception</u>: A favorite dessert for many Americans is *carrot cake*. And the main course can be a *fruit salad*.

As far as cooking is concerned, some things which are technically fruits may be called vegetables because they are used in savory rather than sweet cooking.

Tomato is technically a fruit, but it is universally regarded as a vegetable (because it is not sweet).

Nuts and *pumpkins* will be included in this chapter as fruits.

In the U.S. one buys fruits and vegetables in the <u>produce section</u> of the supermarket.

<u>Produce</u> refers to farm products grown for the markets, especially fresh fruits and vegetables, considered as a group.

The British term is <u>fruits and veg</u> section – "veg" being slang for "vegetables." One can also, in Britain, buy produce at the <u>greengrocer's</u>.

FIGURATIVE USE

The word "fruit" is sometimes used figuratively:
- *There's nothing better than to be able to relish and enjoy the **fruit of one's labor**.*
  (the results of one's work)
- *My sister was thrilled when her idea began to **bear fruit**.*
  (began to produce results)
- *The extra hours he put in at the office turned out to be **fruitful** after all. He got promoted.* (producing results; yielding benefits)

Adjectives used to describe fruits can also be used figuratively:
- *the time is **ripe**; a **juicy** story; a **sweet** success; their relationship turned **sour**, etc.*

SLANG TO DESCRIBE PEOPLE OR THINGS

Apple polisher Someone who seeks favors with a superior

- *Apple-polishers aren't always favorably looked upon by other students.*

Background: To polish an apple originally meant to wash it for sale.

The apple has always been a symbol of knowledge. Since the second half of the 1800s, it has been the tradition for students (especially those in the rural communities) to give their teacher a home-grown apple, usually at the first day of school, as a sign of their gratitude, or with the hope of getting better grades.

Cherry The original slang refers to that part of a girl that is intact before she loses her virginity (crudely often referred to as **pop her cherry**).

Now it is sometimes used to describe something in pristine condition, premium or very cool.

- *That 1965 Mustang is so **cherry**.*

Fruit A derogatory term for a gay man, particularly an effeminate one

Background: According to *Online Etymology Dictionary*, it was first used in 1935, about the same time gay came to mean homosexual in American prisons. Conjecturally, it derives from the light, sweet colorful nature of fruit.

Usage notes:
1. The term is considered outdated by some people.
2. **Fruity** means not masculine; it can also means "daffy" or "goofy," that is, not quite right in the head. It is not as harsh as "crazy" or "insane" or "nut."

Fruit loop A crazy, whacky, goofy person

- *Nancy is a total **fruit loop**.*

Background: A brand of breakfast cereal produced by Kellogg's is called *Froot Loop*. They come in a variety of bright colors and a blend of artificial fruit flavors.

Usage note: Similar words: ***fruitcake; nutcake; looney tunes***

Goober A goofy or silly person

- *Don't act like such a **goober**.*

Background: A goober is a peanut. The term was originally used for a peanut farmer – the implication being that the person was poor and uneducated.

Usage note: The term is now very regional, used only in the American South.

Lemon Any unsatisfactory or undesirable thing, usually said of a defective product, especially a car

- *I wouldn't have paid cash for that car if I had known it would turn out to be a **lemon**.*

<u>Background</u>: The analogy is between the sourness of the lemon (it's the most sour of citrus fruits) and the sour deal one is getting. There is a **lemon law** in most states in the U.S. that forces dealers to repair, replace or refund unless defects are corrected within a certain period of time.

Nut A crazy person
- *That guy is a **nut**.* (Often used as an exaggeration and/or endearment)
- *California is sometimes referred to as the land of **fruits and nuts**.*

<u>Usage notes</u>:
1. Also, a **nut case**; a **nut job**
2. **Nut** can be used to signify a deep passion for or obsession with any thing, for example, a **car nut**; a **health nut**; an **exercise nut**.

See also (AS) NUTTY AS A FRUITCAKE on page 155.

Peanut A small, cute child; also used as a nickname to show affection
- *My little sister is such a **peanut**.*

<u>Of interest</u>: There is a popular comic strip *Peanuts* about a group of youngsters, through which the cartoonist Charles Schulz (1922-2000) poked fun at both juvenile and adult foibles. He originally wanted to name it *Li'l Folks*, but had to change because the title was too similar to another popular comic strip at the time.

Dried-up prune An older man or woman who is sour and bitter because the juices of life in him or her have dried up

Prune face Someone with a wrinkled face and especially with a nasty disposition

Wrinkled old prune An offensive term referring to a woman past her sexual desirability

<u>Background</u>: Prunes are dried plums, well-known for their laxative benefits. The slang epithets mentioned are based on the wrinkled aspect of prunes. This is ironic since prunes are very beneficial to the skin both in terms of preventing aging and general healthiness.

As a side note, the *California Prune Board* changed its name to the *California Dried Plum Board* because the word "prunes" carried a negative connotation about constipation.

See PLUM on page 20.

Pumpkin head Literally, someone with a large head
- *Off the top of my head, some of the well-known **pumpkin heads** in the U.S. are talk show host Rush Limbaugh and the actor George Wendt* (Norm on *Cheers*, a TV sitcom, 1982-1993).

<u>Background</u>: Pumpkins are round and large.

Also used as a term of endearment, to be discussed later

Top banana The boss; the leader
- *Only the **top banana** can make that kind of decision.*

Second banana A supporting person; an assistant
- *The roofer left his **second banana** behind to finish working on my roof.*

Background: Both **top banana** and **second banana** are show business terms, meaning the leading comedian and the supporting comedian respectively. Both have been around since the beginning of the 1900s and are still commonly used:
- *Ed McMahon was the best known, all-time **second banana** to the Tonight Show's **top banana**, Johnny Carson.*

To an American or a European there is something funny about a banana. Perhaps it's the shape. An idea that was frequently used in comic strips, silent movie comedies and in vaudeville and burlesque from the 1900s to the 1940s was that of someone (usually a very dignified man) stepping on a banana peel discarded on the sidewalk and falling – his legs shooting out from under him. An accomplished comedian might be able to do this on the stage without injuring himself. This might have something to do with the title "top banana," but there is no evidence for that. At any rate, two things are obvious: 1.) a banana has no dignity; and 2.), the term means "top banana of the bunch."

Tomato An attractive woman
- *That Kelly's one hot **tomato**.*

Background: This slang term originated in the 1930s. Tomatoes are red, plump, rounded, juicy – in a word, voluptuous – and easily bruised.

Usage note: Though the term is no longer current, most older generation Americans recognize it.

See also HOT TAMALE on page 71.

• •

FRUITS AS TERMS OF ENDEARMENT

Pumpkin seems to be one of the most popular fruit-related terms of endearment in the U.S, used to address children or adults or even pet animals. Its popularity may have come from the fairy tale of *Cinderella* or from a well-known nursery rhyme:

Peter, Peter, pumpkin eater
Had a wife and couldn't keep her
He put her in a pumpkin shell
And there he kept her very well

It could also come from the association of pumpkins and Halloween, a popular festival for children. Whatever it is, people often think that the sound of the word *pumpkin* is cute and cuddling.

Other variants are ***Punkin; Pumpkin face*** (a chubby face); ***Pumpkin head*** (referring to either the shape of the head or the color of the hair similar to that of a pumpkin).

Apple cheeks is probably reserved more for children (referring to the round chubby shape).

Peaches is another common term of endearment.

  - *Hi, **Peaches**! How was your day?*

As an admiring description of someone, it can be used in the singular: "She's a peach!" or "He's a peach!," but as an endearment, a mode of address, it is used in the plural. ("Peach" seems too abrupt.) There is a natural tendency with any noun or adjective used as an expression of affection, to add another syllable, usually a diminutive, so that "sweet" becomes "Sweetie" and "cute" becomes "Cutie." "Peach," however, seldom becomes "Peachy" or "Peachie"; it usually becomes "Peaches."

• •

FRUIT METAPHORS FOR HUMAN CHARACTERISTICS

PHYSICAL APPEARANCES

A woman's body shape can be referred to as a *banana*, *apple* or *pear* and sometimes *avocado*, depending on how her weight is distributed.

Banana-shaped people are tall and thin.

Apple-shaped folks have a large mid-section.

Pear-shaped individuals tend to have larger hips and thighs.

The **avocado-shaped** type is somewhere in between the apple and the pear. It has been said that Cleopatra was a *pear*, Venus De Milo *an apple* and Princess Diana *a banana*.

The body shape many cultures consider as ideal and most desirable doesn't go by a fruit name, however. It is instead called an **hourglass shape**. Women with an hourglass shape are often envied by their friends because hourglasses have well-proportioned upper and lower bodies with a distinctively narrow waist.

And of course there are numerous fruits used to describe a woman's breasts, such as *apples, cantaloupes, grapefruits, lemons* and *raisins* (small breasts), *melons* and *watermelons* (large breasts).

Peach fuzz The fine hair first growing in place of a beard on a teenage boy that is soft and fuzzy

  - *"I don't think I need to shave yet; it's just a little **peach fuzz**," said Tom.*

<u>Background</u>: The name comes from the fuzz (i.e., small, fine hairs) found on the skin of peaches before washing. The fuzz helps protect peaches from being eaten by insects and bugs.

Peaches and cream complexion/skin means bright and clear creamy-colored skin with rosy- colored cheeks, symbolizing good health. To put it another way, it's like what you would find on new-born babies or dolls. Most beauty products promise women this kind of complexion in their advertisements.

<u>Usage note</u>: Also used, ***peachy- glow; peachy-looking skin***

PERSONALITY

Peach

- *She's a **peach**.* (Someone very sweet, nice, wonderful; a sweetheart)
<u>Background</u>: Peaches are sweet – luscious to look at, touch and taste.

Crabapple

- *Don't be a **crabapple**.* (Don't be a crabby person.)
<u>Background</u>: Crabapples are tart and sour, used mainly to make jelly. There's a saying: ***Crabapples make good jelly too***.
The word ***crabby*** meaning, ill-tempered, comes from crabapple.

Clinging vine is an overly dependent person in a relationship.
- *She has been a **clinging vine** all her life. There is no way she can make a decision this big on her own.*
- *I consider myself a take-charge person who could never be anybody's **clinging vine**.*
<u>Background</u>: A vine is any climbing or trailing woody-stemmed plant of which Ivy (also a woman's name) is the best known. Ivy and other vines cling to trees and climb walls.
<u>Usage note</u>: The term is nearly always applied to a woman or a wife.

• •

COMMON EXPRESSIONS

APPLES

An apple a day keeps the doctor away. Eating apples, and fruits in general, will make you healthy.
- ***An apple a day keeps the doctor away** may sound old-fashioned nowadays, but it does have a good deal of common sense and wisdom in its saying.*
<u>Background</u>: It was originally part of a nursery rhyme to encourage children to eat healthy, i.e., to eat more fruits:
"An apple a day keeps the doctor away
Apple in the morning - Doctor's warning

Roast apple at night - starves the doctor outright
Eat an apple going to bed - knock the doctor on the head
Three each day, seven days a week – ruddy apple, ruddy cheeks"

An earlier popular rhyme (first cited in print in 1866) was *eat an apple on going to bed and you will keep the doctor from earning his bread.*

(See EARN ONE'S BREAD on page 61.)

Apples have long been used as symbols of health. They have actually been claimed to be beneficial to humans in many ways. From what I've read, their benefits include weight loss, bone protection, the relief of asthma, lower cholesterol, diabetes management, prevention of Alzheimer's disease, lung, colon and liver cancer. This may help convince skeptics to eat more than just one apple a day.

Usage notes:
1. Sometimes shortened to *an apple a day*
2. Some of the newer twists to the saying:
- *An apple a day keeps both the doctor and dentist away.*
- *An apple a day keeps the doctor away; an onion a day keeps everybody away.*

Apple of discord Something that provokes an argument; a cause of envy, contention or ill-feeling between people
- *When that opinion piece appeared in the Wall Street Journal, it became an apple of discord throughout the financial community in the country.*

Background: It alludes to the story in Greek mythology of a golden apple thrown into a wedding-feast assembly of the gods by the Goddess of Discord, Eris, bearing the inscription, *"For the fairest."* Hera (the wife of Zeus, King of the gods), Athene (the Goddess of Wisdom and War) and Aphrodite (the Goddess of Love) competed for it. Paris, Prince of Troy, was chosen to be the judge. He chose Aphrodite, who then helped him to seduce Helen, the most beautiful woman in the world, and the wife of Menelaus, King of Sparta. Paris carried Helen off to Troy, setting off the Trojan War. All this is told in Homer's *The Illiad*, perhaps the most famous work of poetry in human history.

Apple of one's eye The most beloved or treasured
- *He's the only grandson they have. To them, he's wonderful and can do no wrong; he's the apple of their eye.*

Background: The "apple" here refers to the pupil of the eye, which was once believed to be solid and shaped like an apple. Because injury to the pupil would cause blindness, the expression comes to mean "that which is held dearest."

The term appears a few times in the Bible, *"he kept him as the apple of his eye,"* referring to God's cherishing Israel (Deuteronomy 32:10); also in Proverbs (7:2); Lamentations (2:18) and Psalms (17:8).

Usage note: Notice that it is "eye," not "eyes."

Compare apples to oranges To compare two or more things that are quite different from each other

- *To compare your large truck and my compact car is like **comparing apples to oranges**.*

Usage notes:
1. The two fruits are sometimes used to characterize an odd couple:
   - *They're like **apples and oranges**.*
2. **Compare apples to apples** is to compare two or more things that are as similar as possible without being the same thing:
   - *They compared **apples to apples**, grouping cars of the same year, size and price range, and then tested-driving them.*
3. Also used, an ***apples-to-apples comparison***

Forbidden fruit Anything that is desired but that which is expressly forbidden; an indulgence; a pleasure that is illegal or is believed to be immoral

- *Quit thinking about her; she is already taken - a **forbidden fruit**.*
- *Russian youth saw the late Michael Jackson as a symbol of America's **forbidden fruit**.*
- *In the U.S., drinking alcohol is a **forbidden fruit** for teenagers.*
- *"While **forbidden fruit** is said to taste sweeter, it also spoils faster."* Abigail Van Buren (Dear Abby) (1918-   )

Background: It's a biblical term from the fruit (typically thought of as an apple) of the Tree of the Knowledge of good and evil, forbidden to Adam and Eve. Eve was tempted into eating it. And because both took a bite, they lost their innocence and were expelled from the Garden of Eden.

Usage notes:
1. Often used in the expression: ***Forbidden fruit is the sweetest.***
2. Other similar expressions:
   - ***Stolen water is sweet and bread eaten in secret is the best.*** (Also from the Bible, Genesis 3)
   - ***"Sacred cow makes the best hamburger."*** (Often attributed to Mark Twain)

Get a second bite at the apple To have a second chance at doing something

- *In most court cases, only one bite at the apple is the usual norm. However, the judge in this case allowed the plaintiff to rework the complaint and **get a second bite at the apple**.*

Usage notes:
1. It's the term often used in legal contexts.
2. Sometimes used with the implication that it's not something one deserves or expects
3. Also, ***get a second bite at the cherry***, a British term

In apple-pie order In perfect order

- *The maid came to clean the room and put everything back **in apple-pie order.***

Background: It was first recorded in 1780; the origin remains uncertain. Some believe it comes from the way cooks neatly arranged apple slices on a pie crust. Others say it does not have anything to do with the apples; it's simply an English corruption of a French phrase, *napples pliées en ordre* (meaning, "linen neatly folded").

Usage note: It signifies extreme neatness.

One bad apple spoils the barrel. One bad member can have a negative effect on the group.

- *A formal research has proved that there are toxic workers. Any one of these can drag the overall performance of the team down in a hurry. Yes, **one bad apple spoils the barrel**.*

Background: Once an apple (or any other fruit) has begun to rot, if you leave it in contact with other apples, the rot will spread. Human relationships function the same way. It is an old saying - a 14th century Latin proverb translated as "The rotten apple injures its neighbors."

Usage notes:

1. A modern version is: ***One rotten apple spoils the whole bunch***.
2. ***One bad apple does not spoil the whole bunch*** is the version sometimes used in certain contexts, especially in regards to police corruption or unethical lawyers. When a person is accused of doing something wrong, he or she is looked upon by other members of the group as a bad apple. The implication is that the bad apple has not affected the entire group.
3. A ***bad apple*** is a bad individual among a good group.
   - *Most of his friends are good kids; John is the only one who seems like **a bad apple**.*
4. See also, BAD EGG on page 51.

Rotten to the core Bad or corrupt through and through

- *These politicians are **rotten to the core** with corporate bribes.*

Background: The core is the central part of an apple. "Rotten to the core" means rotten all the way through.

The apple doesn't fall far from the tree. The children are inclined to inherit the traits (good or bad) of the parents.

- *I looked at the father and then the son and thought to myself, **the apple doesn't fall far from the tree** - they have exactly the same kind of mannerisms.*

Usage notes:

1. Other expressions also used: ***Like father, like son*** (or ***like mother, like daughter***); ***a chip off the old block***

2. The saying can be used in a different way:
  - *The apple has fallen very far from the tree. The son is a poor reflection on his well-mannered parents.*

Upset the apple cart To upset things and cause chaos or disorder

  - *Things were running smoothly in the office until the new guy **upset the apple cart** by changing to a new software.*

Background: "Upset" usually means "overturn" or "upend." The usual implication is that someone has upset the apple cart deliberately. This could be easily done; for apple carts -when they existed – usually had only two wheels. When the cart was stationary, its "tongue" rested on the ground. Lifting the tongue would send the piled apples scattering.

Usage note: It can also be used in a different way:

  - *The country was at war and he felt he should **leave the apple cart the way it is**.*

See AS AMERICAN AS APPLE PIE on page 155.

• • • • •

BERRIES & CHERRIES

"It's the berries." (An old expression for something outstanding, like *the bee's knees*, which is also old - from the 1920s)

"You can't have two bites of a cherry." (An old saying meaning, it's impossible to get more out of something than it contains. Typically, one bite is all that it's going to take to eat a cherry.)

Cherry pick To pick and choose; pick the best from the range available

  - *The guy is an A-list actor; he can **cherry pick** the roles that he likes.*
  - *This news network **cherry picks** reports to promote its ideological agenda.*

Background: It alludes to the laborious and selective process of picking cherries. In certain varieties of cherries, the fruits ripen at different time. Therefore, it's necessary to choose between the ripe, red ones which are ready to eat and the green ones which definitely are not.

Usage notes:
1. In basketball, to cherry pick means to hover near one's own basket while plays are being made at the other end of the court waiting for a long pass on a change of possession, enabling the player to score easily before any defenders can reach him.
2. A **cherry picker** is the type of mobile hydraulic crane often used by a utility crew working on poles.

Give someone a raspberry To make a derisive sputtering noise by sticking out one's tongue through pursed lips and blowing out a sharp burst of air

  - *The audience never failed to **give the players raspberries** if they didn't play up to their standards.*

<u>Background</u>: It doesn't have anything to do with the fruit. Raspberry has been used figuratively to mean any sign or expression of displeasure or derision since the 1920s. It's just a silly way to show contempt, disapproval or to say you don't like something. It is often accompanied by various hand gestures such as patting the top of one's head, thumbing one's nose or sticking one's thumbs in one's ears.

One theory has it that it comes from Cockney rhyming slang *raspberry tart* (a pastry) for *fart* (for the sound produced).

<u>Usage notes</u>:

1. It is also known as (*to give someone*) a **Bronx cheer**, referring to the razzing reception that New Yorkers gave the visiting team at Yankee Stadium (in the Bronx).

2. Also, ***blow a raspberry***:
   - *Little Jimmie **blew a raspberry** when he saw liver on his dinner plate.*

3. There are variations for the spelling of this sound (as sometimes seen in comic strips): *thhpptpt!; thbbfpt!; pbbbbbt!; pbththth!*
   - *Oh, yeah!* ***pbbbbbt!***
   Essentially any extended string of p's, b's, t's and h's will successfully convey the idea.

4. There's a different kind of raspberry: you pucker your lips and press them against someone's skin, typically on the stomach or any soft spot like the arm or cheeks. Some parents like to do this to their babies or little children. The intention is to cause ticklish squirming.

   It is called a ***raspberry*** in some parts of the U.S. and a ***zerbert*** in others:
   - *She seemed depressed, but a good **zerbert** cheered her up right away.*
   The term *zerbert* is believed to have been made popular by Bill Cosby on his *Bill Cosby Show* in the 1980s.

Life is just a bowl of cherries. Life is good, really good; everything is well and nice.
- *John is an eternal optimist who thinks that **life is just a bowl of cherries**.*

<u>Background</u>: It is the title of a song from the 1930's.

<u>Usage notes</u>:

1. Another fruit that is associated with a good life is *peaches*. People had been saying **Life is a peach** long before someone started to compare life to a bowl of cherries.

   Also, ***peachy*** (good; splendid):
   - *"How are you?"*
     *"I'm just **peachy**."*
   And ***peachy-keen*** (a humorous way of saying *peachy*, meaning, dandy; swell):
   - *"And how are you doing these days?"*
     *"Why, **peachy-keen**, of course."*
   Peachy-keen can also be used sarcastically:
   - *The shot that Kobe missed - that was just **peachy-keen**!*

2. As a catch phrase, *life is just a bowl of cherries* is often used sarcastically:
    - *"My car broke down on the way to work; my boss yelled at me for being late. Then, I had to deal with some very difficult customers. Sure, **life is just a bowl of cherries**."*
3. Other synonyms are *life is just a bed of roses; life is like living on easy street*.
4. A contrasting viewpoint: *life is not a bowl of cherries; life is no bed of roses; life is not all peaches and cream*; LIFE IS NOT ALL BEER AND SKITTLES (Page 147); *life is the pits* and *I never promised you a rose-garden.*

• • • • •

NUTS

A tough/hard/nut to crack A difficult problem to deal with or a person who cannot easily be persuaded to do something
- *That country has remained **a tough nut to crack** for the U.S. for years.*
- *They may call me **a tough nut to crack** but that's the way I am.*

Background: It alludes to the old days when one had to crack nuts open by hand; some of them did not crack easily.

Usage note: When used with a person, it implies being stubborn or hard to influence or understand. It's not an insult, maybe more of a compliment.

See also (ONE) TOUGH COOKIE on page 158.

Be/go/nuts To be/become crazy; become wildly enthusiastic
- *You're **nuts** if you think I'd go out with you.*
- *The audience **went nuts** when the band started playing that song.*

Usage note: Also, to **be nuts about someone/something**
- *He's **nuts** about his girlfriend/ about opera.*

And, to **drive someone nuts**
- *This debate about health care reform is **driving** just about **everyone nuts**.*

In a nutshell Briefly; in a few words
- *"So, to make sure I understand it right. You will start enforcing all these rules as early as next week?"*
  *"That's it! **In a nutshell**."*
- *I could come up with many different explanations, but my answer, **in a nutshell**, is no.*

Background: Nuts are generally fairly small. A nutshell is small enough to be a symbol for anything brief. There are curious stories of attempts to copy substantial documents into nutshells. The famous Roman orator Cicero is said to have mentioned a parchment copy of Homer's *Iliad* (17,000 lines or over 500,000 letters according to various sources) so tiny that it could literally fit right into a nutshell. There is also a reference to the writing out of the entire Bible in this way in the late 16th century.

The use of a nutshell as a metaphor for something very small appears in Shakespeare's *Hamlet*: Act 2, scene 2: *"O God, I could be bounded in a nutshell and count myself a king of infinite space, were it not that I have bad dreams."*

Usage notes:
1. The phrase connotes the idea of being "short and concise"; often used to introduce a summary.
2. Used colloquially, similar to *in short* and *to make a long story short*
3. A more formal phrase is *in summary*.

No comment from the peanut gallery Phrase used dismissively to a person (or group of people) whose opinions, at least to the speaker, do not count for much

- *We're trying to discuss something very important here.* **No comment from the peanut gallery**, *please.*

Background: The term the *peanut gallery* originated in the 19th century. Literally, it was the balcony at the back of the theater, with the cheapest seats. These were occupied by the rowdiest patrons, who would shout insults or throw peanuts if they didn't like the play or the performers. Peanuts were the cheapest theater snack at the time, costing only pennies. It was popularized in the 1950s by the children TV show *Howdy Dowdy* in which the host, Buffalo Bob Smith, would call the child audience the peanut gallery, presumably to emphasize their smallness and cuteness (see the slang meaning of peanut discussed earlier) and not their propensity to throw things at him.

Usage notes:
1. A very common expression; sometimes used jokingly
2. Variant: **quiet in the peanut gallery**, used as an order
3. Often used when a person contributes his/her opinions on something you think he/she knows nothing about or answers questions you didn't ask him/her:
   - *Oh, great, another* **comment from the peanut gallery!**

Pull chestnuts out of the fire (for someone) To do someone else's dirty job; rescue someone from a difficulty

- *It's not our job to* **pull the chestnuts out of the fire for them**, *especially when they seem unwilling to do anything for themselves.*

Background: It alludes to the ancient fable in which a clever monkey, to avoid burning his own paws (actually a monkey has hands), persuaded a cat to pull hot chestnuts out of a fire for him. The monkey got his chestnuts, but the cat got burned.

Usage notes:
1. Often with the implication that one is being duped or manipulated into doing the job
2. Beyond the original meaning, the word "chestnuts" has degenerated in sports and other crude jargon to be a euphemism for a man's testicles.

Use a sledgehammer to crack a nut To do something with more force than is necessary to achieve the result you want
- *Assigning 10 police officers to deal with a family dispute call was clearly a case of **using a sledgehammer to crack a nut**.*
- *The ban is like **using a sledgehammer to crack a nut**. There must be better ways of solving the problem.*

Background: A sledgehammer is a large, heavy tool with a wood or fiber glass handle and a 16 to 18 pound metal head that is usually used for breaking concrete, or knocking down brick walls.

Most nuts are small; some you can crack open by hand; others simply by using a nutcracker. Using a sledgehammer to do the job is completely unnecessary.

Usage notes:
1. Used when one exaggerates or overdoes things
2. Also, ***crack a nut with a sledgehammer***
3. A similar expression is (to) ***use a shotgun to kill a butterfly***
4. This one is used sarcastically:
    - *Why use a sledgehammer to crack a nut when a steam roller will do an even better job and is fun to drive?*

Work for peanuts To work for very little money
- *Nobody wants to **work for peanuts**, but sometimes you have no choice.*
- *I don't mind **working for peanuts** if I can get some publicity in return for my book.*

Background: Elephants were once trained to work and to do tricks by rewarding them with peanuts. The contrast between the huge size of the elephants and the smallness of the reward strikes most people as grotesque and funny.

Usage notes:
1. Same meaning as CHICKENFEED (Page 87).
2. There is a saying: ***If you pay peanuts, you get monkeys***, meaning, employers who pay low wages cannot expect to recruit good workers.
3. You can also ***buy something for peanuts.***

• • • • •

OTHER FRUITS

Full of prunes Acting stupid; talking nonsense
- *Don't listen to him; he's **full of prunes**.*

Usage notes:
1. An American term; used colloquially
   Prunes are commonly supposed to have a laxative effect.
2. A similar expression: FULL OF BEANS (Page 33).
   Beans produce intestinal gas.
3. Other such expressions: *full of hot air; full of it; full of bull*

Go bananas To be wildly enthusiastic; to be irrational and wild, losing control
- *Susan **went bananas** when she got to meet the president.*
- *Tim **went bananas** when he found out everyone got a raise but him.*

Background: When monkeys are given bananas, they would eat them really fast with tremendous enthusiasm, as if they were losing control of themselves. When one goes "bananas", one behaves like a monkey and degenerates into a confused and gibbering wreck.

This slang expression is relatively new; it started to be used in the U.S. in the late 1960s, according to the *Oxford English Dictionary.*

Usage notes:
1. Also, *drive someone bananas*, meaning driving someone crazy
   - *Being around his mother too long can sometimes **drive him bananas**.*
2. Same meaning as **go nuts** and *drive someone nuts*

Heard through the grapevine Suggesting learning of something through informal and unofficial channels by means of rumor and gossip
- *I **heard through the grapevine** some of us will get laid off in the next few months.*

Background: Soon after the telegraph was invented in the U.S, the term "grapevine telegraph" was coined (sometime in the late 1840s or early 1850s) in reference to the tangled wires that resembled the wild vine.

During the American Civil War (1861-1865), vine-like telegraph wires were strung from tree to tree across battlefields. The messages that came over these lines were often so confusing or inaccurate that soon any rumor was said to come from the grapevine.

The term was immortalized in the Motown song *I Heard It through the Grapevine* by Gladys Knight and the Pips in1967; the most well-known version was sung by Marvin Gaye (1968).

Usage notes:
1. The implication is that the information was passed from person to person, perhaps in a confidential manner among friends or colleagues.
2. Also used: *heard through word of mouth*

If life hands you lemons, make lemonade. Turn something bad into something positive or productive; make the best of what you are given
- *It's no use moaning and groaning. **If life hands you lemons, make lemonade**.*

Background: Literally, you turn something sour into something sweet.

Lemon juice is the liquid you get directly out of the fruit, so it's very sour. Lemonade, on the other hand, is lemon juice mixed with water and sugar.

Usage notes:
1. It offers an optimistic viewpoint, expressing triumph over adversity.
2. Sometimes shortened to *If life hands you lemons...*
3. Similar to *play the cards you are dealt*
4. Variants: *turn lemons into lemonade*
    When life gives you scraps, make quilts.

Low-hanging fruit An easy target; a task or goal that is easily accomplished or an opportunity that is easily seized

- *Our company is so small with very few assets. The only way for us to succeed in a short term is to go after the **low-hanging fruit** first.*
- *People who like to be the first to buy things are the **low-hanging fruit** for our product.*
- *Instead of going for the **low-hanging fruit**, perhaps a better strategy would be to focus on those things that have the most impact.*

Background: It's a metaphor. Fruit which hangs low from the tree is easier to pick; you don't have to stretch or get a ladder.

Usage notes:
1. A typical business jargon, but also used in politics as well
2. Another term, *easy pickings* is pretty much the same concept as *low-hanging fruit.*

Offer an olive branch To offer a peaceful settlement to an existing conflict

- *I think the government should **offer an olive branch** to these protesters for the sake of ordinary citizens.*

Background: Olive trees mature slowly. In ancient Greece, where olive oil was used for soup, lamp fuel and cooking, if an invader destroyed the olive trees, the region was impoverished for up to 20 years. Only in times of peace could the trees produce their fruit; hence, the olive branch was used as a sign of peace or goodwill.

Some say the term is alluded to in the Bible, where the dove comes to Noah after the flood with an olive leaf in its mouth, "a symbol of God's reconciliation with men" (Genesis 8:11).

Plum A desirable or choice thing of its kind (as among positions, appointments, etc.)

- *That job is considered a real **plum** in the broadcasting business.*
- *To be appointed ambassador to this particular country is a political **plum** for him.*

Background: Unlike *prune* with its bad connotations (see under slang), *plum* has been used mainly to connote goodness.

A traditional English dessert is the plum cake, containing plums, nuts, currant and raisins. The plums are especially prized – as is perhaps hinted at by the familiar nursery rhyme:

Little Jack Horner sat in a corner, eating his Christmas Pie
He stuck in his thumb, and pulled out a plum
And said, "What a good boy am I!"

("Pie," instead of "cake," for the sake – one supposes – of the rhyme with "I.")

Also, in seventeenth-century England, the word *plum* was used to refer to the sum of 100,000 pounds (as referenced by Brewer in 1870), a "fortune."

Usage note: Often used as an adjective, meaning "desirable or ideal":
- *She landed a **plum** position with a law firm.*
- *It was such a **plum** role she couldn't turn it down.*

Sour grapes Referring to someone's attitude to belittle or devalue something that one really wants but can't get

> *"How did the job interview go?"*
> *"I didn't get it; the job probably sucks anyway."*
> *"Sounds like a case of **sour grapes**. Everybody knew you really wanted that job."*

Background: The term comes from Aesop's fable, *The Fox and the Grapes*. A hungry fox saw some grapes hanging on a vine above his head. After a few failed attempts to get them, he gave up and said, "*they probably are sour anyway.*"

Usage notes:
1. It has a connotation of resentment and bitterness.
2. There is a distinction to be made between being a **sore loser** and showing **sour grapes**. A **sore loser** shows a lack of class and sportsmanship whereas **sour grapes** is a sign of a lack of honesty with oneself and/or with others.

Turn into a pumpkin To depart; go to bed or otherwise turn in for the night; also used as a curfew

- *I'm about to **turn into a pumpkin**. You can stay up if you like.*
- *She'll **turn into a pumpkin** by 11.00 p.m. You'd better bring her home by then.*

Background: In the fairy tale *Cinderella*, the fairy godmother turns a pumpkin into a carriage to carry Cinderella to the ball, with one condition: Cinderella must leave the ball by midnight before her coach turns back into a pumpkin.

Usage note: Used humorously

• •

OTHER TERMS AND EXPRESSIONS OF INTEREST

Adam's apple A bulge in the throat, mostly seen in men

Background: It is so called from a superstitious notion that it was caused by a piece of the forbidden fruit (typically thought of as an apple) that had stuck in Adam's throat and could not be choked down.

Others say that it is a result of mistranslation from the Hebrew *tappauch ha adam,* which just means "male bump." This explanation is more likely; many such mistranslations from Greek, Latin and Hebrew can be found in modern English.

As sure as God made little green apples Certainly, without a doubt

See also SURE AS EGGS IS EGGS on page 57.

Banana republic Pejorative term (i.e., tending to belittle) first used to describe a small country, especially in Central America, that is politically unstable and has its own economy dominated by foreign interests. The term now applies to countries, states, cities and corporations that are usually dominated by a single strong individual and that are corrupt and poorly run.

- *Any American with proper qualifications can run for a public office, including the presidency, if he or she chooses to. This is the American Republic, not a **banana republic**.*

Background: The term, apparently coined by O. Henry (1862-1910), who wrote numerous comic and semi-comic stories about Central and South America, means that the country's only wealth consisted of bananas – a comically disparaging reference to the country.

Go pear-shaped (British) To turn disastrous; fall apart

- *I was supposed to have a nice dinner with my in-laws but I had a few drinks and it all **went** a bit **pear-shaped**.*

Background: A common explanation is that it seems to relate to training aircraft pilots. At some stage, they are encouraged to do aerobatic loops. It is notoriously difficult to get such maneuvers perfectly circular; often the trainee pilots' loops would appear lopsided and pear-shaped, and hence the connection to failure.

Usage note: According to www.septicscompanion.com, this British expression is usually meant in a rather jovial sense, in a similar way to the American expression *out of kilter* or *off kilter.* You would be less likely to see: "*Well, she went in for the operation but the transplant organ's been rejected and the doctor says it's all gone a bit pear-shaped.*"

Grapes of wrath A dangerous outburst resulting from a group's anger over a situation

Background: "Wrath" is strong, stern anger; vengeance and punishment as the consequence of anger.

The term comes from the New Testament book of Revelation: 14:19 "*And the angel... gathered the vine of the earth, and cast it into the great winepress of the wrath of God.*"

Julia Ward Howe used it in her famous Civil War song, *The Battle Hymn of the Republic* (1862): *"He is trampling out the vintage where the grapes of wrath are stored."*

John Steinbeck made the phrase the title of a novel in 1939 about the plight of dispossessed Oklahomans forced to leave their foreclosed farms for an uncertain future in California.

How do you like them apples? (Rhetorical question) How about that?; What do you think about that?

Background: This old expression has appeared in several movies; the latest was in *Good Will Hunting* (1997) when the character played by Matt Damon says, *"I got her number. How do you like them apples?"* Based on what I've read, the quote really fueled public interest about its exact meaning and origin.

The origin is uncertain. James Rogers (1985) suggests it probably came from a comparison of certain apples with others in a marketplace. Other sources say it originated in World War I with the toffee apples, a kind of trench mortar bomb soldiers used to destroy tanks. A soldier may have exclaimed victoriously, *"how do you like them apples"* after an "apple" took out an enemy.

Usage note: Used to gloat about something you have done, calling attention to your personal triumph

I'm your huckleberry. I'm the right person for the job.

Background: The term was popularized in the movie *Tombstone* (1993); Val Kilmer delivers the line as Doc Holliday to Wyatt Earp.

There's also a line in the song *Moon River* that says,... *"your huckleberry friend, waiting round the bend..."* In this case, the phrase awakens an echo of Huckleberry Finn, the lead character in Mark Twain's novel of the same name (1884), who floats down the Mississippi on a raft with his friend Jim, an escaped slave.

"Huckleberry" was commonly used in the 1800s in the U.S. to denote a small unit of measure, meaning a "tad." A person who was a huckleberry could be a small, unimportant person, usually expressed ironically in mock self-depreciation.

The second and more common usage of" huckleberry" was in the sense of being the exact kind of man needed for a part or purpose.

Old chestnut An old stale joke or often repeated story

- *"Oh no, Larry! Not that **old chestnut** again!"*

Background: The origin is not certain. One suggestion is that it comes from William Diamond's play, *The Broken Sword* (1816), in which one character keeps repeating the same stories. One of them is about a cork tree. He is interrupted each time by another character who says,

"A chestnut, you mean... I have heard you tell the joke twenty-seven times and I am sure it was a chestnut."

Perhaps the term comes from the idea that only a freshly roasted chestnut tastes good. A reheated one is as savorless as a repeated joke (www.idiomdictionary.com).

Play a gooseberry (British) To be an unwelcome, superfluous third person between two lovers

- *Not wanting to **play a gooseberry**, I decided to leave when my roommate's boyfriend showed up.*

Background: The term goes back to the early 19th century. Most sources ascribe it to the actions of some chaperone who had the tact to keep herself out of the way and occupied herself picking gooseberries so that young lovers might enjoy each other's private time.

Usage note: The term is unknown to the Americans, who usually use *a third wheel* (or *a fifth wheel*) to describe this kind of situation.

Raised on prunes and proverbs (Southern saying) Raised to be proper and prudish

Background: "Prunes" here probably comes from *prunes and prisms*, a phrase spoken aloud in order to form the lips into an attractive shape. Mentioned in Charles Dickens' *Little Dorrit* (1857), it was used to teach women an affectedly nice manner of speaking or behaving.

Speak/talk/with a plum in one's mouth (British) Phrase used to describe the way in which someone from the upper class in England speaks, characterized by posh and pompous language and accent. This is called a **plummy accent** or **plummy voice**.

Strawberry mark One of the most common birth marks, it looks like a flattened outline of a strawberry. It usually fades away when the child is about six years old.

The Big Apple Nickname for New York City

Background: The term was popularized by sports writer John Fritz Gerald who used it for his horse-racing column (called *Around the Big Apple*) for the *New York Morning Telegraph* in the 1920s. He first heard the term from stable hands in New Orleans, who referred to New York racetrack as "the Big Apple"- the goal of every trainer and jockey in the horse-racing world.

Jazz musicians in the 30's and 40's made it more popular by using it the same way, referring to the New York jazz scene as "the big time - the Big Apple." In the swing era of the late 30's, the Big Apple was a name of a popular dance.

In the early 1970s, the New York Convention and Visitors Bureau, in an attempt to promote tourism, adopted the Big Apple as a nickname for its city.

Yes, we have no bananas. A nonsense expression that became a popular catchphrase in the 1920s; sometimes still alluded to in pop culture to this day. The word "bananas" may also be replaced by some other fruit.

Background: It was the title of a novelty song by Frank Silver and Irvin Cohn from the 1922 Broadway *Make It Snappy*. The song tells of a Greek fruit-vendor man who can never say "no" to customers. So, even when he doesn't have bananas for people who are looking to buy them, he'd say, *"Yes, we have no bananas."*

2
. . . . . .
Eat Your Vegetables!

"I do not like broccoli. And I haven't liked it since I was a little kid and my mother made me eat it. And I'm President of the United States and I'm not going to eat any more broccoli."
George H. W. Bush, 41th U.S. President (1989-1993), born in 1924

Children notoriously hate vegetables. In American context, ***eat your vegetables***! is a favorite admonition of mothers everywhere at dinner tables. This is often preceded or followed by an obvious reason, *"they are good for you!"* or a reason that doesn't really make sense in the eyes of the little ones, *"there're kids in Africa who are going to bed hungry tonight!"* and even a threat *"or you will never grow!"*

Other favorite vegetable-related "momisms" (a term used for things moms like to say) include:

- *"Eat your carrots so you won't need to get glasses!"*
- *"Green beans will make you strong!"*
- *"All pro basketball players eat squash!"*

It's interesting to note that there are many animated cartoons, fairy tales, rhymes and tongue twisters, as well as popular culture characters that feature certain vegetables.

Bugs Bunny is known for his trademark carrot-munching.

Popeye has been touting the nutritional values of spinach since the 1930s. He gets super strong when he eats a can of spinach, even has a little song he sings along: *"I'm strong to the finish, 'cause I eat my spinach. I'm Popeye the Sailor Man!"* The cartoon became so popular that American mothers exhorted their children to eat spinach and become strong like Popeye.

There are many different versions of rhymes about the value of beans. This is just one of them:

"Beans, beans, the musical fruit!
The more you eat, the more you toot!"

One unique characteristic of beans is that they can grow really fast. And this is exploited in the fairy tale, *Jack and the Beanstalk* featuring magic beans that grow towering beanstalks overnight. The evil giant's castle is at the top of the beanstalks. Jack climbs up them and steals rich treasures from the giant, so he and his mother are no longer poor.

In the late 19th century, a series of tongue twisters were created to help students perfect their pronunciation in a fun way. One of the most popular tongue twisters with a vegetable theme (that people still enjoy reciting) is the following:

"Peter Piper picked a peck of pickled peppers.
Did Peter Piper pick a peck of pickled peppers?
If Peter Piper picked a peck of pickled peppers,
Where's the peck of pickled peppers Peter Piper picked?"

The early 1980s saw the craze for *Cabbage Patch Kids*, the soft-bodied, scrunched-up looking dolls, sold with a given name, birth certificate and adoption papers. The invention was based on the myth that new babies are found under cabbage leaves in a cabbage patch (a variation on the stories that babies are brought by a stork or the British version of them being found under the gooseberry bushes). In the U.S, *"We picked you out of a cabbage patch"* is a common answer parents give to small children when they ask how they came to exist.

The nursery rhyme *Peter, Peter, Pumpkin Eater* and the fairy tale of *Cinderella* and her carriage made out of a pumpkin are mentioned in Chapter 1. Aside from these, there are stories about *Jack Pumpkinhead* and *Jack-O-Lanterns* – a tradition associated with Halloween.

Potatoes figure in a number of children's games.

In *Potato Spoon Race*, each player balances a potato on a table spoon, then runs to a line and back without dropping it.

For *Potato Sack Race*, players race to the finish line while hopping inside burlap bags.

Hot Potato is an elimination game, very similar to musical chairs; players toss a potato (or a beanbag) as fast as possible while music plays, trying to avoid being the last one holding the potato when the music stops. (See figurative meaning of HOT POTATO later in this chapter.)

One potato, two potato is a counting-out method of choosing the player who will be "It" in many games, such as a hide-and-seek or tag. The players put out their hands, formed into fists (to resemble potatoes), and one of them touches each fist in turn, saying:

"One potato, two potato
Three potato, four
Five potato, six potato
Seven potato, more
You are it."

("It" is the person who is singled out to go first.)

The world's (particularly, the U.S.'s) favorite vegetable toy, *Mr. Potato Head*, has been around since 1952. It was originally an actual potato, but is now almost always a plastic model of a potato which can be decorated with a variety of attachable plastic parts such as ears and eyes to make a face. Over the years it has appeared on TV and in such movies as

Toy Story and its sequels. It also has become the spokesperson for the Cancer Society and "Get Out the Vote" group.

The above description is nothing new to English speakers, as it has been part of their lives growing up. For someone like me who grew up in a different culture and came to the U.S. as an adult, it was quite a learning experience. Case in point, I did not know anything about *Jack and the Beanstalk*, or what *one potato, two potato* meant and who *Mr. Potato Head* was until I started to work on this chapter.

• •

ESPECIALLY FOR ENGLISH LEARNERS

SLANG TERMS IN GENERAL

The Americans often shorten *vegetable(s)* to *veggie(s)*. Some people are against it, thinking that it's more like a baby talk. It seems to be in general use nowadays.

In British English, however, a *veggie* means a vegetarian (often spelled with one 'g'—"vegie"; also, "veggy")

A *vegetable* is slang for someone who is comatose.

To *veg (out)* is to take it easy, not do anything:
- *For most college students, winter break is a time for **vegging out** and relying on mom and dad to do the laundry.*

It comes from to *vegetate*.

The basic food for the Americans is MEAT AND POTATOES (see page 78) whereas for the British, it is called *meat and two veg* (no 's'); this same term, however, is also slang for the male genitals.

Rabbit food (or *rabbit's food*) is slang for leafy greens or salad vegetables (think Bugs Bunny eating carrots), used contemptuously by people who hate vegetables. For them, it's something that only HEALTH NUTS (see page 7) and VEGETARIANS (see page 78) eat.

Spud and *tater* are slang for potato.
   Spud derives from the spade-like tool used to dig potatoes.
   Tater is the term used often in the southern part of the U.S.

Bean has a few different slang meanings.
   1. A person's head (the round shape of many beans may be the source for this)
      To *bean someone* is to hit someone in the head, usually with a thrown object. The origin – a ball deliberately pitched at a batter's head, to intimidate him.
   2. The slightest amount, as in *don't know beans*, meaning, don't know anything useful:
      - *Don't trust him with your car; he **doesn't know beans** about fixing cars.*

3. Money, as in **don't have a bean**:
- *Most of my friends are unemployed and **don't have a bean** to spend.*

<u>Note</u>: I am told that lettuce and cabbage – especially lettuce – are often used as slang for paper money (because of the green color of American bills), but I personally have never heard anyone use "lettuce" or "cabbage" in that way. I suspect that this usage has gone out of fashion and is now only used by older persons.

SLANG TO DESCRIBE PEOPLE

Bean counter An accountant; a bookkeeper
- *The **bean counters** are coming in for an audit today.*

<u>Background</u>: The term came into the language in the 1970s. It's an allusion to an overly zealous or fastidious accountant so dedicated to details that he or she counts everything, down to the last small, insignificant bean. Or, it could refer to BEAN, slang for money (see above).

<u>Usage notes</u>:
1. "Bean counter" is almost always used in a disparaging sense – the implication being that accounting is an unglamorous, unimaginative and unheroic profession. But of course "bean counters" have to exist – we couldn't get along without them. For one thing, they correct our mistakes (which may cause some of the resentment against them).
2. Another term also used is *a numbers cruncher*.

Bean pole Someone who is strikingly tall and thin
- *The guy is practically a **bean pole** with chicken legs.*

<u>Background</u>: It refers to a planting practice - you put a pole in the ground and then put the bean stalk around it. Pole beans (as opposed to bush beans), as the name implies, are climbers. They work great in gardens with limited space because you can train them to grow vertically on poles, lattices or fences.

Cabbage head A thick-witted person; a mentally-challenged individual
- *When left on his own, the **cabbage head** started to get lost.*
- *As some people might say, two heads are better than one, even if one is a **cabbage head**.*

<u>Background</u>: The cabbage, a lowly vegetable, resembles a human head in size and shape. But of course it doesn't think.

Carrot top Someone with red hair
- *I'm talking about the **carrot top** over there.*

<u>Usage notes</u>:
1. Used for either sex
2. Also used, a *red head*
3. See also "I'D RATHER BE DEAD THAN RED IN THE HEAD." on page 128.

Comment: "Carrot top" might seem to be a misnomer, because the tops of carrots are green, not red. But, here, the top referred to is the human top, the head – the idea being that the hair resembles the edible part of the carrot, which is a reddish orange.

Cauliflower ear An ear that is thickened and deformed

Background: This condition is caused by repeated blows to the ear and is frequently found among boxers and sometimes among wrestlers. The blows have to be hard enough for scar tissue to form, causing the ear to resemble a cauliflower. One way to prevent cauliflower ear is to wear protective headgear when playing contact sports.

Couch potato Someone who is very inactive and spends most of his or her time on the couch watching TV

  - *With the boon of cable and home video, more people have become* **couch potatoes.**

Background: The term refers to someone lying on the couch as inert as a potato. But it has been suggested that it also refers to the eating of potato chips. The consumption of potato chips by persons lying or sitting on a couch while watching TV is a widespread habit.

The term was coined in the late 1970s with the credit given to both Tom Iacino and Robert Armstrong for a group of TV addicts appearing in the *Doo-Dah Parade* (a parody of the *Tournament of Roses Parade*) in Pasadena, California in 1979.

Couch potato has spawned another expression, **mouse potato** (a play on words between a computer mouse and a couch) coined in the 90's to describe someone who spends too much time on the computer.

Pea brain A dolt; a stupid person

  - *Only a* **pea brain** *like you would make such an assumption.*

Background: A pea is so small that anyone with a brain the size of a pea wouldn't have much intelligence.

Usage notes:
1. Sometimes people use it to refer to themselves in a joking way:
     - *I never used to have a* **pea brain***; I used to have a mind like a steel trap.*
2. Also used jokingly as a term of address:
     - *Listen up,* **Pea brain***!*

Comment: As a side note, I've read that an ostrich, which lives for up to 35 years and weighs about 300 pounds, has a brain the size of a pea but is more intelligent than some other animals with a much larger brain.

Potato head Someone who is not very bright. Often used affectionately

  - *Stop acting like a* **potato head***.*

Background: The phrase is derived from a child's novelty toy, *Mr. Potato Head,* mentioned earlier in the chapter. The very popular actor Tom Hanks has been referred to as *Mr. Potato Head*, because his features are lumpy rather than sharply defined, like those of a matinée idol. It has also been used in reference to the American comedian and actor Don Rickles.

VEGETABLES AS TERMS OF ENDEARMENT/TERMS OF ADDRESS

Certain vegetables are used as terms of endearment in different languages. French has *Mon (petit) chou* (my little cabbage) and *Mon (petit) pois* (my little pea), basically meaning, my darling; Russian has *mya morkovka* (my little carrot); Italian has *cipollina* (little onion) and Spanish has *mi cabasasita* (my little pumpkin or squash). English, on the other hand, seems to go for something sweet, such as confections or DESSERTS (see Chapter 10) or FRUITS (Chapter 1) when it comes to endearment terms.

The one vegetable that is sometimes used for this purpose is **Sweet pea**. Since sweet pea is also the name of a flower, when someone uses it as a term of endearment, is he or she referring to a vegetable or flower? I posed this question to an American friend and got the answer "probably neither;" people use it either simply because of the word *sweet* or they really think the person is sweet.

Sweet pea can also be used as a nickname for either gender. The adopted son of *Popeye* is named *Swee'Pea*.

Other not so common terms of endearment I've heard of are **sweet potato**, **(sweet) pickle**, **tater tot** (usually for small children or even animals).

Of course, with the right intonation, any word can be used to imply love and affection.

Spud is an affectionate term of address for a male friend.

"Spuds" (potatoes) are the most familiar of all foods, especially in rural households and among poor people – they are commonplace, homely, inexpensive and inelegant; and so "spud" is an appropriate nickname for a brother, a nephew or a "homeboy" (a member of one's own gang).

Old Bean is a British term of address, roughly equivalent to the American **Buddy**, **Pal** or **Dude**.

- "*Hello, **Old Bean**, how are you today?*"

This term, popular in the U.S. during the 1920s, may have come from the slang BEAN (see earlier) meaning "head" (and by extension, a person) according to word-detective.com.

COMMON EXPRESSIONS

(As) cool as a cucumber Calm and composed

- *He remained as **cool as a cucumber** when that thing exploded.*
- *Even when everything went wrong, she stayed as **cool as a cucumber**.*

Background: "Cool" here means calm (especially in difficult situations). Cucumbers are cool to the touch. That's why cucumber slices are used to cool down sore eyes. As food, they are usually served cold, at least in western dishes. It has been proved that the inner temperature of a cucumber can be up to 20 degrees cooler than the outside air.

No doubt the phrase has been used because of its alliterative appeal.

Usage notes:

1. Another expression with the same idea is ***cool, calm and collected***.
2. Also, to ***keep a cool head***.
3. Most people consider *as cool as a cucumber* a cliché.

Note to English Learners: Use it when the situation calls for it, but not all the time.

Carrot and stick Describing opposite methods of motivation, incentives and threats; reward and punishment

- *To make Iran stop enriching uranium, the U.S. should use both the **carrot and stick**. It needs to provide incentives such as improved trade and aid packages while at the same time, threaten war if Iran doesn't comply.*

Background: Carrots are not an exclusively human food; donkeys and horses love them too. This expression is based on the idea that there are two ways to get a donkey (or a horse) to move: entice it by dangling a carrot just in front of it while prodding or beating it with a stick from behind.

Jeremy Bentham (1748-1832), an English philosopher, came up with the carrot and the stick theory to apply to humans in the early years of Industrial Revolution around 1800s. He stated that all human actions were driven by efforts to enhance pleasure and reduce pain, and that reward or punishment induced the worker to execute his job.

As a side note, animals, as well as people, often respond better to kindness than to whipping.

Usage notes:

1. Also used as an adjective:
   - *One way to discipline our children is by using a **carrot-and-stick** approach.*
2. Also, ***carrot or stick; more stick, less carrot*** (or vice versa):
   - *We were facing a **stick-or-carrot** dilemma on how to deal with this civil unrest.*
   - *The lawmaker suggested **more stick and less carrot** to get the banking institutions to fix their problems.*

Corny Outdated or too obvious; trite, lacking new ideas; ridiculously sentimental
- *"Why is it not wise to tell secrets in a cornfield?"*
  "Because there are too many ears. Come on! That's a corny joke. Don't you have anything better than that?"
- *The overall movie was OK; it's the love scene that was a bit corny.*
- *I know it sounds corny, but it was love at first sight.*

Background: One theory is that it is a reference to the lack of sophistication of people in the country, where corn is grown. The earliest uses of *corny* were among jazz musicians in the late 1920s to mean old-fashioned or dated style of jazz of the earlier years, likening it to country music, such as bluegrass or square-dance music, something that is associated with country people.

Another theory that most sources seem to agree upon is that seed catalogs sent to farmers in the late 19th and early 20th centuries often contained short jokes, riddles and cartoons scattered throughout the product listings. As the jokes tended to be obvious and trite, they came to be known among farmers as "corn jokes," and, eventually, "corny."

Usage notes:
1. Often used with movies, music or shows, but especially with jokes (the ones that are too often repeated and therefore are not amusing or interesting)
2. Compare with CHEESY on page 49.

Drop someone/something like a hot potato To disassociate from someone or something instantly
- *A lot of sponsors dropped the golfer like a hot potato when the news of his extramarital affairs became known to the world.*
- *Realizing that it was a controversial issue that might alienate his political base, the candidate dropped it like a hot potato.*

Background: A potato that is cooked keeps a lot of heat.

Usage notes:
1. A *hot potato* is something no one wants to handle or be associated with:
   - *The city attorney was given all the hot potatoes that no one else would want to touch with a ten-foot pole.*
   - *Let's see how the new manager handles that hot potato.*

   A *hot button*, on the other hand, is something that creates strong emotions; often used as an adjective:
   - *Abortion has always been one of the hot-button issues in the U.S.*
2. Also, to *toss around like a hot potato*, alluding to a children's game mentioned earlier:
   - *The blame has been tossed around like a hot potato between the state and the federal agencies.*

Full of beans Full of energy
- *You seem to be **full of beans** today; maybe you should relax a little bit.*
- *The kids were so **full of beans** that I couldn't make them sit still.*

Background: The term was originally said of horses and their spirited state after a feeding of beans raised for fodder.

Usage notes:
1. Often used when talking about someone who is almost too joyful, fidgety, giddy, nervous, jumpy, hyperactive

   See also FULL OF PISS AND VINEGAR on page 124.

2. This same phrase can also be used to mean "uninformed, incorrect or exaggerating"

   - *Whoever told you about this was so **full of beans**.*

   See also FULL OF PRUNES on page 18.

Have the IQ of a turnip To have low intelligence
- *How could anyone fall for this scam? That person would have to **have the IQ of a turnip** – a small turnip.*

Background: The turnip, like the potato, the carrot, the beet and the radish, is a root vegetable. The turnip greens can also be eaten like spinach. Historically, turnip was seen as a lowly country vegetable, a poor man's food, providing starch and filler to many dishes. Linguistically, it seems to have gotten a bad rap beginning in the mid 19th century when it was humorously applied to a person, a mild way of calling him or her a knucklehead or an idiot. It is still used in that sense to this day.

Usage note: Most sources say it's British.

I didn't just fall off the turnip truck. I'm not stupid. You couldn't fool me.
- *I've been doing this for almost 40 years. **I didn't just fall off the turnip truck.***
- *We've proved to the world that our players are not new kids on the block. We **didn't just fall off the turnip truck.***

Background: It literally means, I'm not a country bumpkin (i.e., awkward, clumsy, a rustic) who just came from a farm and, on top of that, stupid enough to fall off the truck that I came on.

City people sometimes think that people who live on farms are unsophisticated and stupid.

In the old days, most people living in the country didn't own a vehicle. They had to hitch a ride with the letter-carrier or with whoever was going to town. In this case, it was the turnip truck bringing turnips (and other vegetables) from the farm to the market. One or more people would get a ride by sitting with the turnips in the back of the truck.

Sometimes such vegetables as cabbage or tomato are also used but turnip is often preferred because of the alliteration.

Johnny Carson (1925-2005) was credited for popularizing it as he used it so often on his *The Tonight Show with Johnny Carson* (1962-1992).

Usage notes:

1. A very common expression; said in response to an attempt to cheat or deceive the speaker
2. Variants:
   Do you think I just rode on the turnip truck?
   Do you think I was straight/fresh off the bus?
   I wasn't born yesterday.
   I just didn't come down with the rain, you know!
   I'm not a fool or a newcomer.
   I have more sense than that.
   Do I look like I just got off/was fresh off the boat?

   Sometimes, "fresh off the boat" is abbreviated to F.O.B. It refers to the influx of immigrants to the U.S. from Southeast Asia after the fall of Vietnam in 1974, the so-called *Boat People*. "F.O.B." also means "Free on Board" - referring to items or merchandise being shipped without charge. "F.O.B" in the sense of "fresh off the boat" is a play on words.

3. Also used to question someone (not a nice way to do it, however):
   - *Did you just fall off the turnip truck?*
   - *Did you just get here by boat?*
   - *Are you as dumb as you look?*

Of interest: Here are how other cultures express this same idea:

Irish: *I didn't just float up the Liffey on a lily.* (www. phrases.uk.com)

(*Liffey* is the river that flows through Dublin; *lily* is a shortened form of *lily pad*)

Scottish: *I didn't come down the Clyde in a banana boat.*

(*Clyde* is the river that flows through Glasgow.)

Spanish: *I'm already back from where you are going to.* (*Cuando tú vas yo ya vengo*)

In a pickle   In a difficult or embarrassing situation

- *He was certainly **in a pickle** when his front tire blew out.*

Background: Meat and vegetables can be preserved and flavored by soaking them in barrels of a salty or vinegary solution called pickle. This is a common culinary practice across cultures; just about any vegetable can be pickled including peppers (in the nursery rhyme mentioned earlier). German *sauerkraut* and Korean *kimchi* are well-known examples.

The term *in a pickle* is a translation of the Dutch expression, *de pekel zitten,* "to sit in the pickle" i.e., to sit in cold salt brine. Later, pickle was used to refer to something so treated, such as cucumbers.

Usage notes:
1. Also, (to be) *in a pretty pickle* – adding sarcasm to the situation
2. Other expressions with the same meaning are *in a fix*; *in a jam*; *up a stream without a paddle*
3. Compare with IN A STEW on page 181.
   In a stew means one is in a mental distress – sweating it out, upset and worried.
   In a pickle means that one has got oneself in a difficult situation.
   Of course, if one is *in a pickle,* one might also be *in a stew.*
4. *To be/feel pickled* means to be in a confused state, induced by excessive intoxication from drinking or drugs:
   - *What was I just saying? Sorry! I **was feeling** just a little **pickled.***

Like two peas in a pod Two persons or two things, so much alike that you can hardly tell them apart
   - *I have never seen siblings who look so much alike. They're **like two peas in a pod**.*

Background: In the pod, peas grow close together and you can't usually tell the difference between two peas.

Usage notes:
1. Variant: *as alike as two peas in a pod*
2. *You can hardly tell them apart* is a similar expression.

Of interest: The French would say, *They're like two fingers of the hand. (Ils sont comme les deux doigts de la main)*; in Spanish, it's *to be like the nail and the flesh (ser como una y carne).*

Not amount to/not worth/a hill of beans Amount to very little or nothing
   - *All these ideas **don't amount to a hill of beans** if they don't solve this problem.*
   - *These nice clothes are **not worth a hill of beans** when you work on a farm every day.*

Background: An Americanism, it refers to the planting practice. A handful of bean seeds were covered with a mound of soil making a small hill.

In the era when many households grew their own food, everyone had plenty of beans. Long rows in the garden included so many hills that no one bothered to count them. Therefore, a single hill of beans would be considered so worthless that its value couldn't be estimated.

The most famous use of the phrase comes from the movie *Casablanca* (1942) when Humphrey Bogart says to Ingrid Bergman towards the end of the movie, *"Ilsa, I'm no good at being noble, but it doesn't take much to see that the problems of three little people don't amount to a hill of beans in this crazy world."* ("Not worth a pile of poop" is what Bogart had in mind when using the expression.)

<u>Usage notes</u>:
1. Used to describe something as worthless
2. A newer version some people may use is ***not add up to a can of beans.*** (Real hills of beans are hard to find nowadays; city people are more familiar with canned beans.)

Red as a beet Very red

- *Stop teasing him; don't you see he's **red as a beet.***

<u>Background</u>: A beet is a round vegetable that has a very dark red color. It also goes by other names such as *red beet, table beet, garden beet.* The British generally call the vegetable *beetroot.*

Bortsch (also spelled *borsch*), favored by East Europeans and Russians, is a red soup with the color coming from beet. Beets are so intensely red that their juice can turn other foods on a plate to a red color.

(But not all beets are red. Sugar beets, used to make sugar, are white.)

<u>Usage notes</u>:
1. Often used to describe embarrassment or anger
2. Also used, ***beet red***
3. ***Hot as a hare, dry as a bone, red as a beet, mad as a hatter, blind as a bat*** is the mnemonic (i.e., assisting or intended to assist the memory) used in medical context to describe the side effects of atropine (a name of a plant, also known as belladonna) poisoning (or drug overdose in general), which is fever, dry mouth, delirium and blurred vision.
4. ***Beeturia*** is the passing of red or pink urine after eating beets. It affects 10-14 % of the population. (Wikipedia)

<u>Comment</u>: Beet is not the kind of vegetable that is common the world over. People of certain backgrounds may have difficulty understanding the concept of this expression because they don't know what beets look like. I was that way (even though I have lived in the U.S. for quite a long time) until I started thinking of the (canned) beets I liked to put in my salad.

Small potatoes A person or thing regarded as unimportant or insignificant

- *This political scandal will look like **small potatoes** compared to a long list of crimes being committed by some lawmakers.*

<u>Background</u>: When sorting potatoes for sale, the smallest ones are typically tossed aside as being not good enough to sell.

<u>Usage note</u>: Often used in comparison to something else; similar in meaning to the British SMALL BEER (See page 148).

Spill the beans To disclose a secret, usually by accident or imprudently, often ruining some surprise or other plan

- *It was supposed to be a surprise birthday party. Who **spilled the beans**?*
- *I might as well **spill the beans** now; you are going to find out about it soon anyway.*

Background: One folk etymology attributes it to the ancient Greek voting system of gathering beans in a jar (a white bean meant yes and a black bean meant no); occasionally, the jar was knocked over and the beans were spilled. However, this theory is not possible since the phrase first came into use in the early 20th century in the U.S.

"Spill" meaning "to let something out" dates to the 1500s. The beans in this idiom may just be filler, in such variants as ***spill your guts*** for telling secrets, or just ***spill*** for talking about confidential material. Beans are very common food and many people have spilled beans while cooking at some point in their lives. This somehow was transferred to cover the spilling of information that should have remained secret.

Usage notes:
1. Used often by the police in their interrogation of the suspects:
   - *OK, **spill the beans**!* (Confess and tell the truth!)
2. Another idiom with similar meaning is ***let the cat out of the bag***
3. There is a difference between ***spill the beans*** and RAT SOMEONE OUT (See page 45): *Spill the beans* means to tell about something; *rat someone out* means to tell about someone. ***Rat someone out*** usually implies a betrayal of a person; ***spill the beans*** does not imply betrayal; it just refers to the revealing of information.

You can't get blood from a turnip. You can't get something from someone, especially money, that he/she doesn't have.

- *They can't raise any more taxes. Nobody has the money. **You can't get blood from a turnip!***

Usage notes:
1. Also used, ***You can't squeeze blood out of a turnip.***
   You can't get blood from a stone.
2. You can also use it in a different way:
   - *We might be able to **squeeze blood out of a turnip** before we could get real answers from him.*
3. Used for impossible situations; for the merely difficult ones, ***it's like pulling teeth*** is used

• •

OTHER TERMS AND EXPRESSIONS OF INTEREST

Beans that talk behind your back (Southern expression) Beans that give you intestinal gas

Beanie A small, brimless skull cap, cut in gores (i.e., a triangular piece of material used to produce the desired shape) to make it fit the head, worn by boys in the U.S.

Background: The term must have evolved from the American slang BEAN for head (see earlier).

Beantown Nickname for Boston

Background: Boston baked beans is a classic American dish consisting of navy beans cooked slowly with molasses and salt pork.

Colonial Puritan women baked beans on Saturday to avoid cooking on the Sabbath and served them for Saturday dinner and as leftovers on Sunday breakfast and lunch. So ingrained is the association between Bostonians and beans that the city is called Beantown.

Can of corn (Baseball term) A fly ball that's very easy to catch

Background: The term is from the late 19th century. The standard theory traces it to the practice of old-fashioned grocery stores where canned goods were stored on high shelves and tipped down with a long pole. An experienced store clerk would have no trouble catching the tumbling cans with an open hand or apron, thus the term.

Usage note: Its extended meaning is "an easy accomplishment":

- *That test was a **can of corn**.*

Cool beans! Excellent! Wonderful!

Background: Slang among American teens in the 70's – 80's, it may have come from *cool*, another slang for "awesome, good." It's still in use, though not as popular as it once was.

Cornrow An African-American hairstyle originally from Africa that reemerged in the U.S. in the early 1970s. The hair is parted into numerous uniform rows (like a cornfield) and each section is tightly braided flat to the scalp.

Down to beans and chili Very poor; down to one's last penny

Eggcorn phenomenon Words or phrases used by mistake usually because they are homophones (words pronounced the same as other words but different in spelling and meaning), such as know and no; see and sea; bear and bare. It occurs in any language and is often committed by the native speakers themselves. Here are some examples:

The correct version	*The eggcorn version*
VEGETABLE-RELATED	
Acorn	Eggcorn
Asparagus	Sparrow grass
Beanstalk	Bean stock
Cole slaw	Cold slaw
Cornrow	Corn roll

OTHER FOOD-RELATED

Bed and breakfast	Bread and breakfast
Paprika	Pepperika
Skimmed milk	Skimp milk
Sour grapes	Sore grapes
Tartar sauce	Tarter sauce
Yolk	Yoke

Even a blind squirrel finds an acorn once in a while. Even the disadvantaged get lucky sometimes.

- *It's well-known that John is a lousy free-thrower, but he made one yesterday and helped his team win the game. **Even a blind squirrel finds an acorn once in a while**, I guess.*

Usage note: Variants:
- *Even a blind hog roots up a few acorns once in a while.*
- *Even a blind chicken finds a grain once in a while.*
- *Even a broken clock (watch) is correct twice a day.*

Fine words butter no parsnips. Flattering words or fine promises alone are useless.

Background: Parsnips are like carrots in texture, though not as sweet. They are good as a carrot substitute in clear soups.

Usage note: There are many other sayings along similar lines.
The following are taken from *Cassell's Dictionary of Proverbs*:
- *Fair words fill not the belly.*
- *Fair words will not make the pot boil.*
- *Fair words make me look to my purse.*

Also from the same source, a contrasting view is expressed in such sayings as:
- *Fair words shake wrath.*
- *Fair words cost nothing.*
- *Fair words hurt not the tongue.*
- *Fair words break no bones.*

Garden-variety Something that is ordinary, not special in any way

- *It's just a **garden-variety** fridge but it works fine.*
- *This is not a **garden-variety** insider-trading case. It is the largest one ever charged criminally.*

Background: It alludes to a common plant, rather than a specially bred hybrid.

Usage note: The British would say **common-or-garden.**

Know one's onions To be highly knowledgeable in a particular field

- *It's obvious he can't handle that assignment; he doesn't **know his onions**.*

Background: An American expression from the 1920s. Other similar ones from the same period are *know one's oats; know one's apples, know one's eggs*. (www.worldwidewords.org)

Usage note: No longer in common usage; a more common expression is *know one's stuff*.

"May you grow like an onion, with your head in the ground." A Yiddish saying, more like a curse, meaning "May you drop dead, head first!"

Rhubarb A heated dispute; a brawl

- *John got caught up in a rhubarb last night.*

Background: It was popularized in baseball by broadcaster Red Barber who used it in the late 1930s to 1940s to describe game-stopping melees. It was later applied to a similar fracas anywhere.

The allusion of the term is unclear. Some think it derives from the tangled appearance of stewed rhubarb. Another more likely theory is that in British theaters and stage plays, extras were instructed to mutter "rhubarb" over and over to simulate a restive and noisy crowd, and that "rhubarb" eventually came to be theatrical slang for "commotion."

Usage note: In the U.K. and Australia, *rhubarb* is slang for rubbish, used in response to a comment or a dubious statement.

Salad days The days of youth, where one is "green" (without experience) but fresh and hopeful; the connotation is a sense of crisp and fresh youth, with boundless optimism.

Background: Shakespeare coined it in *Anthony and Cleopatra* (Act 1, Scene 5).

Usage note: The term is sometimes quoted but not commonly used in everyday language.

The Corn Belt The major agricultural region of the mid western U.S. that produces much of the U.S. corn crop and soybeans

3
· · · · ·
Dairy and Eggpressions

"I don't care how many pails of milk I lose, as long as I don't lose the cow."
Proverb

ESPECIALLY FOR ENGLISH LEARNERS

TERMINOLOGY

Dairy (noun) is a place where milk and milk products (such as butter, cream and cheese) are processed or sold.
- *His family owns a **dairy**, so he's grown up working in a dairy his whole life.*
- *Our **dairy** has been producing simply the best milk for nearly a century.*
  Also used as an adjective:
- *I'm sure you can find some cottage cheese in the **dairy** section of the supermarket.*

Milk comes from such mammals as cows, goats and sheep.

Milk can be classified as whole milk (or regular milk); low-fat milk; non-fat milk (an old term is skim/skimmed milk).

Some people are lactose intolerant, meaning they have trouble digesting milk, or milk products.

In New Zealand, an independent convenience store is often referred to as a dairy; in Australia, a milk bar.

Eggs are from chickens, ducks and geese, among others.

Eggs have a different chemical composition from dairy; someone can eat eggs if he or she is allergic to dairy and vice versa.

The whole egg (or regular egg) consists of egg white and egg yolk.

People tend to be more health-conscious in recent years and often go for egg whites or Egg Beaters (egg substitute products) instead of regular eggs.

In English-speaking countries, eggs are usually eaten as part of breakfast and they can be cooked in many different ways. A typical question a server in the restaurant would ask customers is: *How do you want your eggs?* or *How would you like your eggs cooked?* The answer can be one of the following: sunny-side up; over-easy; over-medium; over-hard; over-well; poached (cooked in water); basted (a little bit of water and covered with a lid); soft-boiled; HARD-BOILED; SCRAMBLED. For the figurative uses of these last terms, see HARD-BOILED (p.53) and HAVE SCRAMBLED EGGS FOR BRAINS (p. 57).

Eggs can also be served omelet style (or, omelette, the French spelling).

An omelet is made from beaten eggs quickly cooked in a pan with oil or butter, usually folded around a filling such as cheese, vegetables and meat. See YOU CAN'T MAKE AN OMELET WITHOUT BREAKING EGGS on page 55.

Dairy and eggs are often linked together for several reasons. Both are animal products from farms. In the supermarket they are shelved next to each other since both need refrigeration. A lot of recipes also call for both dairy and eggs. Also, vegans (i.e., strict vegetarians) don't eat dairy products and eggs, out of concern for animal welfare.

The linkage of dairy and eggs can be seen in such expressions as:

Butter-and-egg man A wealthy, unsophisticated man who comes to the big city, spends money lavishly and becomes an easy prey of gold-diggers and unscrupulous people. The term is immortalized in a song sung by Louis Armstrong (1924):

"*Now she wants a **butter-and-egg man***
 From way out in the west
 She wants somebody, who's workin' all day
 So she's got money — when she wants to play"

George S. Kaufman also used it as the title of a Broadway comedy in 1925.

Butter-and-egg money Supplemental income for family; extra money stashed away for an emergency; personal spending money

 - ***Butter-and-egg money** is what you must have to fall back upon in case you should lose your job, so don't risk investing it; you might lose it all.*

Background: Before WWII, butter and eggs were produced by small farmers. The farmer's wife usually did the butter-churning and supervised the hens and the money received from selling them was considered hers.

Besides butter and eggs, farm women also sold garden produce, fruits and nuts from the wilds, homemade items of fancywork (like quilts and featured pillows) and baked goods.

Butter-and-eggs (*plants*) Plants with flowers in two shades of yellow, the pale one of butter and the deeper one of egg yolks

 - *While on our morning walk yesterday, we saw this small patch of **butter-and-egg** wild flowers growing among other plants.*

SLANG, EUPHEMISMS, ETC.

Big cheese (Slang) An important or influential person; the boss

 - *Who is the **big cheese** around here?*
 - *The **big cheese** said he would give us a raise next month.*

Background: The *cheese* here has nothing to do with the dairy product. It came from the Hindi *chiz* meaning *thing*. Anglo-Indians used *chiz* quite a bit in their speech and the word became quite popular in England in the 19th century (e.g., they would say *real chiz* instead of *real thing*). The English later replaced *chiz* with the more familiar *cheese*.

When the Americans got hold of the expression in the early 20th century, *real cheese* became *big cheese* – the Americans seem to have a habit of putting *big* before nouns to convey the idea of wealth and power, for example, **big gun, big shot, big wheel, big kahuna** (in Hawaii – a native medicine man or priest) and **bigwig** (during the 17th and 18th centuries, when everyone wore wigs, an aristocratic or wealthy person would wear a larger and more luxurious wig than a middle-class commoner; so a *bigwig* was someone of position and power).

Usage notes:
1. The term is not always complimentary; it can be said sardonically to describe a self-important person.
2. See also THE BIG ENCHILADA (Page 69); BIG FISH (Page 103).

Comment: I've read that it's the kind of word you wouldn't use if the person is around, but I think it depends on the context. I've heard people say, "*Well, you're the big cheese*" (meaning "You're the boss, the person in charge").

Butterball Slang for a chubby, fat person, used derogatorily or affectionately
- *She is obese, a fat balloon, a **butterball**. No doubt about that.*
- *Oh! My little chubby **butterball**!*
  (Comparable to the Spanish *Mi gordito/mi gordita*)

Background: The term can be taken literally as a lump of butter or as a plump turkey (*butterball* is a brand name of turkey sold in the U.S.). People who use this slang probably refer more to the latter.

Butterface (Slang) *She has a butterface* means everything is good "but her face."

Background: It doesn't have anything to do with edible butter.

Americans tend to pronounce *butter* with the *d* sound. When one says *but her face* really fast, it just sounds like *butterface*. This slang seems to be popular among younger generations.

Butterfingers A clumsy person, especially one who is prone to drop things
- *You, **butterfingers**! You dropped the ball again!*

Background: It refers to the slippery, greasy nature of butter.

Cheeseball Meaning tacky (not tasteful or fashionable)
- *This music video is a freaking **cheeseball**.*
- *What a **cheeseball** this guy is!*

Cheese eater Slang for an informant
- *That **cheese eater** told the police about all our plans.*

Background: In the past, the "cheese eaters" was the name the Catholics used for the Dutch Protestants in retaliation for being called FISH EATERS

(See page 116) by the Protestants. (The Dutch have long been associated with dairy. The Netherlands, despite its tiny size, has been and still is one of the world's leaders in cheese exports.)

Another term for the underworld slang *cheese eater* is **rat** (rats eat cheese), used as both a noun and verb. To **rat someone out** is to betray one's associate(s) and tell on them to authorities:

- *Judas was probably the ultimate **cheese eater**. According to the Bible, he **ratted** Jesus **out** on Wednesday and Jesus was crucified on Friday.*

Cheese-head A nickname, sometimes used disparagingly, for a person from Wisconsin; also the name of a foam hat shaped like a large wedge cheese, worn by fans of Green Bay Packers, which is a Wisconsin football team

Background: It alludes to the large volume of cheese production in that state. The term was originally used to refer to Dutch immigrants, many of whom settled in Wisconsin. It was considered to be a cruel racial insult.

In the sports context, *cheese-heads* were used in a derogatory sense by Illinois sports fans referring to opposing Wisconsin sports fans.

In 1987, Ralph Bruno hand-made the modern cheese-head symbol by cutting a triangle out of the upholstery of his mother's couch, burning holes in it and painting it yellow. He wore it as a hat to a Milwaukee Brewer's game. The cheerful response from the crowd gave him the idea of turning his silly hat-making into a money-making novelty business.

Since then, the Wisconsin fans have embraced the term ***cheese-head*** with great pride.

Cream (verb) (Slang) To triumph over someone quite decisively; to damage or destroy severely

- *We **creamed** our rivals on their home court.*
- *I've been **creamed**, but I've decided I'm going to take the high road.*

Background: It alludes to the idea that cream always gets whipped (or beaten).
Usage notes:
1. Often used in a game or other contest
2. Other synonyms are ***whip, beat.***

Cut the cheese A euphemism for flatulence, known colloquially as *farting* or *passing gas* or *breaking wind*

- *What's that smell? Who **cut the cheese**?*

Background: Presumably it comes from the strong odor released when one cuts a fresh slice from a piece of stinky cheese, such as Limburger.

Toe cheese also smells bad, but the term itself refers to the shreds and particles of dead skin, often sweaty, that are found between the toes.

Egghead (Slang) An intellectual

- *These **eggheads** may be experts in their field, but they lack common sense.*

<u>Background</u>: The term was first used in England merely to describe a bald person, but soon was extended to intellectuals, probably related to the idea that baldness is a supposed sign of high intelligence. Because heads with this characteristic resembled eggs, people with high forehead came to be called *eggheads.*

The term was popularized in the United States during the 1952 presidential campaign between Dwight D. Eisenhower and Adlai E. Stevenson. The Eisenhower camp used it to describe Stevenson who was an intellectual and also bald. Although great intelligence is normally considered a good thing, Stevenson's critics used it against him by claiming it meant he was out of touch with the common people. The irony of the situation was that Eisenhower was even more bald.

<u>Usage note</u>: Usually a term of mild derision as used by anti-intellectuals

Milk toast (Slang) One who cannot stand up for oneself; spineless; having no backbone

- *He may act tough but he's just a **milk toast** who wants people's attention.*
- *He did what he was told because he was **milk toast**.*

<u>Background</u>: Milk toast is a breakfast food – buttered toast, sometimes sprinkled with cinnamon or sugar, served in hot milk. It was once a popular COMFORT FOOD (See page 207) for kids and the ailing.

There is also **milksop**, a similar dish made with untoasted bread. It has been used figuratively to mean "a sissy, a weakling, a wimp" since Chaucer's time. (14th century)

In 1924, the cartoonist H.T. Webster created a one-panel comic, *The Timid Soul*, which was featured every day in newspapers until 1953. The hero was *Caspar Milquetoast*, who was hopelessly and even fantastically timid. The comic was popular because Webster treated Casper with affection.

<u>Usage notes</u>:
1. A pejorative term, used mostly for men
2. Also spelled, **milquetoast**

Say cheese! Smile
- *Ready? Everybody, **say cheese!***

<u>Background</u>: It is a photographer's traditional request of someone whose picture is about to be taken, the reason being that the way saying the word "cheese" makes one's mouth form a smile.

• •

COMMON EXPRESSIONS

MILK

It's no use crying over spilt milk. Don't fret over mistakes; what's done is done.

- *Come on! Stop thinking about it. **It's no use crying over spilt milk**.*

Usage note: Variants:
- *There's no point crying over spilt milk.*
- *You can't pick up spilt milk.*
- *Don't cry over spilt milk.*

Of interest: To express this same idea, the Japanese would say *fallen blossom doesn't return to the branch*. Also, *broken mirror cannot be made to shine*.

Milk (verb) To get milk from an animal; to take advantage or extract as much of what you want out of someone or something as possible
- *"If you don't **milk** every day, the cow will dry up."* Unknown
- *The old lady was **milked** out of her retirement savings by a con man.*
- *The news network is **milking** the exclusive rights for this interview for all it's worth, spreading out excerpts over five separate news programs during the two days.*

Usage notes:
1. As for human milk, one would say (*the mother*) **nurses her baby** or **breastfeeds her baby**.
2. **Milk the (time) clock** refers to needlessly staying on the clock after working a shift, to add extra hours to your paycheck. The phrase applies to people who are paid by the hour.
   - *Everybody knows that Susan likes to **milk the clock.***

Milk run A task or trip that is very easy to accomplish, or that is routine
- *Don't worry, these pilots are very experienced and have done this so many times before. This flight will be just a **milk run** for them.*

Background: The term probably comes from the route, with frequent stops, followed by a truck delivering bottles of milk to homes in the old days. During World War II, the term was also appropriately used by bomber pilots to describe a mission without difficulties or losses.

I've read that during the Vietnam war, *a cakewalk* or *a walk in the sun* were the common terms for such missions.

Why buy the cow when you can get the milk for free?/for nothing? Why pay for something that is free? Why make a long-term investment when the benefits are available without having to do it?
- *If you go live with him now, he'll just assume there is no hurry to get married.* **Why buy the cow when you can get the milk for free?**

Background: Owning a cow requires care, feeding and shelter. Why would anyone go to the trouble and expense of owning the cow, if one could get the milk without it?

Elvis Presley was known to have used this expression in the 1950s.

The saying is usually applied to sex, from a male perspective: why get into a committed relationship with a woman as long as she will keep having sex with you anyway?

It is a not-so-flattering analogy to a 'living together' arrangement, instead of marriage. The practice became popular in the late 70's in the U.S.

Usage notes:
1. Sometimes shortened to *Why buy the cow...*?
2. Also, *why buy a cow when milk is so cheap*?

• • • • •

BUTTER, CREAM AND CHEESE

"The bread never falls but on its buttered side." An old saying
(If something goes wrong, the outcome is likely to be as bad as possible.)
"After cheese comes nothing." An old saying
(Cheese was thought to make a fitting end to a meal; it was used as a kind of medicine to facilitate the digestion of other foods.)

As different as chalk and cheese/like chalk and cheese Two people or two things superficially alike are entirely different in their personalities or qualities.

- *The two women are both married into the Japanese royal family and both seem like traditional wives but they are actually **as different as chalk and cheese**.*
- *I never understand how they can stay married this long; they're **like chalk and cheese**.*
- *These two technologies are **like chalk and cheese**. But it's hard to say which one is superior.*

Background: On the surface, some white cheeses look similar to chalk (freshly-made chalk, not something made for the blackboard) but their taste, texture and value are very different.

Usage notes:
1. A very old British expression, comparable to the American *as different as night and day*
2. The opposite would be LIKE TWO PEAS IN A POD (See page 36).

Bread and butter The source of one's income; one's livelihood

- *Waiting on tables is my **bread and butter**; writing is my hobby.*

Background: Bread and butter are basic to one's diet and so working, even at a menial job, means one can afford them.

Usage notes:
1. Also used as an adjective:
    - *China's **bread-and-butter** exports include such things as clothes and household items.*
    - *She's your **bread-and-butter** client, so you'd better take good care of her.*
2. There's a saying, ***Don't argue with your bread and butter.***

See also, KNOW WHICH SIDE YOUR BREAD IS BUTTERED ON on page 50.

3. **Bread-and-butter letter** is a letter one writes to thank the hosts for their hospitality (and also for the food they provided) during one's stay at their house. It's an American term from the early 20th century. It is equivalent to our modern day "a **thank-you note**."

4. **Bread and butter!** is an exclamation used when two people walking together are momentarily separated by someone or something (such as a tree or a telephone pole) coming between them. After one says *bread and butter!*, the other is supposed to reply, *toast and jam!* or *cheese and crackers!* This is just a superstition. Some believe that if they don't say it, they'll have a fight later. The idea behind it is that *bread and butter* are inseparable after you put them together. And so are *toast and jam* and *cheese and crackers.*

Butter up To flatter someone lavishly with the intention of getting something

- *She sure knows how to **butter up** the boss without being too obvious.*

Background: The link between butter and flattery is easy to understand. Just as butter on bread and other food makes them taste better, honeyed words given to a person often help oil the process of persuasion and make things go smoother.

Usage notes:
1. Other synonyms are to **kiss-up to** and to **brown-nose** (crude language).
2. See also FINE WORDS BUTTER NO PARSNIPS (Page 40).

Butter wouldn't melt in his/her mouth Describing someone who appears to be so sweet and innocent but is capable of doing unpleasant things

- *She may look as if **butter wouldn't melt in her mouth** but she really is a cruel person.*

Background: This is a very old expression. It appeared in John Heywood's *Book of Proverbs* (1546).

Referring to hypocrisy, the term is applied to someone who is so excessively proper and demure that his or her demeanor arouses suspicion, meaning one is nowhere near as virtuous as one seems. A person who is disingenuous and playing innocent is considered cold and calculating, so cold that butter in his or her mouth could not melt.

Cheesy In poor taste; cheap, shoddy, shabby

- *The gift she gave me was really **cheesy**.*
- *I would never watch that show; it seemed so **cheesy**, sensationalistic.*

Background: It is probably an allusion to the unpleasant smell of over ripe cheese.

Usage notes:
1. Very common
2. Other synonyms are *lame; chintzy.*

Cream of the crop The best of anything
- *This group of students was the **cream of the crop** of their graduating class that year.*
- *These apples are the **cream of the crop** of this orchard.*

Background: The term is comparable to (and is often said to have derived from) the French **crème de la crème** directly translated to "cream of the cream." It means the best of the best.

Milk, if left to itself, undergoes a process in which the lighter fatty portions of the milk float to the top, due to their lesser density. They are then skimmed and packaged as a separate product called cream, which is richer than milk and therefore more expensive.

Some people think **cream of the crop** is an awkward expression (i.e., a mixed metaphor) because milk isn't exactly a crop.

There's no doubt that it was adopted for its alliterative appeal.

Usage notes:
1. The phrase is especially appropriate for groups that come in cycles — graduates and political candidates, for example.
2. Other similar expressions are **pick of the bunch** and **flower of the flock** (At first glance, **flower of the flock** would seem to make no sense, as a **flower** belongs to the plant world and **flock** to the animal world; but the *Oxford Encyclopedic Dictionary* defines flower as "the best or best part of whatever is being described.")
3. The French term, **crème de la crème** is also used in English, usually to mean the wealthiest or the most socially prominent people in society.
   - *There's a certain pecking order in Hollywood. The **crème de la crème** still get the major roles. Newcomers have to work harder to get to that level.*
4. A related expression is to **skim off the cream/cream off** meaning to take the best of something:
   - *This is a free market, so everyone is allowed to **skim off** whatever **cream** they can.*
   - *Not that many teams can afford to **cream off** all the young talents from across the world like we do.*
5. There is an old saying: **The cream always rises to the top** meaning that anyone who is exceptionally gifted will distinguish himself or herself from others and be acknowledged as such; excellence always becomes evident eventually:
   - *There's going to be adversity and obstacles. Believe in your talent. Continue to work hard. Eventually you will get noticed. **The cream always rises to the top.***

Know which side your bread is buttered on To know what's good for you, what's advantageous to you and what's not and act accordingly
- *"Be sure to be really nice to my mother when you see her tonight. She lets us stay here without charging any rent."*
  *"Don't worry. I **know which side my bread is buttered on**."*

Background: This is another very old expression mentioned in John Heywood's *Book of Proverbs*. Bread tastes better with butter than without. And usually, bread is buttered on one side, not two. Metaphorically, one would want to choose the side with the butter on.

Usage note: A related expression is **don't butter your bread on both sides** meaning don't be greedy. It comes from the idea that if you butter your bread both sides, you might drop it; and at least you will have greasy fingers.

• • • • •

EGGS

"When arguing with a stone, an egg is always wrong." African proverb

Bad egg Someone who is malicious, surly, aggressive or "difficult," but of course it could be used for just about any negative judgment one makes about a person.

Good egg A good-natured, trustworthy and thoroughly reliable person
 - *She turned out to be a **bad egg**. What a shame!*
 - *He looks like a **good egg**. I'll take a chance on him.*
 - *Be a **good egg** and go to the market for me, will you?*

Background: Literally, a good egg is one that is fit to eat. There is no way, however, that you can tell from the outside of an egg if it is good or bad; you have to crack it to find out. So, it's a natural metaphor to call someone who at first sight seemed OK but actually is not, *a **bad egg**.*

Usage notes:
1. The expression **last one in is a rotten egg** has nothing to do with an actual egg – it's just a children's call for everyone to join immediately and whole-heartedly into any activity (such as a game or a race) that is taking place:
   - *Come on! The **last one in** the pool is **a rotten egg**!*
   - *Little Jimmie is so competitive that his favorite phrase is **last one in is a rotten egg**. He'll even yell that trying to get to the lunch table first.*
2. To a child, being called a **rotten egg** is a great insult.

Don't put all your eggs in one basket. Don't risk all you have on just one thing; don't rely too much on one resource.
 - *A rule of thumb in investment is that you need to diversify. **Don't put all your eggs in one basket.***

Background: It alludes to the fragility of the eggs. If the eggs are in one basket and you drop the basket, all the eggs are likely to break.

Figuratively speaking, if something goes wrong in one area of your life, at least you can salvage the rest of your treasures or have other things to fall back on to.

<u>Of interest</u>: There's also a newer version: ***Put all your eggs in one basket, and then watch that basket.*** The quote is almost universally attributed to Mark Twain, but it was actually first used by Andrew Carnegie in his address to students at Curry Commercial College, Pittsburgh, PA, June 23, 1885. Twain's usage was later and he probably picked it up from Carnegie. (freakonomics.blogs.nytimes.com/2009/05/08)

Don't try to teach your grandmother how to suck eggs. Don't try to teach someone who has more experience than you or is an expert in that area.

- *You're just a newbie; he's a guru. I'm sure he knows how to program. Like my dad always used to say,* ***don't try to teach your grandmother how to suck eggs.***

<u>Background</u>: It seems like an odd phrase with an absurd image because few people now have direct experience with egg-sucking, though the meaning is quite clear.

The fact is you can make a hole in both ends of a raw egg and suck out the insides.

Some think that the term originated at a time when false teeth were less common than they are now and raw or soft-boiled eggs were a preferred form of nourishment for many old people. One could then see this egg-sucking as being something that grandmothers would know about already. However, when a child learned this, it was the kind of thing the child wanted to teach to someone else, especially Granny.

Others think it comes from the Easter egg dyeing tradition – you suck out (or blow) the insides of the egg with a straw and later decorate the egg.

In the U.S, Easter eggs (other than those made of chocolate or marshmallow) are mostly known and used in Easter egg hunts (such as the Easter egg hunt on the White House lawn every year), usually for the amusement of children. These eggs are not usually hollowed out; they have been left in their native stage or have been hard-boiled.

<u>Usage notes</u>:
1. This is an old expression, now not much used.
2. Variant: ***Don't teach your grandma/granny/ to suck eggs.***
3. It can sometimes be phrased differently, for example:
   - *I don't need someone to teach me how to suck eggs.*
   - *I know it might seem like I'm teaching you how to suck eggs, but it's important that you do it properly.*
4. See also NEVER OFFER TO TEACH A FISH HOW TO SWIM (Page 105).
5. ***Suck an egg!*** is another way of saying: "shut your mouth"; "stop bothering me!"; "go do something else (something stupid or menial)"
   - *Oh! Why don't you go* ***suck an egg!***"
   Also, ***go fry an egg!; go fly a kite!***

Egg on To urge someone on; dare someone to continue doing something, usually something unwise

- *Stop **egging** him **on**! He's got in enough trouble already without your encouragement.*
- *He didn't want to drink any more, but his friends **egged** him **on**. So he did until he got completely drunk.*

Background: It has nothing to do with a hen's egg. It comes from an old English word, "egge" meaning the sharp edge. So *egg on* has more of a sense of poking someone with a sharp stick.

Hard-boiled Streetwise, tough and unsentimental; type of fiction (or movies) which portrays crimes and violence in an unsentimental, matter-of-fact way

- *Drill sergeants are notorious for being **hard-boiled**.*
- *He is one of the most famous of the **hard-boiled** fiction writers of our time.*

Background: A hard-boiled egg is an egg that is boiled until the yolk is solid.

According to straightdope.com, the term was first used in American Army World War I training camps, with the meaning of "tough, and often violent." By 1920, the connection between hard-boiled eggs and no-nonsense personalities was cemented.

In 1924, there was a movie comedy about a would-be tough guy called *A Ten-Minute Egg*. P. G. Wodehouse was also fond of describing a particular forbidding character as a *twenty-minute egg*. Right around this time, *hard-boiled* started to become a literary term, referring to a genre of crime novels about rough, cynical men and women in a corrupt and violent world. The masters of hard-boiled detective fiction are Raymond Chandler (1888-1959); James Cain (1892-1977) and Dashiell Hammett (1894-1961).

Have egg on one's face/with egg on one's face To feel foolish or to be embarrassed at something one has done or the way one has done it

- *I still **have egg on my face** for making a scene in the restaurant and later finding out my boyfriend was with his niece and not another woman.*
- *He didn't have his facts straight before he went on TV with that story. So, he ended up **with egg on his face.***

Background: There are three theories about the origin of this phrase. It could be an allusion to audiences pelting performers they don't like with raw eggs. Or it might originally have been a reference to working farm dogs that steal eggs and eat them – the remains of the egg (the yolk and shell about their muzzles) of course giving them away. But most likely source is simply the common experience of someone eating an egg and then discovering, to his embarrassment, that he has left traces of the egg (usually the yolk) about his mouth and chin.

Usage notes:
1. Very common
2. No article is needed before *egg* when using the expression.

Kill the goose that lays the golden eggs   To destroy a source of future revenue out of impatience or greed for immediate wealth
- *The candidate, seeing the high-technology as one of the main engines of prosperity, wanted the Fed to keep hands off it as much as possible, so the government **doesn't kill the goose that's been laying the golden eggs.***

Background: The saying comes from Aesop's fable *The Goose that Laid the Golden Egg*: The farmer and his wife had a magic goose that could lay golden eggs, but only one per day. As they grew rich, they grew greedy, wanting to get all the golden eggs at once. So the farmer killed the goose and opened it only to find nothing. The moral: greed often overreaches itself.

Usage note: It has become a metaphor for any action that promises an immediate reward but proves (or will prove) disastrous.

See COOK ONE'S GOOSE on page 175.
WHAT IS SAUCE FOR THE GOOSE IS SAUCE FOR THE GANDER on page 126

Lay an egg   To fail miserably; make a humiliating error, especially in a public performance
- *We had great hopes for our new show. Unfortunately, it **laid an egg** – but we'll keep trying.*
- *His joke **laid an egg**.*
- *"If I have to **lay an egg** for my country, I'll do it."* Bob Hope (1903-2003)

Background: On the surface, this usage is somewhat puzzling. How did laying an egg become synonymous with making a mistake? A chicken would consider that a great accomplishment.
The meaning of this phrase, as it turns out, is based on the resemblance of an upright egg to a 0 (zero).

Usage notes:
1. **Goose egg**, in many sports, means a score of zero (0); in cricket, it's **duck's egg** (often shortened to **duck**).
2. Other terms to denote a score of zero are a **donut** in some sports:
   - *We won the game. We got 21 points; they got a big **donut**.*
   Or a BAGEL (See page 70); also 0 (zero) and **zip**
   - *We won 3 to **zip**.*

Nest egg   Savings set aside to be used in the future, either for retirement or for a 'rainy day'
- *Our **nest egg** is still small. Hopefully, it will get a lot bigger by the time we are ready to retire.*

Background: The allusion is to a real or artificial egg placed in a hen's nest to encourage it to lay (more) eggs in that same nest.

Walk on eggs/eggshells To act with the greatest of caution in a tricky or sensitive situation, especially to avoid hurting or provoking someone

- *I always felt like I was **walking on eggs** when I worked with her. She tended to get upset about every little thing without any good reason.*

Background: According to www.grammarphobia.com/blog, the original, 18th century version involved the whole egg, not just the shell "to tread on eggs". The eggshell version showed up more than a century later and is by far the more popular form today.

Of interest: Spanish, French, Italian and German express this idea the same way (i.e., using 'the egg' image) In Norwegian, on the other hand, it would be "walk in the salad."

What came first, the chicken or the egg? Phrase used as shorthand for situations where it's impossible to determine what actually came first or which of two events caused the other

- ***What came first, the chicken or the egg?** Was it the housing crisis or the economic meltdown?*

Usage notes:
1. Very common
2. Also, ***it's a chicken-and-egg situation*** (or ***question*** or ***thing***) meaning, it seems that each thing needs to be done first before the other thing can be done.

WHAT DO YOU WANT? EGG IN YOUR BEER? See on page 144.

You can't make an omelet without breaking (a few/some) eggs. Reaching a goal may require some sacrifice or unpleasantness.

- *Supporters of the war often justify the collateral damage - the killing of innocent people - by saying that **you can't make an omelet without breaking a few eggs**.*

Background: The saying is often attributed to Maximilian Robespierre (1758-1794), the architect of the Reign of Terror (1793-1794) who first said it in 1790, alluding to the excessive zeal of his followers in overthrowing the French monarchy.

Others ascribe it to Napoleon Bonaparte (1769-1821) who used it to justify the carnage he caused in attempting to build his empire.

It was also a justification used by Lenin regarding the killing of millions of Russian citizens during his push to produce a better communist state.

As one can see, the original use of the expression was to rationalize actions that were less than noble (i.e., to justify atrocities).

Usage notes:
1. It's a stock phrase used as a response to the claim that the end justifies the means.

2. Variants:
- *You've got to crack a few eggs to make an omelet.*
- *How do you make an omelet without breaking eggs?*

• •

OTHER TERMS AND EXPRESSIONS OF INTEREST

Butter my butt/buns/and call me a biscuit! (Southern expression of surprise) Isn't that something?

- *Well, **butter my butt and call me a biscuit!** Look who's here!*

Cheese it! Shut up! Stop what you' re doing! (especially something illegal or inappropriate); lay low!

Background: A warning among criminals since at least the early 19th century, it is now outdated, seen mostly in old comics as ***cheese it! the cops!***

Columbus' egg/egg of Columbus A genius idea or discovery that seems simple or easy after the fact

Background: It refers to a popular story of how Columbus, having been told that discovering the Americas was no great accomplishment, challenged his critics to balance an egg on its end. All tried and none succeeded. Columbus then took the egg, tapped it until the shell cracked a bit and flattened it. Now the egg could be placed on the table without falling over. In another version, the challenge took place while Columbus was seeking funding for the trips and was told it was impossible. Once he proved he could make an egg stand upright, he was granted funding.

Since then, ***Columbus' egg*** has become synonymous with an ingenious solution found outside the box of conventional thinking. It has also become a metaphor widely referenced in Portuguese and Spanish cultures.

Cottage-cheese thighs Slang for cellulite

Background: Cottage cheese is a soft white cheese with a distinctive lumpy texture; cellulite is the lumpy substance that is commonly found on the thighs, stomach and butt.

Curate's egg Something that is partly good and partly bad and therefore not wholly satisfactory

- *Like the **curate's egg**, the details of his speech were good in parts.*

Background: A curate is a British word for an ordained minister who is an assistant to a vicar or parish priest (www.worldwidewords.org).

In 1895, the British humor magazine *Punch* published a George du Maurier cartoon entitled *True Humility*. It depicts a curate dining at his bishop's house. The bishop remarks that his guest has been served a bad egg. The curate, desperate to remain polite and not offend his superior, replies, *"Oh, no. I assure you parts of it are excellent."*

The joke is that there's no such thing as partially rotten egg. The cartoon was actually poking fun at deference and the extremely repressed nature of British polite society at that time.

Usage note: This is a British term not commonly known to the Americans.

Good cheese on the ball (Sports term especially golf and baseball) Phrase used when one hits or pitches the ball hard. It implies a lot of power and speed.

Guns-and-butter policy The phrase is generally associated with President Lyndon B. Johnson (in office between 1963-1969) – his attempt to prosecute the war in Vietnam without sacrificing domestic programs.

Background: It originated as *guns before butter* and was used by two Nazi politicians in 1936.

Joseph Goebbel: *"We can do without butter, but despite all our love of peace, not without arms. One cannot shoot with butter, but with guns."*
Hermann Goring: *"Guns will make us powerful; butter will only make us fat."*

Guns before butter comes to mean the economic sacrifices that a nation at war must make. When the term was later used in the U.S., it was changed to **guns and butter**.

Ham and egg (Golf term) Playing well with a golf partner either because of complementary skills or offsetting luck, just like a good combination of ham and eggs breakfast

Have scrambled eggs for brains To be a scatterbrain; can't think straight, confused, all mixed up

Usage note: Also used, ***One's brain is turning into scrambled eggs.***
And, ***One's brain feels like scrambled eggs.***

Land of milk and honey Paradise; a place which has plenty

Background: It alludes to the enormous benefits and necessities of honey and milk to humans.

In the Old Testament, the Promised Land (now Israel) is described as "a land flowing with milk and honey" (Exodus 3:8).

Milk of human kindness Compassion

Background: It was coined by Shakespeare in *Macbeth*, Act I, Scene 5: Lady Macbeth complains that her husband is too full of the *milk of human kindness* to kill his rivals.

Raised on sour milk (Southern saying) Bad-tempered, always complaining

Sure as eggs is eggs Absolutely sure

Background: Some say it comes from *sure as x is x*.

That makes the cheese more binding. That's an interesting development.

The moon is made of green cheese. (Sarcasm) Used to illustrate silly nonsense and extreme gullibility, along the same line as WHEN PIGS FLY (page 93)

Background: It is an old saying dating back over 500 years ago, mentioned in John Heywood's *Book of Proverbs* (1546). Heywood was probably sarcastic when he said it.

Since the real composition of the moon should be a well-established bit of knowledge, anyone who would honestly believe it was made of green cheese would clearly be seen as ignorant or gullible.

Want some cheese to go with that whine? (Sarcasm) Used when someone is whining incessantly

Background: It's a wordplay on wine and cheese tasting but is meant in a derogatory manner.

4
......
Our Daily Bread (and Rice, and Others)

"Para el hambre no hay mal pan." Spanish saying
(Literally, for hunger, there is no bad bread. In other words, ***beggars can't be choosers****.*)

*"For every (rice) grain left in the bowl, children are told, there will be a
pockmark on the face of their future spouses."* Chinese saying

"Eating bread crusts will make your hair curly." Old English saying
(The leverage parents everywhere use to get kids to clean their plate and
eliminate wasted food.)

Most cultures have a starch that is staple food. The Asians eat a lot of rice
and noodles; the Mexicans and many Latin American peoples go for rice
and beans. The Europeans and most western cultures, on the other hand,
have bread.

How important is bread? According to the Bible, bread is ***the staff of life***,
meaning a very basic food that supports life. I've read that there are no
less than 400 references to bread, leavened and unleavened (as well as the
rituals involved in eating it) in the Old and New Testaments. Some of the
notable ones are:

Break bread To share a meal with someone, signifying a sense of sharing
and camaraderie; a way of signaling peace or making up

- *The Opposition Party leader will **break bread** with the president as part
of a reconciliation effort between the White House and his Party.*

Give us this day our daily bread. From the Lord's Prayer. Matthew 6:11.
The words "daily bread" mean daily food or one's livelihood.

Man does not live by bread alone. Deuteronomy 8:2-3. Physical nourishment
is not sufficient for a healthy life; man also has spiritual needs.

Cast your bread upon the waters (for you will find it after many days)
Ecclesiastes 11:1. This is a rather ambiguous saying. Some people think it
means you should do good without expecting any reward or even gratitude;
others interpret it as meaning you should do good deeds and you will
receive back blessings.

See also CRUMBS FROM THE RICH MAN'S TABLE and MANNA FROM HEAVEN
later in the chapter.

. . . .

ESPECIALLY FOR ENGLISH LEARNERS

TERMINOLOGY: The differences between the British and American terms

BRITISH	AMERICAN
biscuits (sweet)	cookies
biscuits (savory)	crackers
buns (sweet, individual cakes, sometimes with dried fruits, e.g., Chelsea bun, currant bun, hot cross bun)	muffins (cup-shaped, baked in muffin pan; usually sweet, e.g., a blueberry muffin)

Note: The Americans have cinnamon buns (which are very common) and sticky buns that are sweet too.

baps (soft bread rolls used for making sandwiches)	hamburger buns (this is odd to the British ears as the British think of "bun" as being sweet)

Note: *Baps* is also crude British slang for a woman's breasts.

scones	biscuits (unsweetened breakfast or dinner pastries, e.g., biscuits and gravy)

Note: *Scones* and *biscuits* look the same superficially, but the tastes and textures are quite different.

crumpets have dimpled tops but smooth pancake-like bottoms; not split, they are made from batter and have a rubbery texture.	English muffins (round, flat, split bread made from dough, eaten - in place of toast - as part of American breakfast)

Notes:
1. *Crumpet* is also (sometimes crude) slang for an attractive woman; *a bit of a crumpet* means "a sexually available woman."
2. It has been said that the people who came up with *Thomas' English Muffins* were inspired by what was sold door-to-door or in the streets in the 1800s England by a "Muffin Man" as mentioned in the nursery rhyme *Do You Know the Muffin Man?*

    "Oh, do you know the muffin man,
    The muffin man, the muffin man,
    Do you know the muffin man
    That lives in Drury Lane?"

    The question is what exactly was the muffin man selling? Sweet buns or crumpets? (Or fairy cakes or teacakes?)

I've read that people in the north of England call crumpets "muffins" whereas people in other regions may call them "pikelets" (thinner kind of crumpets, more like mini pancakes)

3. In the U.S., *muffins* and *English muffins* are two different things.

SLANG USE

Bread Money

- *"Can you loan me some **bread**? I'm so broke right now!"*

Background: The idea behind this slang term is that one needs bread in order to live and money is needed to buy it.

The British point of view is that it comes from the Cockney rhyming slang *bread and honey*, hence *money*.

Usage note: To **earn one's bread** (British: to **earn one's crust** or to **earn a crust**) is to earn one's living.

Breadwinner is the wage earner; someone who BRINGS HOME THE BACON (See page 94).

Dough Money

- *I need some **dough** to pay my rent.*

Background: Dough is a mixture of flour, water (or milk) and other ingredients. It is too stiff to pour (as opposed to BATTER; see later) but pliable enough to knead. Dough is used to make bread. For this reason, it also becomes slang for money. The conventional humorous explanation is that dough is *kneaded*, and money is also *needed*.

Usage notes:
1. To be **rolling in dough** means to have more money than you need.
2. To **rake in the dough** means to make a lot of money.
    Other slang terms one can use are (to) **make a lot of moolah**; **make big bucks**; **make a killing**.
1. Also used, **dough-re-mi** (from the musical notes *do-re-mi*)
2. Other slang for money: **scratch, greenbacks, bucks, legal tender, cash, long green**
    Someone with a lot of money: **well- off, well-heeled, loaded, flush**

Breadbasket The general stomach area

- *He punched the bully right in the **breadbasket**.*

Background: This slang term has been around since the mid 1700s.

It is likely that there is some connection between the basket used to hold bread and the "basket" (i.e., the stomach) where the bread ends up after a person eats it.

From the 20th century on, the term has also been used to refer to an agricultural area, especially one that supplies grain production; for example, *The Midwest states of the U.S. are the nation's **breadbasket***.

The comparable term used in Southeast Asia is **rice bowl**, as in *The Delta of the Chao Phraya River is Thailand's **rice bowl**.*

MILK TOAST See page 46.

Muffin top A roll of flesh overhanging the waist; caused by wearing pants that are too tight

- *I know she's cute, but look at the **muffin top** on her!*

Background: It refers to the cake-like American-style muffin. The "muffin top" is the mushroom bit that spills over the side of the muffin tin. When people not sufficiently slim wear low-rise, hip-hugger pants (or skirts) or midriff-baring tops that are too small, the resulting spillage of flesh at the midriff is said to resemble a muffin top.

The term originated as Australian slang in the mid 2003, but has since become popular in other English-speaking countries.

Usage Notes:
1. A pejorative term, used mostly with women
2. **Spare tires** and **love handles** are the usual slang terms for that excess fat when it is not being squeezed by a too-tight pair of pants.

Toast (To be) in deep trouble; in a very bad shape

- *If Dad finds out about this, we're **toast**.*

Background: Literally, a **toast** is a slice of bread that has been heated until the outside is brown and crisp. It is used as slang in the sense of "to be done; finished (for good)."

Usage note: Another slang often used is (to be) DEAD MEAT (See page 78).

White-bread (adjective) Bland; dull and boring (but also familiar and comforting); also used to describe a place's demographics as predominantly white

- *The TV moms in the '50 and '60 sitcoms were incredibly **white-bread** women.*
- *After her acting career was over, she went back to a **white-bread** existence in her hometown.*
- *The audience in this tiny, **white-bread** town reacted to the senator's speech by constantly cheering and clapping.*
- *Because of its diversity, I wouldn't call it a **white-bread** neighborhood.*

Usage notes:
1. Its usage is similar to the term (PLAIN) VANILLA (See page 164). They both signify plainness and blandness.
2. The phrase is, over time, taking on more and more derogatory connotations. It is often used as a racial slur, referring to a white person.
3. A **cracker**, on the other hand, means a native of Georgia (nickname) and is equal to a class of poor whites in southern states.

"BREAD" USED AS A VERB OR ADJECTIVE

To **bread (fish or meat)** To cover or dress it with bread crumbs
- *For best results, you should **bread** the pork chops before you cook them.*
- *I love **breaded shrimps**! Too bad I can't eat a lot of them because of my high cholesterol.*

Usage note: Not to be confused with another cooking term: **batter**. As a noun, **batter** means a beaten mixture of flour and liquid (usually eggs and milk); to **batter** is to coat food in batter prior to frying, for example, the fish in *fish and chips* is usually **battered** and deep-fried.

• •

COMMON EXPRESSIONS

A few sandwiches short of a picnic Said of a person who is not completely mentally sound
- *Don't pay attention to him. He's **a few sandwiches short of a picnic**.*

Background: The word "sandwich" means two or more slices of bread with a filling of meat, cheese or any other food between them. It is named after the fourth Earl of Sandwich, an English nobleman of the 18th century, who invented it so he could eat without leaving the gambling table.

The phrase alludes to sandwiches as the American quintessential picnic food.

Usage notes:
1. It is one of those "Fulldeckisms" – humorous and witty ways to say someone is dumb, named after the classic *a few cards short of a full deck*. Here are some more of the food-related ones:

   A few noodles short of a happy bowl
   A few french fries short of a happy meal
   He's one chopstick short.
   His biscuits aren't all baked.
   Eats soup with a fork

   There are hundreds and hundreds of them. People seem to have a lot of fun with this type of expressions, so new ones are invented all the time.
2. See also NOT THE SHARPEST KNIFE IN THE DRAWER on page 187.
3. See SANDWICH GENERATION later in this chapter.

Baker's dozen A group of thirteen
- *Make it a **baker's dozen** and I'll take it.*
- *The book "Your Favorite Seuss: A **Baker's Dozen** by the One and Only Dr. Seuss" is a volume of 13 classic Dr. Seuss stories.*
- *The local team made it a **baker's dozen** after last night's victory. It takes its record to 13-0 overall.*

<u>Background</u>: A *baker's dozen*, also known as a long dozen, had its origin in 13th century England: bakers typically gave an extra item when selling a dozen of something to safeguard against penalty for light weight.

Most baked goods today are sold on a per item basis, rather than a weight basis.

Best thing/greatest thing/since sliced bread Best to come on the scene in a long time

- *My aunt told me she has been using a microwave to cook all kinds of food. For her, it's the **best thing since sliced bread.***

<u>Background</u>: Bread used to be sold in unsliced loaves. Pre-sliced, packaged bread has only been available since the late 1920s or early 1930s. It was truly the culmination of a century of techno-innovations as it needed electricity, a uniformed sized loaf of bread, a plastic wrap and a toaster to build up the demand.

It's hard for us to imagine it nowadays, but sliced bread was a true convenience. People didn't have electric knives and other gadgets in their kitchen in those days, so cutting the loaf of bread was a chore.

Apparently the phrase comes from a 1930s marketing campaign for *Wonder Bread*. Since it was coined, people have often wondered, *what was the best thing before sliced bread?*

<u>Usage notes</u>:
1. Said in praise of an invention or breakthrough that has had a real impact on our daily lives
2. It can also be used humorously or sarcastically about someone or something (some new, over-hyped gadget, for example):
   - *The way he talked about her, you would think she was the **greatest thing since sliced bread.***
   - *You may think that Facebook and twitter are the **best things since sliced bread**. A lot of people don't even (care to) know what these two things are and manage to live quite happily.*
3. Variants: ***the best thing ever; the most wonderful thing in the world***
4. Also used, ***next best thing since sliced bread; better than sliced bread***
5. Instead of *sliced bread*, you can basically use anything you think is really innovative, for example, *indoor plumbing; hula hoop* or *microwave popcorn*.

BREAD AND BUTTER See page 48.

Bread and circuses Offerings, such as benefits, handouts and petty amusements intended to avert potential discontent or distract attention from a policy or situation; any kind of crowd-pleaser, especially offered by the government

- *This "Government money for your car" program was a good example of **bread and circuses** designed to distract people's attention from the underlying economic crisis of our country.*

- *These politicians are dreaming up more **bread-and-circuses** ploys to gain support from their constituents.*

<u>Background</u>: The term was first used by Juvenal, a Roman satirist (circa 100 AD) in his *Satires*. Deploring the decline of Rome, where people once took a great interest in government, he wrote that now the populace cared for only two things, *panem et circensus* (bread and circus games).

<u>Usage notes</u>:
1. It is a general term for government (often unsound) policies that seek short-term solutions to public unrest.
2. Often used as a synonym for ***political manipulation***
3. The term has become proverbial to describe those who give away significant rights in exchange for material pleasures:
   - ***Bread and circuses** is the phrase that accurately describes the political situation in this country.*

<u>Of interest</u>: Spanish has the corresponding expression, *pan y toros* (*bread and bulls*, the latter referring to the sport of fighting bulls which is very popular in Spain).

Bread and roses Phrase symbolizing both life's necessities and its pleasures
- *We must have both **bread and roses**. One without the other never will be enough.*

<u>Background</u>: Politically, the term is associated both with Labor and the Woman's movement.

It originated as a title of a poem written by James Oppenheim, published in *American Magazine* in December 1911. It was then used as a slogan during the textile strike in Laurence, Massachusetts during January – March 1912. The strikers, led to a large extent by women immigrants carrying signs that read *We want bread and roses, too*, demanded not just decent treatment at work, but the right to dignity and a better quality of life (*bread* meaning the money to live; *roses* meaning shorter work hours to enjoy life).

The strike, now often known as the *Bread and Roses Strike*, was settled on terms generally favorable to the workers. The notion of *bread and roses* has become a cry for justice and dignity for women around the world.

Bread and water Minimal fare to stay alive
- *They practically lived on **bread and water** for weeks because they were so broke.*
- *Is it possible to lose weight by going on a **bread-and-water** diet?*
- *A woman convicted of severely neglecting her horses got a 30-day jail sentence with three days on **bread and water**.*

<u>Background</u>: *Bread and water* is the plainest and cheapest possible diet and therefore, something one would have to settle for in poverty. It is often chosen in abstinence (as in fasting for religious or health reasons) and has also become known as a staple for prisoners.

Giving *bread and water* as a punishment has been a common practice among military personnel. It has been said that the reason the British Royal Navy used that particular sentence was not simply to deprive their sailors of food, rather that the diet caused horrible constipation. The bowel disorder was the real punishment.

Of interest: A comparable expression in Thai is "rice and fish sauce," a phrase my late mother always used as we were so poor when I was growing up.

Crumbs from the rich man's/someone's/table Any small act of charity or generosity from the rich to the poor
- *When you are so poor and hungry and in need of money, sometimes you have to settle for* **crumbs from someone's table**.

Background: Crumbs are little bits of bread or other food that sometimes fall off onto the table while one is eating. Usually, crumbs are for dogs, birds and other animals.

This is an old expression that has a biblical reference. In Luke 16:19-31, Jesus tells of Lazarus, a beggar who lay outside the gate of a rich man, hoping to be fed with crumbs that fell from the rich man's table (which never happened).

Usage note: A related expression is to **throw someone a crumb** meaning to give the smallest amount to pacify someone.
- *The Roman 'bread and circuses' is based on the idea that if you* **throw the masses an occasional crumb** - *some food or joy, you can get away with tyranny.*

Crusty Harsh, surly, rude, testy, touchy, brusque
- *The* **crusty** *old man didn't even acknowledge my hello when I walked past him.*

Background: Literally, "crust" is the brown, hard outer portion or surface of a loaf or slice of bread (also the dough or pastry shell of pizzas or pies) whereas a *crumb* is a small particle of the bread, either from the crust or the inside of the loaf.

A crusty person often seems unfriendly at first but is really kinder and more caring than he or she seems.

Usage notes:
1. To **have a lot of crust** is slang meaning "have a lot of nerve; have a lot of gall"
   - *The guy* **had a lot of crust** *showing up at the wedding without an invitation.*
2. **Crusty** also has a slang meaning of someone or something that is ugly, gross, nasty or unappealing:
   - *That girl is so* **crusty** *looking!*
   - *Susan decided that he was too* **crusty** *for her to go out with.*
3. **Crusty** as a noun is British slang for a tramp or homeless young person with poor cleanliness.

Fifty lashes with a wet noodle A playful scolding meaning "shame on you for messing up"

- *"Sorry I forgot to bring you the book I promised you."*
  *"**Fifty lashes with a wet noodle** for you!"*
- *The teacher told her students jokingly that she would give them **fifty lashes with a wet noodle** if they were caught misbehaving.*

Background: Fifty lashes with a whip is enough to kill or at least cause great pain. Hitting someone with a wet noodle definitely does not have that effect. In fact, it would be difficult or impossible since, being wet, it is completely floppy and really has no form or stiffness.

This is an expression that Ann Landers (1918-2002), an American advice columnist, seemed to have popularized (See also WAKE UP AND SMELL THE COFFEE on page 138). She would use it to scold people if she believed they had done something mean or just plain stupid.

Usage notes:
1. The number of lashes in the expression can be changed to any other number the speaker likes.
2. A *wet noodle* is also slang for "wimp."

Half a loaf is better than none/no bread. It's better to have something than nothing at all.

- *"How did the lawsuit go?"*
  "I'll probably get less than what I'd asked for."
  *"At least you get something. Look at it this way, **half a loaf is better than none**."*
- *"If you don't believe that **half a loaf is better than none**, you will always be hungry."* Anonymous

Usage notes:
1. This is a very old saying that is still in common usage.
2. Other food-related variations to this saying:
   Half an egg is better than an empty shell.
   Even a few crumbs are better than nothing.
   If you have no bacon, you must be content with cabbage.

Like white on rice Following someone/something very closely; all over someone/something

- *"What a defense! He has been on the guy **like white on rice**,"* said the announcer after the defensive back knocked the ball out of the receiver's hand.

Background: Until the health food craze of recent years, when people talked about rice, it was generally presumed that it would be white rice. So the term is used to talk about things that traditionally go together, like ***stink on a skunk*** or ***ugly on an ape***.

Usage notes:
1. Often used in American football to emphasize how close one player is to another. You can't get any closer than white on rice – the two are inseparable.
2. Compare with LIKE A DUCK/A CHICKEN/ ON A JUNE BUG on page 89.

Manna from heaven An unexpected gift or aid, often a valuable or desperately needed one
- *The sight of the rescue team was **manna from heaven** for the injured hikers.*
- *The 10 million-dollar donation from one of its patrons was like **manna from heaven** for a library greatly in need of repairs.*

Background: The term comes from the Bible (Exodus 16: 14-36). God sent down manna to feed the Israelites when they ran out of food while wandering in the desert after leaving Egypt. This bread, white as coriander seeds, tasted like flat cakes made with honey.

Noodle (around) To improvise on a musical instrument, especially as a warm-up exercise; to toy or experiment without a particular direction
- *There's nothing wrong with **noodling around** to find the key and the melody; it's what many musicians do a lot of the time.*
- *He **noodled** for a few weeks before coming up with this ad campaign.*

Background: The noun "noodle" as slang means the human head (as in **use your noodle**) or a stupid person (sometimes called a **noodlehead**). It possibly comes from an older word, "noddle" (which meant "head").

The edible "noodle" comes from the German word "nudel," which is probably a variant of "knodel" (a dumpling, literally, a small knot) (www.grammarphobia.com/blog).

Usage note: In some parts of the U.S., such as Arkansas, **noodle (around)** is the term used in hand fishing – to feel around and see what you can find, i.e., to catch fish bare-handed.

On the bread line With no money at all
- *Even in a country as rich as ours, there are a lot more people living **on the bread line** now than there were ten years ago.*

Usage notes:
1. A **bread line** is a line of needy people waiting for handouts of bread and other food from charity.
   See also SOUP KITCHEN on page 76.
2. To be **below the bread line** is to be below the level which is officially considered to be extremely poor:
   - *People in Zimbabwe are so destitute that many are **below the bread line**; they cannot even afford basic food to survive.*

Take the bread out of someone's mouth To make it impossible for someone to earn a living, especially by taking their work away

- *Our employer is **taking the bread out of our mouth** by cutting down our hours.*

Background: "The bread" here is a metaphor for money earned as wages.

The big enchilada A very important person, especially the highest-ranking individual in an organization; one who is in charge; something of high value

- *The guy is **the big enchilada** in the State Department.*
- *Florida is obviously going to be **the big enchilada** in this year's primary election. It will immediately be very important in picking both Democratic and Republican presidential candidates.*

Background: This slang term was popularized by President Nixon's aide, John Ehrlichman. In the Watergate tapes released in 1973, Ehrlichman was heard referring to Attorney General John Mitchell as "the big enchilada."
Usage notes:
1. Used with "the"
2. See also BIG CHEESE on page 43; BIG FISH on page 103.

The whole enchilada The whole deal; the entirety of something, especially something impressive or outstanding

- *I wouldn't mind having your job - good pay, short hours, a week off every three months - **the whole enchilada.***

Background: *Enchilada* is a tortilla roll with a filling typically of seasoned meat and served with a chili sauce. Its name means "seasoned with chili" The slang *the whole enchilada* came into the language in the early 1960s.

Usage note: There are a lot of expressions in English to describe the idea of "everything," for example, ***the whole nine yards; the whole shootin' match; the whole ball of wax; the whole kit and caboodle*** (the whole lot of persons or things); ***the whole shebang*** (the structure of something, as of an organization or affair) also, ***the whole bag of tricks.***

Trail of breadcrumbs/breadcrumb trail(s) Clues or traces; navigational aids

- *The police can now retroactively bug your cell phone for your **breadcrumb trail** if they can justify that it's relevant to an ongoing investigation.*
- *People don't abruptly bail out of long-term relationships; there's almost always a **trail of breadcrumbs** marking their path out the door.*

Background: It's a reference to the Hansel and Gretel story from the Brothers Grimm. The evil stepmother sends Hansel and Gretel into the woods hoping they would lose their way and never return. As they explore the forest, Hansel scatters a trail of breadcrumbs to mark their path. Unfortunately for them, the hungry birds swoop down and gobble up their trail markers. And the children are lost and alone in the woods...

<u>Usage note</u>: ***Breadcrumbs*** or ***breadcrumb trails*** is now commonly used as a computer term - a navigation technique typically appears horizontally across the top of a webpage. Breadcrumbs provide links back to each previous page that the user navigated through in order to get to the current page.

Toasty Pleasantly or comfortably warm; characteristic of or resembling toast

- *It was freezing outside, but we felt snug and **toasty** by the fireplace in our house.*
- *Consult with us; we'll help make a relationship **toasty** warm, not toast.*

<u>Usage note</u>: A related expression is (***as***) ***warm as toast***, used both literally and figuratively:

- *Their home is **as warm as toast** since embracing eco-friendly heat pump technology.*
- *I'm **warm as toast** in this new outfit.*
- *He's **warm as toast** and sweet as sugar. That's my little boy.*

Upper crust The highest social class or group

- *These people were not part of the true **upper crust** of society. They just acted like they were.*
- *The terrorist accused of trying to set off a bomb on Christmas Day was reported to come from the **upper crust** of Nigerian society.*

<u>Background</u>: It alludes to the top layer of crust, as of a pie.

<u>Usage notes</u>:

1. A synonym often given is ***upper class*** (the aristocracy or the wealthy class).
2. Other terms used are ***the elites; elite social class*** and ***the swells*** (socially prominent people).

• •

OTHER TERMS AND EXPRESSIONS OF INTEREST

Bagel (verb) (Sports term) Slang for zero

- *We **bageled** our opponent last night.*

<u>Background</u>: A bagel is a firm-textured, ring-shaped roll of yeasted wheat briefly dipped in hot water to give it a hard sheen prior to baking. Originated as a Jewish food, it has become popular throughout the U.S. since the 1990s.

The slang meaning is evoked supposedly by the bagel's round shape.

<u>Usage notes</u>:

1. To ***bagel*** in tennis is to win a set 6-0.
2. ***Breadstick*** (often considered a type of cracker), on the other hand, is tennis jargon for winning (or losing) a set 6-1: the straight shape of the "1" resembling the straight shape of a breadstick.

Bun in the oven Euphemism for being pregnant
- *Guess what? She has another **bun in the oven**.*

Background: It was first used in the mid 20th century.
A bun = a baby; the oven = the womb
A bun (or roll) grows while baking, thus the analogy with a fetus growing.

Usage note: Some other slang terms for "pregnant" are:
- (To be) **knocked up** A semi-vulgar expression
- **A baby bump** A British term often used in the U.S. celebrity-oriented news media
- **Preggers** Also British term meaning, "with child"

Cry hunger with a loaf of bread under your arm To feel sorry for yourself when you really have a lot to be thankful for
- *Movie studios claiming poverty? That's **crying hunger with a loaf of bread under your arm**. They are only going to make a few millions less, just pocket change for them.*

Comment: I had not heard of this expression before until I came across it while looking for something else. From what I've read, it's an old saying – a quite descriptive one, indeed. It reminds me of another expression, to **cry poor mouth**, meaning to constantly complain about how poor you are.

Doughboy The nickname first applied to the infantry of the U.S. army during the Mexican-American War of 1846-1847, then to all American troops of any combat branches sent to Europe during World War I.

Background: The most often-cited theory is that the brass buttons on the mid 19th century infantry uniform resembled the doughboy dumplings eaten by soldiers and sailors of earlier times, and the name was transferred from the pastry to button to soldier.

During World War II, the troops were alternately known as the *Yanks* and *GI's*.

Yank – Slang for Yankee, a native or inhabitant of New England, later came to mean anyone from the U.S.

G.I. – Government Issue (the standard issue of shoes, blankets, hair-cut, etc.)

The **Pillsbury Doughboy**, on the other hand, is an anthropomorphic wad of dough used to sell products for the Pillsbury Company – "anthropomorphic" meaning the ascription of human form or attributes to something that is not human.

Hot tamale American slang for a very sexy woman

Background: A tamale is a Hispanic dish consisting of corn meal and a variety of fillings wrapped inside a corn husk.

I could sop you/him/her/up with a biscuit. Phrase used to mean that a person is so sweet and appetizing the she (or he) appears to be delicious

Usage notes:
1. Another expression also used in this sense is *I could just eat you up (with a spoon).*
2. Sometimes used as a pick-up line (a line used to entice the person you are interested in) by men

Is it bigger than a bread box? Phrase used to gauge the size of something or what some surprise object may be

- *John: "I have a birthday present for you, but you can't open it until tomorrow."*
- *Jane: "Is it bigger than a bread box?"*

Background: A bread box is where you keep your bread so it stays fresh. Bread boxes are usually big enough to fit one or two average sizes loaves of bread. They were a common household kitchen item until the bread started to be sold commercially.

This catch phrase was the creation of Steve Allen, a guest panelist on the TV game show *What's my line?* in the early 1950s. The object of the show was to guess the occupation of a mystery guest. This meant that panelists often had to ask questions about a product produced by the guest.

Pretzel logic Twisted or circular reasoning that does not make sense or does not explain the situation rationally

- *According to this government proposal, we are required to buy health insurance but will be taxed on health insurance that's too expensive (i.e., too good). This sounds like **pretzel logic**.*

Background: European in origin, a pretzel is either a bread (soft inside) or a sweet pastry - both with the same characteristic shape: a rope of dough formed into a loop, and an extra twist given to the ends. The shape is supposed to represent the human shoulders with arms folded. (Some say it represents arms crossed in prayer.)

The analogy is between a pretzel looped in a certain way and ideas that are looped without an outcome.

Usage note: It is an American term, used mostly in political contexts.

Sandwich generation Middle-aged adults who care for growing children and aging parents at the same time

Usage note: To **sandwich** means to insert or squeeze something between two other things:
- *At the crowded party, he was **sandwiched** between two beautiful girls.*

Twisted like a pretzel In a contorted position

- *He was **twisted like a pretzel** trying to hit the tennis ball.*

Use your loaf Use your head

Background: It's from Cockney rhyming slang *use your loaf of bread: head.*

5

· · · · · ·

what's Cooking in the Kettle?

"A good wife and a wholesome cabbage soup, what more could you want?"
Russian saying
"Troubles are easier to take with soup than without." Yiddish saying

ESPECIALLY FOR ENGLISH LEARNERS

Kettle means a large pot, used for making soup or boiling stuff. It can also refer to a teakettle (a container with a lid, a handle and a spout, used for boiling and pouring water).

What's cooking in the kettle? is the kind of language found on restaurant menus. It simply means *"what kind of soup do you have today?"*– a typical question posed by customers to their server.

In some fancy or high-class restaurants, the term **soup du jour** (special soup of the day) may be used instead.

· ·

COMMON EXPRESSIONS

Alphabet soup A metaphor for an abundance of abbreviations or acronyms
  - *Pentagon Adds MISO To **Alphabet Soup**.* (npr.org, 7-2-2010)
  - (Note: MISO here stands for Military Information Support Operations. It's a play on words. *Miso* is the name of a Japanese soup.)

Background: Literally, *alphabet soup* is a broth with pasta in the shape of letters of the alphabet (novelty soup; sometimes useful for young children to learn their letters).

The term took on a figurative meaning when it was used in a mildly derogatory sense to criticize the proliferation of government agencies during Franklin D. Roosevelt's administration. When FDR took office in 1933, he feverishly created program after program to give relief, create jobs and stimulate economic recovery for the U.S. They came to be known by their acronyms (words formed from the initial letters of a title or words in a set phrase). Many critics remarked that these New Deal programs reminded them of *alphabet soup*. For instance, Alfred E. Smith, a Democrat disenchanted with Roosevelt described the government as *"submerged in a bowl of alphabet soup."*

Chowderhead (Slang) An idiot; a dummy
  - *Geez, what a **chowderhead**! He came up with stupid remarks again!*

<u>Background</u>: On the surface, one would think that it had to do with *chowder soup*, i.e., someone who acted like his or her brain was mashed into chowder soup. However, most word experts conclude that there is no relation between the two. *Chowderhead* traces back to an old English word "jolterhead" (sometimes spelled "cholterhead") that meant someone who acted as if his brain had suffered some sort of jolt.

<u>Usage notes</u>:
1. Alternative spellings are **chowder-head** and **chowder head**.
2. **Chowderhead** is also a mild derogatory name for someone from the North East (especially Boston, Massachusetts). That is where the best clam chowder is from.

Fog thick as pea soup Any type of thick fog
- *The fog was **thick as pea soup** and at times it was hard to see the cars right in front of you.*

<u>Usage note</u>: Also, **a pea-soup fog; this fog is pea soup** and the slang term **soup**
- *Better drive slowly. It's hard to see anything through the **soup**.*

See SOUPY later in this chapter.

From soup to nuts From beginning to end; including or covering everything
- *Our company provides technical support **from soup to nuts**.*
- *This department store sells everything **from soup to nuts**.*

<u>Background</u>: An American term, it comes from the way formal dinners in the mid 20th century were served, beginning with a soup course and ending with the nuts (as snacks to go along with alcoholic drinks).

<u>Usage note</u>: It seems to be used quite a lot in the technology and business sectors.

In the soup In big trouble
- *Economist: We're **in the Soup** of Recession.* (www.kdka.com, 2-20-09)

<u>Background</u>: This is also an Americanism, coined in the late 19th century. There are so many colorful theories as to the origin of the phrase, ranging from a waiter spilling soup on a customer to a losing baseball team dressed in waiter suits.

According to www.word-detective.com, it could be an allusion to the idiom **in hot water**.

Souped up Used to refer to something that has been modified to increase power or efficiency
- *If you want a **souped up** car and choose to do it yourself, you'd better check first which car accessories are street legal. It can save you money and an encounter with the police.*

<u>Background</u>: According to www.worldwidewords.org, the term must at root derive from "super" as in *supercharger*, a device known from 1919 to increase the pressure of the fuel-air mixture in an engine to improve its performance.

Also, there's a connection with the foodstuff, which accounts for the shift in spelling. *Soup* has at times been used as a slang term for such liquids as nitroglycerine mentioned in newspaper reports about criminal activity. And in the past, it was slang for stimulants injected into horses to make them run faster.

Usage notes:
1. It has been used in relation to car and motorcycle engines since the 1930s.
2. It is now used with any kind of gadget:
    - *President Obama is going to get his blackberry – the souped-up blackberry will soon arrive in his hands.* (www.blogrunner.com, 1-20-09)

Soupy Watery like soup; foggy or cloudy
    - *This oatmeal is too soupy; I like it really thick.*
    - *We had to drive in soupy weather all morning.*

Too many cooks spoil the broth. If too many people try to take charge of a task, they end up making a mess of it.
    - *First, let's decide who's going to be in charge here. Too many cooks spoil the broth.*

Usage notes:
1. Often shortened to *too many cooks...*
2. TOO MANY FINGERS SPOIL THE PIE (See page 156) also expresses the same idea.
3. **Broth**, a flavorful liquid made by simmering meat or vegetables in water, also appears in other sayings; for example, *every cook praises his own broth* and *good broth may be made in an old pot.*

• •

OTHER TERMS AND EXPRESSIONS OF INTEREST

Duck soup Something that is easy to do
    Background: No one seems to know its origin, though some suggest that it may have come from another expression SITTING DUCK (See page 90) meaning "an easy target." Or it could originally mean something like "as easy as eating duck soup" – similar in this respect to a PIECE OF CAKE (See page 153).
    In any case, The Marx Brothers (Groucho, Harpo, Chico and Zeppo) popularized the term when they used it as a title for their movie in 1933.
    Usage note: It is no longer current.

Jewish penicillin A nickname for chicken soup which for centuries has been lauded as a cold remedy
Jack Canfield and Mark Victor Hansen, taking advantage of the belief in the medicinal benefits of this soup, named their series of inspirational books *Chicken Soup for the Soul*. The first one came out in 1993. Their overall enterprise has become quite a success.

Soup and fish Slang for men's formal dress, specifically white tie and tail coat – a tuxedo

> Background: It is a 19th century Americanism. One dons a **soup and fish** for a high-class social occasion such as a formal elaborate meal, starting with soup and followed by fish before one gets to the main course of meat.

> Usage note: The term is no longer current.

Soup kitchen and **soup line**

> - *Our governor is in line at the* **soup kitchen**, *begging for a federal loan.*
> - *The giant automaker stepped up to the* **soup line** *for the government handout.*

> Background: During the Great Depression (1929-1934), many Americans had nothing to eat and would stand in line at a soup kitchen to get a free hot meal.

Why soup? Because it could be made with whatever was in the kitchen and could be stretched to feed more people by adding more water. Plus, it was easy to cook and serve.

Soup kitchens had been around even before the Great Depression. They went back to the Potato Famine in Ireland in the 1840s.

There are still soup kitchens in the U.S. serving prepared food of any kind to the poor, the homeless and the disadvantaged. They are mostly in big cities and often run by charity groups.

Soup Nazi (and other *–nazi* compounds) Term used to describe someone very controlling, authoritarian or inflexible

> Background: It comes from the TV sitcom *Seinfeld* (1989-1998), in an episode about a small take-out owner who makes such great soups that people line up around the block to buy them. He is nicknamed the **Soup Nazi** because of his strict rules that customers have to follow when ordering soups. If he's not pleased with the way they present themselves at his soup counter, he yells, ***"No soup for you! Next!"***

According to the *Oxford English Dictionary*, the term *safety nazi* (someone who is obsessed with safety) has been around as early as 1982. Another term, *grammar nazi* appeared a few years before *soup nazi*. But because *Seinfeld* was such a popular sitcom, the term that it created – the *Soup Nazi* (or *soup nazi*) has helped to popularize these types of words a great deal:

> - *The guy is a* **hot dog nazi**. *He doesn't even allow ketchup on his hot dogs. If you don't like it, leave. He has such a large clientele that he doesn't care about your business.*

The phrase **no soup for you!** also became a catch phrase right after the show. It is used when someone changes his or her mind about giving something to someone else. The word "soup" may be replaced with something else.

> Usage note: Many people prefer to use the word *-police* instead of *-nazi*, as in **grammar police**; **food police** and **fashion police**.

Spare your breath to cool your porridge Don't waste your time talking.

Background: *Porridge* is a general term for any type of boil-until-mushy grain or legume (e.g., peas, beans, lentils).

Back in the medieval times in Europe, porridge was cooked in a large kettle by the lower classes who would, each day, add new ingredients to the batch leftover from the days before. Peas were a regular ingredient as is captured in this nursery rhyme:

"*Pease porridge hot, pease porridge cold*
  Pease porridge in the pot, nine days old"

Some people think that the porridge in this nursery rhyme is what we now call split pea soup.

Porridge and *pottage* were originally interchangeable terms. In the 17th century, they started to have distinctive meanings, with *pottage* keeping its original association with vegetable soup and porridge referring to cereals, primarily oatmeal.

Pottage is rarely used now, except in the expression **sell one's birthright for a mess of pottage**, meaning to accept some trivial financial or other gain but to lose something much more important:

- *It's shocking that he **sold his political birthright for a mess of pottage** – fifty thousand dollars in bribes. Is that all his asking price?*

("A mess" is a prepared dish of food. It also refers to meals served in the military.)

It is associated with the exchange of his birthright by famished Esau for a meal of lentil stew from his twin brother, Jacob, as described in Genesis 25:29-34. Esau later regrets the trade.

Usage notes:

1. *Porridge* now has a more restricted meaning. The British use it for oatmeal. They also have *plum porridge*, a grainy soup made with spices, wine and dried plums. It would evolve over centuries into a dessert Christmas pudding.
   Americans usually don't use the word *porridge*. They use either the actual name of the grain (e.g., oatmeal, grits, cornmeal mush, cream of wheat or rice) or simply refer to it as hot or cooked cereal.

2. *Pottage* and *broth* also appear in some versions, i.e., **spare** (or, **save**) **your breath to cool your pottage** (or **broth**).

"Waiter, there's a fly in my soup!"

Most Americans are familiar with the *"waiter, there's a fly in my soup"* joke (with punch lines like *It's OK, sir, there's no extra charge; Now that fly knows a good soup.*)

But do you have any idea how long this joke has been around?

According to Benjamin Zimmer (www.languagelog.com), magazines and newspapers began running variations on the "fly in the soup" joke in the late 1880s. He cites some of the jokes he had found in the newspaper archive databases. His theory is that the joke could be the origin of the metaphor IN THE SOUP (see earlier) which first arose at about the same time.

6

·····

The Meats That We Eat

"Poor men seek meat for their stomach; rich men stomach for their meat."
English Proverb

MEAT

Dead meat Slang for someone doomed to ruin or defeat

- *If this campaign ad doesn't work, we're **dead meat.***

Usage notes:
1. Very common
2. See also TOAST on page 62.

Get to the meat of something To get right to the essence or substance of something

- *You should **get to the meat of your lecture** as soon as you can to hold the interest of your audience.*

Usage note: We also talk about **more meat on the bone** or the **meaty** part of just about anything besides food:
- *If he wants to get elected, he has to put **more meat on the bone**. He has to be more specific about his policies on the economy, health care and the war on terror.*
- *It was such a **meaty** role that when it was offered to her, she took it right away.*

Meat and potatoes Basic or fundamental part(s)

- *Music, especially the oldies, is the **meat and potatoes** of this radio station.*

Background: A basic American meal consists of meat and potatoes (and a vegetable).

Usage notes:
1. The term a ***meat-and-potatoes*** person can be used literally and figuratively. If one is talking about food, it means a person just prefers 'plain' food, nothing fancy. In its figurative sense, it means someone who is pretty down to earth, no-nonsense, no-frills or, as in another expression, ***no bells and whistles***.

   However, ***meat and potatoes*** can be mildly derogatory. It implies that one is not very adventurous or open to new things:
   - *He's a **meat-and-potatoes** guy; we could never get him to try Thai food.*
2. A **meat eater** is a person whose diet consists mainly of meat; the opposite is a **vegetarian.**

Meat grinder A metaphor for a destructive process
- *We all know we are walking into a* **meat grinder** *when we play this team next Sunday.*
- *This job – not just for me, but for everybody – is a* **meat grinder.**

One man's meat is another's poison. Different people like different things; what's good or works for one may not be good or may not work for another.
- *My sister really loves being a nurse. I wouldn't care for that kind of work at all. Well,* **one man's meat is another's poison,** *I guess.*

Background: "Meat" originally meant food of any kind, and this is the sense used in this context: what some people eat as food may be poisonous or tastes very bad to other people.

Usage notes:
1. A very old saying that is still in common use
2. Used in response to someone's distaste or shock regarding someone else's likes, hobbies or literally the food they are eating
3. Other more recent expressions with the same meaning:
   One man's trash is another's treasure.
   One man's garbage is another's art.
4. Also, **there's no accounting for taste.**
      different strokes for different folks
      whatever floats your boat
5. This one is just for fun:
   One man's fish is another man's poisson. "Poisson" is the French word for "fish." As used here, it's a pun (a play on words) on the English word "poison."

Throw/toss out/red meat To attempt to satisfy or to excite the base or followers
- *He* **tosses out red meat** *to conservative activists better than the other Republican candidates.*
- *When delivering a lecture, it doesn't hurt to* **throw red meat** *to your audience now and then. But that may depend on what kind of audience you have.*

Background: You throw out red meat (that is, raw meat) to lions to feed them, if they are in a zoo or circus, or distract them from eating you. Figuratively, you throw "red meat" to your audience to give them something appetizing to chew on while you continue to dish out something else.

Usage note: Very common in American political contexts

BEEF

ESPECIALLY FOR ENGLISH LEARNERS

TERMINOLOGY

Beef is the meat from cows.

Cow is the generic term for the animal, but is mostly used to refer to a mature female one.

Heifer is a young female cow.

Both bulls and steers are males. A steer is a sterilized (or "castrated" or "neutered") bull and can no longer reproduce; it is kept mainly for beef. (I once came across this line: *"Quit milking it, children. It's a steer!"* It would be hard to understand the joke if you didn't know the difference between a cow and a steer.)

An ox (the plural is oxen) is a mature female or castrated male, most likely trained (though some never get trained) to work (as in transport and haulage), and at the end of its life, inevitably used for meat. Note: ox and oxen are very seldom used in the U.S.

Cattle (no "s") is the collective term.

A calf is a young cow. The plural is calves.

Bovine is the scientific term for the species to which cows belong. It includes oxen, buffalo and bison.

IN CASE YOU DIDN'T KNOW

Cow is an offensive term when used about a woman, but, aside from being sexist, it doesn't usually have a sexual overtone, except negatively: the implication being that she is unattractive.

She's a real cow. (She's overweight, lacking in intelligence, grace and manner.)

Other adjectives used are *silly/fat/lazy/dirty*.

Some people might use a **heifer** instead of a *cow*.

I'm not sure what the male equivalent would be. My husband did suggest *he's as big as a whale/ a horse;* still it doesn't seem to have the same insulting sense as a *cow* does.

• • • • •

COMMON EXPRESSIONS RELATED TO COWS AND BEEF

All sizzle but no steak A person or thing that fails to measure up to its description or advanced publicity

- *The guy is **all sizzle but no steak.***
- *In spite of all the ads and positive reviews, the movie turned out to be **all sizzle but no steak.***

Usage notes:

1. Other expressions used in this sense: ***more flash than substance; all style and no substance; all talk, (but) no action; all hat, (but) no cattle***

2. The expression **sell the sizzle, not the steak** (or **don't sell the steak, sell the sizzle**), one of the all-time marketing mantras, was created by Elmer Wheeler, a legendary salesman and motivational speaker in the 1930s. It means that while the features ("the steak" – how it's designed, what it does) of a product are important, that is not normally what gets someone's initial interest and makes the sale. A good salesperson would emphasize the benefits ("the sizzle" - how it's useful) of that product instead.

Beef up To strengthen

- *One way to **beef up** your resumé is to take a few computer classes.*

Background: It alludes to the idea that one builds up more meat and muscles in one's body to make one stronger.

Usage note: It's a very common expression and can be used in just about any context.

Don't have a cow! Calm down!; chill out!; don't freak out!

- ***Don't have a cow!** I didn't steal your book; I just took it by mistake.*

Background: From what I've read, this expression has been around since either the 1950s or 1960s. Bart Simpson (of the TV cartoon dysfunctional family) did help to popularize it a great deal in the earlier episodes of *The Simpsons*.

Usage notes:
1. Used humorously to someone who seems to be overreacting to something bad that you've done (in the sense that it might create the same agony and pain as literally giving birth to a cow)
2. The positive form, to **have a cow** (or to **have a fit**) is sometimes used in anticipation of an emotional response:
   - *I thought my husband was going to **have a cow** when he found out I wrecked his car, but he seemed to be taking it OK.*
3. Both are considered slang and are used only in very informal contexts.

Grab/seize/the bull by the horns To take control of the situation; tackle the problem or task directly

- *Some investors are risk-taking, ready to **grab the bull by the horns.***

Background: This expression is evidently inspired by a form of bullfighting. In order to bring down a bull, you have to grab the horns and twist one into the ground, thus stopping the bull.

Have (a) beef with To have a complaint, problem or an argument

- *I don't **have a beef with** your position. So let's just leave it at that.*

Background: No one knows for sure how "beef" became slang for "argument" or "complaint." Robert Palmatier (2000) suggests that it comes from the noisy "complaints" cows make when they have waited too long to be fed, milked or led back to the barn.

However, www.word-detective.com has a different theory. Since **beefy** is slang for a large, muscular man, it is likely that 'beef' in "have (a) beef with" is a sort of shorthand to describe a complaint that might well escalate into a beefy, muscular conflict.

Usage notes:

1. Also, **What's the beef?** (What's the source of complaint?):

- *I don't know* **what his beef is**. *But whatever it is, I'm sure somebody will hear it.*

2. *Have a beef with vs. have a bone to pick with*

A *beef* is an angry or indignant complaint. The person with the beef has been offended and the beef could escalate into a loud quarrel, physical violence or a lawsuit.

To *have a bone to pick with someone* or to *pick a bone* is to make a specific complaint, perhaps about a small matter. It could lead to a dispute, or even a serious quarrel but not necessarily. *Pick a bone* has a delicacy - you are picking a sharp bone from the carcass of a chicken, a duck or a fish, a delicacy that is foreign to *have a beef with.*

Hit the bull's eye To be exactly correct

- *His comments about the company's problems hit* **the bull's eye.**

Background: "The bull's eye" is the small central circle on a target toward which people throw darts or shoot arrows or bullets. Why a bull instead of a cow or any other animal? Nobody knows.

Kill the fatted calf To pull out all the stops in celebrating someone or something

- *We'll* **kill a fatted calf** *when John is back from his military service.*

Background: It is an allusion to Jesus' parable of the prodigal (i.e., recklessly extravagant) son, who left home and wasted everything in riotous living but nevertheless was welcomed back by his father who ordered a fatted calf to be killed for the celebration (Luke 15: 11-32).

One interpretation of this parable is that we should never turn our back on people who are willing to admit they were wrong, but instead should welcome them as joyfully as ever. The father in this parable is God himself; we humans who have sinned are the prodigal son; the fatted calf is Jesus Christ.

Usage notes:

1. Some people use the phrase sarcastically to a person who did them wrong:

- *"Well, so you think I should* **kill the fatted calf** *just because you said you were sorry?"*

2. "Fatted" is the obsolete form of "fattened" and is now found only in this context. (www.users.tinyonline.co.uk.com)

Like a bull in a china shop Phrase used to describe people who are really clumsy or destructive in either a literal or figurative sense

- *Ron is **like a bull in a china shop**. Don't let him near those plants.*
- *The guy has assumed a political post that needs delicate moves, but he acts **like a bull in a china shop**.*

Background: This is a vivid simile. A bull being really boisterous, clumsy and strong (as opposed to a china shop being a fragile place) would just run into anything, smashing everything in its way.

The Discovery Channel's *Mythbusters* program once put this expression to the test. They placed shelves full of china inside a bull pen and released the bulls inside it. Surprisingly, the bulls actively avoided the shelves. A few dishes were knocked to the ground when as many as four bulls were running around, but overall they proved surprisingly nimble.

Some people argue that the bull-in-the-china shop myth was not really tested since the test done was not in a shop but in a yard that the bulls were more familiar with.

Sacred cow A person or thing that cannot be tampered with, or criticized, for fear of public outcry

- *He's widely acknowledged as one of America's great songwriters. But he's also the most sacred of music industry's **sacred cows**. I think he's simply overrated.*
- *Social Security is a **sacred cow** in America. Any member of Congress who does anything that would harm Social Security faces death at the hands of angry voters, especially senior citizens.*

Background: The term comes from cow worship in Hinduism - cows are considered holy and their slaughter is banned throughout most of India. They are allowed to roam around freely in a country where food supply has been a problem. This strikes many Westerners as silly and has led to the use of *sacred cow* as a term for any commonplace institution, object, idea or political process that is treated as if it were untouchable.

See also HOLY COW! later in the chapter.

Usage note: Such immunity from criticism is often looked upon as being unreasonable. The term is usually used cynically.

Until the cows come home For an extremely long time

- *You can apologize to them **until the cows come home**, but that is not going to change their low opinion of you.*

Background: Cows are sluggish by nature; they walk slowly unless being hurried along. Once out in pasture to eat grass, they won't make their way back to the barns until very late just in time to get milked again.

Usage notes:

1. Often used to describe something that is futile or unproductive

2. There's a Southern expression: *He'd rather wait until the cows come home*, meaning he is a procrastinator.

Where's the beef? An all-purpose phrase questioning the substance of an idea, event or product

- *The president's speech does sound good, but **where's the beef?***

Background: The phrase started off as a commercial for *Wendy's* fast food hamburger chain in the early 1980s. In the commercial, an older woman would go from one fast-food place to the next questioning the tiny piece of meat in a huge hamburger bun using the punch line *where's the beef?* (She finally finds the most meat at *Wendy's*, of course).

The phrase became an instant hit and was almost immediately transferred to other things, such as politics. During the Democratic primary debate between Walter Mondale and Gary Hart in 1984, Mondale used it to question Hart's "new ideas." Since then, *where's the beef?* has become one of the Hall of Fame political clichés.

• •

CHICKEN

ESPECIALLY FOR ENGLISH LEARNERS

TERMINOLOGY

Chicken (or poultry) is the meat from chickens. The breast and wings are white meat; the thighs and legs are dark meat.

Chicken is a general term; adult male chickens are known as roosters (in the UK, cocks). Females over a year old are hens and younger females pullets. Babies are chicks.

IN CASE YOU DIDN'T KNOW

In the U.S. *chick* is a common term used by men to refer to a young woman. This may sound offensive to some women, but other women sometimes use it in reference to themselves (*The Dixie Chicks*, a country music group, for example).

(I've heard that in England and Australia, the term often used is *bird*; in Scotland, it's *hen*.)

There are also *chick-lit* (i.e., literature) and *chick-flicks* – the books and movies that cater to women's needs and interests.

Chickadee is a term of endearment used by a man or by parents for their girls. A *chickadee* is any bird of the tit family. They are very small, have dark crested (or crowned) heads and are very common in the U.S. W.C. Fields (1880-1946), an American comic and actor, made this term famous in his 1940 movie *My Little Chickadee*.

A *chicken* when used as slang, means a coward, though not a harsh one. (Chickens are considered cowardly; the young ones especially, are very timid.)

- *"Come on! Don't be such a **chicken**! Go ahead and do it."*

There's a saying among rodeo people: *"Don't eat chicken the night before the big (rodeo)day, because* YOU ARE WHAT YOU EAT!*"* (See page 194.)

A **chicken-hearted** (also chicken-livered) person, therefore, is someone who acts cowardly.

To **chicken out** is to back out of something because one is afraid:
- *I **chickened out** of that business deal when I realized how risky it was.*

To **play chicken** is to take part in a game of physical hazard in which the first person to lose his or her nerve and withdraw from a dangerous situation is the loser (i.e., "the chicken" – the coward).

One such game is car racing, where two cars race towards each other to see who will swerve away first. An example: in the movie *Rebel Without A Cause* (1955), starring James Dean, there is a scene where two young men race their cars towards a cliff — the first one to turn aside is the chicken.

Figuratively speaking, it means to engage in mutual challenges and threats, hoping the opponent will withdraw before actual conflict:
- *Both leaders **played** a little high-stakes **chicken** with each other at the tail end of yesterday's economic talks. It's not clear who won –or who blinked.*

A **hen** as slang, means a woman, especially a fussy or nosy old woman.
A **hen house** is a house shared by several females (and females only).
A **hen's night out** is slang for a female social gathering (without men);
also for a pre-wedding celebration (also called, *a bachelorette party*).

To be **as fussy as a hen with one chick** (or **chicken**) is to be over anxious and absurdly fussy about small matters like a hen that never leaves an only chick alone.

Another related term is a **mother hen**, a person who worries and watches over other people especially in an overprotective, annoying way:
- *Our football coach often fusses over the players like a **mother hen**.*

The term **henpecked** is used in a derogatory sense to describe a husband dominated by his wife. It also applies to boyfriends.

In the chicken social hierarchy, all roosters are normally dominant to all hens. Occasionally, the rooster at the bottom of the rooster pecking order will actually overlap the pecking order of the hens. He will become submissive to one or more of the dominant hens.

• • • • •

COMMON CHICKEN-RELATED EXPRESSIONS

As scarce/rare/as hen's teeth Rare to the point of non-existence; very difficult to obtain
- *These records were extremely hard to find. They were **as scarce as hen's teeth**.*
Background: It refers to the fact that hens don't have teeth.

*"**Does a chicken have lips?**"* (Sarcasm) Stating the obvious like *"Duh!"* or *"Why are you asking such a stupid question?"*
- *"Was that calculus exam difficult?"*
  *"**Does a chicken have lips?**"*

Background: Chickens, like all other birds, have beaks. They survive by eating worms, seeds and small bits of vegetable matter, pecking them up from the ground with their horny beaks. They have no use for lips.

Usage notes:
1. Very common
2. Other similar expressions:
- *Is the Pope Catholic?*
- *Is the sky blue?*
- *Do fish swim?*
  Basically, you can make up anything you like.

Don't count your chickens before they're hatched. Don't assume something will be successful before it has happened.
- *You should wait until you actually get the promotion before making all those plans. **Don't count your chickens before they're hatched!***

Background: This proverbial advice is generally attributed to Aesop. In his fable *The Milkmaid and Her Pail*, a farmer's daughter is daydreaming about her profits from the milk (to be sold for eggs hatching into chickens) while walking to town with a pail of milk balanced on her head. She is so deep in her daydreams that she ends up spilling all her milk.

See also DON'T GUT YOUR FISH TILL YOU CATCH THEM on page 116.

Live like a fighting cock To live in luxury
- *We all thought he was wealthy. We had that notion because he was **living like a fighting cock.***

Background: Fighting cocks are well-fed in order to increase their size and strength. In some Asian countries, like Thailand and the Philippines, fighting cocks live a much better life than their food-destined counterparts. They are expensive to buy and are treated accordingly.

Usage notes: There are also other common expressions about "cocks" in English:
1. **Cock of the walk** is someone who dominates others within a group:
   - *The guy acts like he was the **cock of the walk**.*
     "The walk" is a place where the fowls are bred. A cock (rooster) would never allow any other cocks within this space.
2. A **cocky** person is someone who is arrogant and overbearing.
   Also, there's a saying: *He's like a cock, always crowing.*
3. A **cock-and-bull story** is an absurd or otherwise incredible story fabricated to deceive (or, possibly, to amuse). A common answer to

such a story is *"That's (a bunch of) bull!,"* which is a truncated or abbreviated obscenity. Note: it may sometimes be the only appropriate response, but it is always meant to be offensive.

4. *I felt like a duck at a cock fight* means "I had no stake in what was going on." A more common variation is *I have no dog in that fight.*

No spring chicken A woman past her prime

- *She's **no spring chicken** but she still dresses like she was 18.*

Background: A spring chicken is a young chicken, having tender meat and ready for eating.

Usage notes:

1. It often implies someone who fails to act one's age.
2. Some dictionaries use it to describe men. So, the term might not be gender-specific after all.

Run around like a chicken with its head cut off To be panic-stricken, rushing about in a disorderly way and failing to get anything done

- *I was **running around like a chicken with its head cut off** trying to get everything ready in time for the party.*

Background: It refers to the fact that a decapitated chicken may continue to run and flap its wings wildly for some time, although to no purpose (because it is dead!).

Scratch out a living To earn barely enough money to live

- *I somehow managed to **scratch out a living** during those tough years without having to borrow from my parents.*

Background: Chickens need to scratch to get their food (they are known for being industrious).

Usage notes:

1. It also gives us *chicken scratch* – unreadable or barely-readable handwriting.
2. A very little amount of money is often referred to as *chickenfeed*, because the grain scattered to chickens is small and cheap.

Taste just like chicken Phrase used when people try to get you to taste strange, exotic, new foods

- *"Come on! Eat this, it **tastes just like chicken**."*

Background: The reasoning behind it may be that chicken has a very basic taste compared to other meats, so it serves as a good measure to judge other meats by. Besides, most people have eaten chicken and know what chicken tastes like. The message this phrase conveys is that the taste is actually good, or at least it's blandly inoffensive.

From his perspective, Ogden Nash, an American light verse poet (1902-1971), has this to say:

> *"A gourmet once challenged me to eat*
> *A tiny bit of rattlesnake meat*
> *Remarking, "don't look horror-stricken*
> *You'll find it **tastes a lot like chicken***"
> *It did*
> *Now chicken I cannot eat*
> *Because it tastes like rattlesnake meat"*

The chickens come home to roost. A person's offenses and wrongdoings may eventually come back to cause trouble for himself.

- *You're sowing so much hatred and vengeance in your life that I can assure you that **your chickens will come home to roost** very soon.*

<u>Background</u>: Its full form is *curses are like chickens; they always come home to roost.*

Chickens which stray during the day return to their roost at night.

The sky is falling. Term used to denote a hysterical or mistaken belief that disaster is imminent

- *In the difficult economic environment we're experiencing, cries of **"the sky is falling"** may prove to be a self-fulfilling prophecy.*

<u>Background</u>: It comes from a nursery story about *Chicken Little* who, after being hit on the head by an acorn, ran around crying, "The sky is falling! The sky is falling! The moral of the story is: don't treat a small accident, injury or misfortune as if it were The End of the World. And the lesson to children is: "Don't lose your head because of some hurt or loss – life will go on."

<u>Usage notes</u>:
1. The term is used in a derogatory sense.
2. A **Chicken Little** also comes to mean a confirmed pessimist or an alarmist - a person who panics at the first sign of a problem.
   - *Don't be a **Chicken Little**! Try to focus on the possibilities!*
   - *I wonder how many entrepreneurs have succumbed because of 'a **Chicken Little**' mentality.*

See WHAT CAME FIRST, THE CHICKEN OR THE EGG? on page 55.

• •

COMMON DUCK-RELATED EXPRESSIONS

"You aren't the only duck in the pond."
(It's an old saying meaning "it's not all about you.")

Dead duck A person or thing that is beyond help, redemption or hope

- *One more missed opportunity and this business deal is a **dead duck**.*

There's an old saying: *"Never waste powder on a **dead duck**."*

Get/have/all one's ducks in a row To get all one's facts straight and all the small details accounted for before embarking on a new project

- *If you want the bank to approve your home loan early, you have to first **get all your ducks in a row**: a good credit history, a record of steady income and a down payment of at least $10,000.*

Background: There are a few plausible theories for the origin of this phrase. The first is from early variation of bowling, where the pins were called "ducks." To get started, you had to get your ducks in a row.

Another theory suggests that baby ducklings usually swim in a straight line behind the mother duck. If the ducklings stray too far, the mother will get them back in line; that is, get her ducks in a row.

It's also possible the term comes from the natural flight formation of ducks as they move through the sky. The most efficient arrangement is a V-formation behind the leader, which allows each duck to take advantage of reduced wind resistance (www.wisegeek.com).

Usage note: It is a common phrase in any type of negotiation.

If it walks like a duck and quacks like a duck, it's a duck. If you behave a certain way, it doesn't matter what you say about yourself, you are how you act.

- *He has all the earmarks of a pathological liar. You know what they say: **if it walks like a duck and quacks like a duck, it's a duck.***

Usage note: Sometimes simply shortened to *if it walks like a duck*

Comment: I've heard it used a lot on TV by the legal experts in discussing who "the suspect" might be in a certain case.

Lame duck An elected official on the way out, especially when a new one has been elected but not sworn in yet

- *Even though he was a **lame duck**, the president still worked very hard to secure his place in history.*

Background: The phrase was originally 18th century London business slang referring to investors who were unable to pay their debts.

Usage note: It's possible that some people may use this term to refer to a weakling, an ineffectual person, or someone who is not at the top of his or her abilities.

Like a duck/chicken/on a June bug To be absolutely on or after someone or something

- *She jumped on that comment **like a duck on a June bug**.*

Background: Ducks and chickens love to eat insects and worms. So when a duck sees a June bug, it will move at warp speed to try to gobble the bug down before it flies away.

<u>Usage notes</u>:
1. Used to describe someone doing something very quickly
2. *Like a duck on a June bug* is different from LIKE WHITE ON RICE
   (See page 67): one is striking or jumping on; the other is sticking with.

Like water off a duck's back   Criticism or advice that has no effect on a person
- *The bad reviews just rolled off the actor **like water off a duck's back.***
- *I tried to convince my sister to take that job, but my advice was **like water off a duck's back.***

<u>Background</u>: It refers to the fact that duck feathers shed water.

<u>Usage note</u>: It can be used in a positive or negative way.

Sitting duck   An easy target; a person in an exposed situation – open to attack and easily disposed of
- *Out in the unfamiliar terrain, the soldiers were like **sitting ducks** to the enemy.*
- *Women are generally **sitting ducks** to aggressive car salesmen (and mechanics).*

<u>Background</u>: A duck on the ground or floating on a pond - a sitting duck - is far easier to shoot than a flying duck.

It's now illegal to shoot ducks on the ground; it's certainly unsportsmanlike.

Take to something like a duck to water   Phrase used if someone has a natural talent for something and enjoys it
- *It was her first time teaching little kids, but somehow **she took to it like a duck to water.***

<u>Background</u>: Ducks like water.

<u>Usage note</u>: Similar in meaning to TAKE TO SOMETHING LIKE A FISH TO WATER (page 105)

• •

PORK

ESPECIALLY FOR ENGLISH LEARNERS

TERMINOLOGY

<u>Pork</u> is the meat from pigs.

<u>Swine</u> (no "s" at the end, even when used as a plural) is a generic term, referring to the pig family in a general way. It's also formal. It is used in connection with swine flu (influenza) and in citations from the Bible and fairy tales.

<u>Pig</u> is a young domestic swine.

The (really) young are called either <u>piglets</u> or <u>shoats</u>.

A <u>hog</u> is a domesticated pig raised for slaughter.

A mature female hog is called a <u>sow</u>.

A mature male hog, usually but not always castrated, is called a <u>boar</u>.

Both are sold as market <u>hogs</u> at 5-7 months of age and at weights of 220-260 pounds.

IN CASE YOU DIDN'T KNOW

A **porker** is an obese person; it implies someone who doesn't even try to do anything about his or her own weight.

A **pig** is a selfish or unpleasant person; also derogatory slang for a policeman.

A **hog** is someone who takes more than his or her proper share:

- *If I put too much food on my plate, I feel I look like a **hog** to others.*

There are all kinds of hogs: for example, a road hog, a conversation hog or a bathroom hog.

Also used as a *verb*: to **hog** something:

- *The guy likes **to hog** other people's **limelight**.*

Linguistically speaking, pigs are not generally treated kindly in the English language.

They are often associated with greed, obesity and gluttony.

Besides what has been mentioned so far, there are such expressions as:

As fat as a pig To be unusually overweight or obese

To **eat like a pig** To eat greedily and noisily, referring to bad table manners

To **pig out** is to gorge oneself on one's favorite food, usually done after a period of restraint from overeating:

- *I try to eat healthy, but every once in a while I enjoy **pigging out**.*

To **make a pig of oneself** is to eat too much:

- *I really **made a pig of myself** at the party last night. I couldn't help myself because everything tasted so good.*

And their lack of cleanliness:

The equating of pigs with filth can be seen in the expression **as happy as a pig in mud/poop/slop/shit** and in the underlying meaning of **sweat like a pig** – to sweat profusely.

On the surface, the expression *sweat like a pig* is illogical as pigs have ineffective sweat glands. That's why they need a good mud wallow where they can roll around to cool themselves off. People often associate heavy sweating with being filthy and associate pigs in their mud wallows with filth; they then somehow link the two together.

• • • • •

COMMON EXPRESSIONS

Cast pearls before swine To share something of value with those who have no appreciation for it

- *Don't waste your time! Trying to explain those concepts to him would be like **casting pearls before swine**.*

Background: Pearls are considered to be things of great value; swine are considered to be lowly animals.

The term comes from the Bible (Matthew 7:6). Its original meaning, according to one interpretation, is that followers of Jesus should pass his message on to those most likely to accept it.

Usage note: It can apply to thoughts, wisdom or even physical objects.

Don't buy a pig in a poke. Don't make any kind of deal until one has checked things over.

- *Since the candidate refused to answer any of the questions about the city's issues, the voters should look elsewhere. **Don't buy a pig in a poke!***

Background: "A poke" is a bag. It's a term no longer in much use. Literally, it means don't buy a pig in a poke until you have actually seen what is in the bag.

Usage note: Variant: ***Never trust a pig in a poke***

Eat/live/high on the hog To live well and prosperously

- *He's a millionaire; he can **eat high on the hog** at all times.*
- *She's been **living high on the hog** since she got the promotion.*

Background: The hog's upper parts (the sides, upper legs and shoulders) are the tastiest part and therefore, the most expensive.

Usage note: Also used, *eat/live/high off the hog*

Everything but the oink (Using) every last bit of something; wasting nothing

- *As pork connoisseurs like to say, you can eat **everything but the oink**.*

Background: No other animal provides us with a wider range of products than swine. According to www.foodservice.com, hog by-products are used in the production of clothing, shoe adhesives, fertilizers, bone china and even pharmaceuticals.

Comment: The first time I came across this expression, I couldn't guess what it meant because I had no idea that "oink" is the usual way the grunting of a pig is represented in English. Of course, other cultures hear the pig's grunts differently. Where I came from (Thailand), it sounds more like "ood ood."

Go hog wild To be out of control; so wildly excited as to be irrational or lose good judgment

- *Try not to **go hog wild** and spend all your paycheck on your shopping today!*

Background: It refers to the way hogs become wildly excited when aroused.

Go (the) whole hog Go all out, above and beyond; deeply into something
- *I've stopped eating meat and dairy for a while now; maybe I should* ***go whole hog*** *and become a vegetarian.*

In hog heaven In a state of utter bliss and contentment
- *My husband was* ***in hog heaven*** *over his new car.*
- *I would say that a hog rolling in mud is* ***in hog heaven***.

Background: (U.S. slang) No one seems to know its origin. It's likely just another one of those alliterative little phrases that we like so well.

Put lipstick on a pig To try to make someone or something look appealing or attractive when it quite clearly will not work or will only deceive the dumbest of people
- *It was just an old car with a new paint job that the salesman tried to pass it off as new. Talk about* ***putting lipstick on a pig!***

Usage notes:
1. Used to convey the message that making superficial or cosmetic changes is a futile attempt to disguise the true nature of a person or a product
2. Another expression used in this sense is ***look like a sow in a dress.***

Root, hog or die Phrase used to express the idea that one must do what is necessary to stay alive
- *He found out that* ***'root, hog or die'*** *was the law of combat. You took whatever you could. You had to fend for yourself or you didn't make it.*

Background: It's an old country expression. Domestic hogs were turned out to fend for themselves in the woods thus lowering the farmers' feeding cost. The hog had to "root" for its food or die.

Slicker than a greased pig Said of someone who is slick or sneaky
- *That politician took in so much money that his hands were probably* ***slicker than a greased pig.***

Background: Pigs run surprisingly fast. They can outrun people in just a few seconds. Many county fairs have greased pig catching contests. The impossibility of getting hold and keeping hold of such a slippery pig is the idea behind this expression.

When pigs fly/And pigs may fly. No way that is going to happen.
- *"Do you think you'll ever ask her out?"*
  " Sure, ***when pigs fly***.*"*
- *"Maybe we should elect this guy. He sounds like he can fix the economy."*
  *"**And pigs may fly**.*"*

Usage notes:
1. Used for humorous effects in response to someone's wishful thinking
2. Also, ***when pigs have wings; and pigs will/would/might/ fly***.

3. Other expressions with the same meaning:
   When hell freezes over!
   In your dreams!

You can't make a silk purse out of a sow's ear. You can't make a good quality product using bad quality materials.

- *You can't make a silk purse out of a sow's ear. This is also true with clothes. You can't make a good suit out of poor materials or poor workmanship.*

Usage note: Also, *you can't turn a sow's ear into a silk purse.*

• •

BACON, BALONEY, HAM, SAUSAGE, ETC.

Baloney! Nonsense! Any untruth, from an exaggeration to an outright lie in your face

- *The guy is just full of baloney. He doesn't know what he's talking about.*
- *Don't give me all that baloney!*

Background: *Baloney* (In England, *boloney*) was originally Bologna (Italy) sausage; just as a *frankfurther* is a Frankfurt (Germany) sausage and a *hamburger* is a Hamburg (Germany) sausage. Another name for a *frankfurther* (also called a *hot dog*) is *weiner*, a word derived from Vienna (or Wien), Austria.

(**Weiner** and **weenie** are also comic terms for the male appendage – especially where boys are concerned).

Baloney sausage is generally made from low quality scraps of meat cuts (In the U.S., the meats used can be chicken, turkey, beef or pork.), and that may be the origin of the slang term.

Usage notes:
1. There's a catch phrase **No matter how thin you slice it, it's still baloney** meaning, regardless of how many clever points or fine distinctions you're trying to make, what you're saying still retains its basic characteristics; i.e., is still false or is still nonsense.
2. Also used, **phony baloney** (either as a noun or adjective)

Bring home the bacon To earn money that supports one's family; to accomplish something

- *Now that Linda has a steady job, she can bring home the bacon.*

Background: According to www.worldwidewords.org, the phrase was first recorded at a 1906 famous boxing match between Joe Gans and Oscar Nelson for the light weight championship. The *Oxford English Dictionary* dates it from 1924. However, the term is widely believed to have come from the much older fairground contests of catching a greased pig, in which the winner was awarded the pig. Bacon was a valuable commodity then. If you had enough money to bring home bacon, something that wasn't common on the dinner table, then you were making good money.

Usage note: It's an equivalent to another modern-day expression, **bring home the paycheck.**

Ham it up To overact; showing expressions and emotions more obviously than is realistic; to be over the top; excessive

- *She likes to **ham it up** for the camera.*

Background: A ham actor enjoys his own performance and so has a natural tendency to overact. He thinks he is giving a great performance. It might be mentioned in this connection that the supposed ambition of every actor, ham or not, is to play *Hamlet* in the Shakespeare play of the same name. This does not mean that *Hamlet* is the source of "ham," but the closeness of the play and of a part that calls not just for good acting but great acting must have contributed to the widespread acceptance of the word "ham."

Hot dog Someone who is skilled or proficient in some field, especially in such sports as surfing, skateboarding or skiing

- *He thinks he's a **hot dog** but he's not.*

Usage notes:

1. Now it is more often used when someone is considered to be showing off:
- *While he's a skilled surfer, some of his critics said he's too much of a **hot dog**.*
2. Also used as a verb, to **hot dog** is to perform a dangerous or difficult act or stunt as a display of skill or daring.
3. **Hot dog!** is an exclamation of delight or enthusiasm.

Also, its jocular extension: **hot diggity dog!** is used to express extra excitement or anticipation

Comment: I was told that the term is still around though I have not heard anyone use it.

People who enjoy eating sausage and obey the law should not watch either being made. Because both require long and tedious processes to come up with the final product(s).

Also, if you see how sausage is actually made, you might lose some of your taste for it.

And the legislative process often involves compromise and deal-making and can become disillusioning and even ridiculous.

Background: The saying is generally attributed to Otto von Bismarck, first Chancellor of Germany (1871-1890).

Usage notes:
1. It is a very common saying in political contexts.
2. Variations:
   There are two things you never want to see being made: sausage and the law.
   Laws are like sausages – it is better not to see them being made.

Save one's bacon To rescue one from a difficult situation or harm
- *Our boat capsized in the storm. Luckily the lifeguards came just in time to **save our bacon.***

Background: According to one theory, it was originally "save one's bacon from the fire." What this suggests is that the bacon has fallen into the stove or the fireplace or has been too long in the skillet and must be retrieved immediately or it will be burnt to a crisp. It now usually refers to retrieving a bad situation or even saving one's own skin.

What am I, chopped liver? How come they overlooked me as if I'm not important?
- *How come they didn't invite me to their party?* **What am I, chopped liver?**

Background: Chopped liver is delicatessen food. It's calf or chicken chopped liver (chicken is traditional) used as sandwich spread, appetizer or side-dish. Johnny Carson often resorted to this expression on *The Tonight Show.*

Usage note: Used when one feels left out, often humorously

• •

TURKEY

ESPECIALLY FOR ENGLISH LEARNERS

TERMINOLOGY

Male turkeys are called toms; females hens.
Only male turkeys make a gobbling sound.

IN CASE YOU DIDN'T KNOW

Gobble, gobble is a common expression, and understandably so, for anything turkey-related.

Turkey Day is Thanksgiving Day.
(The Americans love to celebrate their Thanksgiving by feasting on turkey.)

In American slang, a **turkey** is someone who is incompetent, naive, stupid or inept. There's also a popular workplace quote: *"How can I soar like an eagle when I am surrounded with turkeys?"* Turkeys fly badly and only for short distances. This expression is not so much about intelligence (although that is necessarily involved) as about ability and performance.

Turkey is also frequently used to describe a play or movie, etc. that is very poor artistically and a financial flop.

COMMON TURKEY-RELATED EXPRESSIONS

Cold turkey Abruptly quitting an addictive substance, or any habit, without tapering off

- *He had to quit smoking **cold turkey** when he realized he had difficulty breathing.*

Background: One speculative theory is that it comes from ***talk (cold) turkey***. Another says it derives from the comparison of a cold turkey carcass and the state of a withdrawing addict – the cold sweats and goose bumps. Yet another suggestion is that the fact that cold turkey is a dish that needs little or no preparation may have given rise to this term.

Usage note: You can *go, quit, give up* or *kick a habit **cold turkey.***

Talk turkey To get down to facts or to the heart of the problem, no joshing around

- *Now is the right time to **talk turkey** about our national debt.*

Background: There are several debatable theories as to its origin. One is that the first contacts between the American Indians and the settlers often centered on the supplies of wild turkeys, to the extent that the Indians, whenever they met the whites, would always ask, *"You come to talk turkey?"* (www.worldwidewords.org)

Others think that it derives from the hunter's practice of making a gobbling noise so that the stupid turkey would answer with a gobble and give away its whereabouts. (www.randomhouse.wotd.com)

Another theory sounds more like a joke than a documented fact. It is a story of a white man and an Indian who went hunting together. They shot several birds, among them crows and turkeys. When it came time to divide the bag, the white man, thinking to take advantage of the Indian, always arranged the counting in such a way that he got the greater amount (or all the turkeys, depending on what version you read). Justifiably annoyed, the Indian protested, *"Stop talking birds, let's talk turkey!"*

Usage note: Other expressions with similar meaning: ***make no bones about something***; ***not mince words***

• •

OTHER TERMS AND EXPRESSIONS OF INTEREST

Bleed like a stuck pig To bleed profusely

Background: When a pig is slaughtered, its large artery in front of its heart is 'stuck' or cut with a sharp knife instantly, so that it will bleed to death very fast. This is done because a pig, if frightened, will release a hormone that can spoil the meat and leave it tasting very bad. So, a quick and thorough bleed is one of the basic steps in putting out high quality meat.

Cash cow A business or a segment of a business that produces a large, regular and predictable cash flow. Cash cows are often 'milked' to support new or struggling segments of the company. A good example of a cash cow business is the self-storage industry.

> Background: Its metaphor is rooted in the notion of a dairy cow that can be milked on an ongoing basis with little expense after being acquired.

> Usage note: The term is sometimes used sarcastically by sales people to describe a customer or an organization that has no control over its spending, especially government departments such as Defense and Social Security.

Chicken hawk A politician or a bureaucrat who now advocates war but once took special efforts to avoid military service (i.e., chickened out then but sounds hawkish now)

> Background: Originated during the Vietnam War, the term implies that chicken hawks are the ones who lack the experience and moral standing to make decisions about going to war.

> Usage note: In some parts of the U.S., the term refers to a gay man who prefers adolescent sexual partners. It has also been used for a straight man who seeks adolescent girls. (www.wordspy.com)

Chicken in every pot The Republican Party slogan in 1928 (The person who was reported to have said it first was Henry IV, king of France from 1589-1610.)

The full slogan was *a chicken in every pot and a car in every garage*. It was a promise to bring about prosperity for everyone.

The slogan was closely associated with Herbert Hoover (1874-1964), who won the election to become the 31st President of the United States (1929-1933). Because of the Great Depression that began in 1929, however, he never was able to fulfill his campaign promise.

Cow eyes Large, beautiful, innocent and/or/ docile eyes

> Usage note: To *make/cast/cow's eyes* (or to *cast sheep's eyes*) is "to look coy or docile yet clearly intend that the person looked at will find the looker attractive." (www.paininenglish.com)

Cow pie A piece of cow manure, called a pie because of its round and flat shape

> Usage notes:
> 1. Other terms also used are *cow patties*; *cow flop*; *cow plop*; *pasture patties* and *meadow muffins* (in Texas). In a dried state, meadow muffins become cow chips which can be used as fuel or in throwing contests.
> 2. **Road apple**, on the other hand, is the droppings of a horse (because they are round and somewhat hard).

Fine day for ducks Drizzly weather (because ducks like water)

> Usage note: Also, *a nice day for ducks/nice weather for ducks/nice weather if you're a duck*

Hogwash Meaningless, ridiculous talk; nonsense
- *"Do you think video games promote violence?"*
  "Hogwash!"

Background: The term comes from a "hogwash," a bucketful of kitchen scraps and leftovers given to pigs.

Holy cow! (Exclamation of surprise) A euphemism for "Holy Christ!"

Background: Cows are sacred to Hinduism. Travelers driving in India frequently have shouted at them the words *"Holy cow!"* as a warning not to hit a cow in their path.

On the *Batman* television series of some years back, Batman's side-kick, Robin, the Boy Wonder, was in the habit of exclaiming *"Holy Cow, Batman!"* when anything startling occurred.

Independent as a hog on ice Technically independent but powerless to act, just like a pig trying to move on slick ice will keep falling without getting anywhere

There's a Southern saying: ***He looks like a hog on ice***, meaning he's clumsy.

Madder than a wet hen Phrase used to describe someone who is raging mad

Background: Supposedly, chickens don't mind being in the rain but they don't like a bucket of water thrown at them or to get dumped in water. (Sometimes farmers will do this to their hens a few times to get them to lay new eggs.) By some accounts, chickens get extremely mad if they have to swim out of water, something that they are not good at.

Meatball (Slang) A stupid, clumsy, boring, slow-witted or uninteresting person. The term refers mostly to the physical appearance of the person. It's not as insulting or derogatory as ***meathead*** - someone who doesn't have any brains (since he has only meat in his head).

In the 70's sitcom *All in the Family*, Archie Bunker, a bigoted loading dock worker, often addresses his liberal son-in-law as *Meathead*.

Meat wagon Slang for an ambulance

Mutton dressed/dressed up/as lamb Middle-aged or elderly women who dress or act like they were much younger than they actually are, thereby attracting ridicule

Background: Lamb is meat from a very young sheep; mutton (the term mostly used in England) is lamb butchered at an older age.

Pecking order The social hierarchy among animals of the same species living in close proximity. Chickens, for example, establish a pecking order within minutes of being brought together in a coop – each pecks subordinate chickens and submits to being pecked by dominant ones.

<u>Usage note</u>: The term can also be used to refer to any other types of hierarchy:
- *As a Hollywood couple, they are at the top of the **pecking order**, each capable of commanding top projects and top dollars to go with it.*

Piece of meat A person of the opposite gender (usually women) viewed as a sexual object to satisfy one's sexual urge

<u>Usage notes</u>:
1. The term is often used with regard to night clubs and bars. One gets a *piece of meat* at a **meat market**, a place where the objective of a good number of people who frequent it is to find sexual partners.
2. Also used as a reference to lack of respect:
   - *She felt his eyes on her and felt like a **piece of meat**.*
3. You can also use a ***piece of meat*** to describe a person regarded merely as strong or useful physically, such as a laborer or a prizefighter, as in this Yiddish saying *"You are a **piece of meat** with two eyes."* (Used humorously or as an insult.)

Piggy (pig) in the middle A person caught up in a disagreement where he or she belongs to neither side but is affected adversely by the situation
- *I feel like a **piggy in the middle** whenever my parents have big arguments. And they've been doing a lot of that lately.*

<u>Background</u>: The term derives from an old children's game where two or more players throw a ball to each other and the person in the middle has to try to intercept it.

Pork barrel spending Government projects that benefit people in a particular area and make the politician representing that area look good to his or her constituents

<u>Background</u>: *Pork barrel* is a barrel used to store pork.

<u>Usage note</u>: A very common American political term; sometimes abbreviated to ***pork***

Rubber chicken circuit (Political term) The endless series of public luncheons and dinners needed to raise funds. The food served often includes chicken, which is cooked hours earlier and then reheated, giving it a rubbery texture. Professors and authors also have to endure the dull food of lecture tours.

Strange duck (or **queer duck**; **odd duck**) An eccentric person

Tenderloin Figuratively, the part of a city notorious for vice, crime and corruption

<u>Background</u>: Beef tenderloin is the cut from the cow's middle, the muscle that hangs beneath the central spine (between the sirloin and ribs). It is the most tender and most flavorful and therefore the most expensive cut.

The term alludes to the luxurious diet of corrupt police officers getting easy money from bribes.

To bed with the chickens and up with the rooster Classic expression — it alludes to the fact that chickens go to sleep at sundown and a rooster crows at first light.

Ugly duckling A person who lacks physical charm or appearance when young but develops later into a real talent or beauty

Background: The term comes from a tale by Hans Christian Andersen about a duckling who is rejected by the mother duck because he's so ugly. He later turns out to be a beautiful swan.

Why did the chicken cross the road? (the answer to which is "*to get to the other side*") is supposed to be one of the oldest and most famous joke riddles still in use in the English language. Its first known appearance in print was in 1847 in the *Knickerbocker*, a NY monthly magazine. (Wikipedia)

Comment: The first time my husband posed me the question, I could not answer it. I guess I tried too hard to come up with a clever answer. I was told later that the humor of the riddle comes from the fact that the answer is so obvious and straightforward and not tricky, as with most riddles.

7
......
Fish and Other Seafood

Humans have relied on seafood as a source of protein for thousands of years, even before they learned how to used clubs to hunt for animals. It's no wonder then that fish and other sea animals show up in a lot of sayings and expressions in English as well as in many other languages.

ESPECIALLY FOR ENGLISH LEARNERS

TERMINOLOGY

Fish vs. Fishes

Fish can be used both as a singular or plural form.

- *We caught four **fish**.*

One exception is the expression ***loaves and fishes***, which refers to the miracle performed by Jesus when he fed a crowd of thousands with only five loaves and two fishes (Matthew 14: 14-21).

- (*Most*) **fish are** *cold-blooded.* (referring to the creatures in the sea)
- **Fish is** *good for you.* (referring to the meat of the fish)

When you are talking about more than one kind or species of fish, both *fishes* and *fish* are used:

- *varieties of tropical **fish***
- *all the **fishes** of the sea*

The names of many kinds of fish are both singular and plural: s*almon, cod, carp, tuna, halibut, perch, flounder* and *mackerel,* to cite a few examples. But the plural of *shark* is *sharks* and the plural of *octopus* is *octopi.*

Most citizens of the sea are cold-blooded; the warm-blooded marine mammals always take an 's' for the plural: *whale, whales; dolphin, dolphins; porpoise, porpoises.*

The shellfish I can think of use the plural form: *clams, crabs, lobsters, scallops, shrimps, oysters.*

Caviar, on the other hand, is usually uncountable.

DIFFERENT MEANINGS OF THE NOUN "CATCH"

We talk about the fisherman and his **catch**:

- *He shared his **catch** with the others.*

Restaurant businesses often use the line **Our catch for today is...** (the name of the fish) to advertise their special fish for each day. It implies that the fish is fresh (i.e., it has just been caught). Whether this is true or not is another story.

If someone has caught a large number of fish (or a number of large fish), we say he has had **a good catch.**

Figuratively, **a (good) catch** is a person desirable as a dating partner or a spouse

- *Throughout much of my 20's, I wasn't what most people would consider **a 'catch'** since I was both heavy and insecure.*
- *The guy is too good **a catch** to pass up.*

• •

COMMON EXPRESSIONS

FISH AND WATER

"The best fish swim near the bottom." English proverb
(Nothing of worth can be gotten without trouble.)

Many other languages also have the same saying, including French, Chinese and Japanese.

"Only dead fish swim with the tide." Scottish proverb
(Don't compromise your values and integrity but go your own way.)

A big fish in a small pond An important or powerful person only in a limited area (because there is little or no competition)

- *At the moment he's **a big fish in a small pond** since he's in the amateur ranks, but by turning pro he'll be a very small fish in a big pond.*

Usage notes:
1. An American expression; the tone is fairly neutral - it simply describes a person's abilities or influence in relation to his or her surroundings. Oftentimes, though, it implies that the person is content with this situation.
2. There is also an expression: **Better a big fish in a small pond than a small fish in a big pond.** This one seems to indicate the degree of ambition in a person.
3. A **big fish** is slang for a person of importance.
   - *He works at the White House and I think he's quite a **big fish.***

   The term is often used to refer to some kind of a ringleader, to be hooked by law-enforcement officials:
   - *The police caught a very **big fish** involved in an international prostitution ring.*
4. **Small fry**, on the other hand, means a person or persons of little importance or influence. It can also mean small children:
   - *I'm getting tired of being a **small fry**. Maybe I should start looking for a job and do something with my life.*

*- The FBI was busy chasing the **small fry**, but let the big fish get away.*
The young, especially newly-hatched fish is called "small fry."

One always says ***small fry*** (never "small fries"), even when referring to more than one person or object. It is sometimes used as an adjective, for example: *a **small fry** politician.*

Cold fish A cold, aloof, unresponsive person

*- People often portray her as a **cold fish**. But she is not. She's a very caring person, someone who always reaches out.*

Usage notes:
1. The term is used in a pejorative sense to describe someone who gives the feeling of coldness and deadness.

   In the Czech language, such person would be called "a dead fish!"
2. Often with sexual undertones:
   *- She's such a **cold fish**. No one would want to date her.*

Drink like a fish To drink too much alcohol

*- He's a kind person. But he **drinks like a fish** and therefore is not very reliable.*

Background: The term probably originated in the belief that fish, which breathe through their open mouth (it's their way of extracting oxygen from the surrounding water, with the help of their gills), are constantly drinking.

Usage notes:
1. It is usually used in a derogatory sense.
2. ***Swim like a fish***, however, is a compliment. It means that he or she swims as well as a fish.

Like a fish out of water Awkward and uncomfortable in an unfamiliar situation or environment

*- Most of us will feel **like a fish out of water** when we go to a foreign country for the first time.*

Background: It alludes to the fact that water is fish's natural environment. They need water to survive; they cannot breath air and will die very quickly if left out of water too long.

Usage notes:
1. This is a very old expression that is still commonly used.
2. In such languages as French, Spanish, Chinese and Czech, there is an expression which can be translated into English as "like a fish in (the) water." English doesn't seem to have an exact equivalent. The one expression that comes close to it is (*to be*) ***in one's element***, which means doing what one enjoys or is good at in a familiar and comfortable situation or environment:
   *- My husband **is completely in his element** whenever he talks about his favorite topic — old cars.*

Another 'fish-related' expression with similar meaning is to **take to something like a fish to water** - to do something with ease, and possibly enjoy it:

- *Have you noticed that a lot of young people nowadays **take to music like a fish to water?***

See also TAKE TO SOMETHING LIKE A DUCK TO WATER on page 90.

Like/as easy as/shooting fish in a barrel Ridiculously easy

- *Learning how to use a computer nowadays is **like shooting fish in a barrel.***

Background: A barrel is a large, round bulging conical container, traditionally made of wood with a flat top and bottom of equal diameter, used for storage and shipping.

It's easy to shoot the fish swimming in confined space, such as a barrel (as opposed to the ones swimming in the stream).

Usage notes:
1. It's a standard expression used to describe something that is so easy that success is guaranteed.
2. Another expression used in this sense is LIKE TAKING CANDY FROM THE BABY (See page 158).
3. Or, to use a basketball term, *like a slam dunk* (i.e., forcing the ball through the basket from above)

Comment: From my standpoint as an English learner, the problem lies in the word "barrel." Once I found out what it meant, it was easy for me to understand this expression.

Live in a goldfish bowl To live under public scrutiny

- *Most celebrities **live in a goldfish bowl**. The more fame they seek, the less protection from the media they get.*

Background: A goldfish bowl is a small, round glass bowl where goldfish are kept as pets. This is often considered inhumane – it's not good for any type of fish to live in a bowl – no filtration, no oxygen, and the fish's waste will eventually kill the fish.

The implied message of the term is that one has absolutely no privacy. His or her life is always on display for everyone to see, just as you can see the goldfish through the transparency of the glass bowl.

It can apply to any public figure. Some people have to live their lives that way because of the nature of their work or because of who they are or who they are associated with.

Never offer to teach a fish how to swim. Don't give needless advice to someone wiser and more experienced than you are.

- *Don't try to tell me how to do my job. I've been working here a lot longer than you have; I know what I'm doing. Haven't you heard of the saying 'never offer to teach a fish how to swim'?*

<u>Usage notes</u>:

1. There are many other expressions with the same meaning:

- DON'T TRY TO TEACH YOUR GRANDMOTHER HOW TO SUCK EGGS. (Page 52)
- *Never teach your grandmother how to knit.*
- *Don't teach the dog to bark.*
- *Old foxes want no tutors.*
- *The old fox needs not to be taught tricks.*

2. It's also possible to play around with this expression:

- *Watch me! I'll try to teach this fish how to swim.*
- *He has just taught a fish how to swim!*

<u>Of interest</u>: Here are how some other languages express the same idea:

Japanese: *Sell Buddhist chants at the gates of Paradise*
(Also, *Preaching to Buddha*)
Russian: *Do not teach a pike to swim; a pike knows his science.*
(Also, *Eggs cannot teach a hen.*)
Thai: *Like teaching a crocodile how to swim*

• • • • •

FISH AND ITS FRESHNESS

"Fish is the only food that is considered spoiled once it smells like what it is."
P.J. O'Rourke, American humorist and political commentator (1947-   )

A fish begins to stink at the head. Any problem in an organization can be traced back to its leaders; any corruption or incompetence starts from the top down.

- *If a child is missing from the school, the principal has to be responsible for it, whether he or she personally knows that child or not. After all, **a fish begins to stink at the head.***
- *There are many factors contributing to his failed presidential candidacy – bad advisors, bad campaign organization, for example. But above all, it was the candidate himself. Like they say, **a fish begins to stink at the head.***

<u>Background</u>: It's a common belief that the freshness of a dead fish can be judged by the condition of its head. Similarly, when the person in charge is rotten, the rest will soon follow.

This saying (sometimes with a variant "rot" instead of "stink") appears in many languages. I once read that an estimated 36 European languages have it. One question that is rarely asked is whether it is literally true. According to an expert on fish cited by William Safire in his article *Rot at the Top*, there is no biological evidence to support this saying - everything would decompose at about the same rate, though probably the stomach, or any injured part of the fish would start to smell first.

Another fish pathologist I've read of has a more specific opinion: "when a fish rots, the organs in the gut go first." This idea seems to be supported by professional fish buyers who, before deciding on their purchase, would want to check the condition of the belly of the fish first.

Usage notes:

1. Whether *a fish begins to stink at the head* is a good metaphor or not remains open for discussion. It is, however, popularly used, especially when training people in management or leadership positions, or talking about success or failure of companies and organizations.
2. A curious variant in this same area — one that accepts responsibility for whatever has gone wrong — is *the buck stops here*, coined by Harry Truman, the 33rd U. S. President (in office between 1945-1953).

Fish and guests smell after three days. Don't outstay your welcome.

- *I never feel comfortable staying at someone's house for long. I guess I'm a firm believer in 'fish and guests smell after three days.'*
- *We already liberated these people. It's time we got out of their country. Remember the old saying: 'fish and guests smell after three days.?'*

Background: This expression is usually attributed to Benjamin Franklin.

Guests are nice to have for a while. But they can wear you out if they hang around too long, just like fish which will go bad easily.

Usage notes:

1. A very common saying
2. Other variations are:
   - *Fish and company stink after three days.*
   - *House guests are like fish; they begin to smell after three days.*
3. The 'three days' in the saying is not to be taken literally. It simply denotes the idea that the shorter the stay, the better.

Of interest: According to the *Dictionary of Ichthyology*, this is a saying in many European and Asian countries with variations such as "the fish and guests being *poisonous, odious, old, wearisome, smelly, stinky*," etc. but all giving three days as the limit.

Fishy Suspicious; questionable

- *Certain elements of her whole story seem a bit fishy to me.*
- *Something about him is fishy.*

Background: It means that it has a faint, unpleasant smell — as most fish do (even before they go bad).

Usage notes:

1. Interestingly, saying that something smells or tastes *beefy* or *fruity* is a compliment, whereas *fishy* means the opposite.
2. Mainly used to describe things or situations; sometimes applied to a person to suggest that he or she does not seem trustworthy:
   - *He seems very fishy to me.*

Green around the gills Looking ill; nauseated
- *After eating ice-cream the whole afternoon, Jane was **green around the gills**.*
- *When he got off the roller coaster, he looked really **green around the gills**.*

Background: The color 'green' is often associated, among other things, with sickness.

Gills, a breathing organ for fish, is also an old word for the skin around the jaw line, chin and ears.

Usage notes:
1. Used when someone is about to faint or throw up, often from the effects of overeating or motion sickness
2. Also sometimes used, ***blue around/about the gills***

• • • • •

FISH AND FISHING

"Fish where the fish are." A common saying among salespeople
(To sell what you are selling, you have to be talking to the right crowd.)

"Catch no more fish than you can salt." (Don't take on more than you can handle, the *fish* version of DON'T BITE OFF MORE THAN ONE CAN CHEW; see page 201.)

Cast a wide net To seek potential candidates, customers, materials, etc. from a large area
- *The president needs to **cast a wider net** and show that he wants a quality Cabinet, not just a familiar one.*
- *As a new small business owner, you have to decide sooner or later whether you want to **cast a wide net** or aim at a niche market.*

Background: The "net" here is a fishing net. The wider the net is cast, the greater the number of fish that can be caught.

Fish for To search for something by feeling one's way; to seek something in a sly or indirect way
- *She **fished for** coins in both pockets to put in the parking meter.*
- *The guy always **fishes for compliments**. That is just disgusting!*
- *Not knowing what to put in his term paper, John tried to **fish for ideas** from the instructor.*

Usage note: ***Fish for compliments*** is a very common expression.

Fish in troubled waters To try to take advantage of a confused situation to gain one's end
- *It was wartime and they **fished in troubled waters** by selling their electronic communication systems to both sides.*
- *While the company was on the brink of bankruptcy, John angled for a promotion, **fishing in troubled waters**.*

Background: Fish reputedly bite better in rough, or "troubled," water.

Usage note: Some people may interpret it to mean " to put yourself in harm's way in what you want to do":
- *John is thinking about selling illegal drugs to get money for his college tuition. That is just like **fishing in troubled waters.***

Of interest: The Chinese would say, "to loot a burning house."

Fish or cut bait To get serious and participate in this more important activity or make yourself useful in some lesser way
- *It's time to **fish or cut bait**. Do you still want to be in charge of the project?*

Background: "Cut bait" means cutting up dead bait. (Some people use it as if it meant to **throw in the towel**: to cut the bait off the fishing-line and go home.)

The allusion is to the nature of fishing in a cramped boat – everyone has to do his or her share; either one should be actively trying to catch fish or cutting up bait for others to use.

Usage notes:
1. Often used as an order and spoken with urgency to an indecisive person to make a choice one way or the other
2. A similar but very vulgar expression is ***poop/piss/or get off the pot.***

Fish out To extract something; to retrieve something, usually with some effort or difficulty
- *It took her a while but she finally was able to **fish out** her ring stuck behind a dresser drawer.*

Background: The term means "done in a manner similar to the actions of fishing."

Fish story A boastful, exaggerated story
- *Don't pay attention to him. He's just spinning another **fish story** of his to impress people.*
- *"Do not tell **fish stories** where the people know you; but particularly, don't tell them where they know the fish."* Mark Twain

Background: It alludes to the tendency of fishermen to exaggerate the size of their catch, especially **the one that got away**, i.e., the one they almost caught:
- *If you think this fish is big, you should have seen **the one that got away**. It was twice as big.*

There is also a saying, ***Every fish that escapes appears greater than it is.***

Usage notes:
1. ***The one that got away*** is often used figuratively to refer to a romantic interest or something good that one nearly had or that nearly happened:

- *As it turned out, she was **the one that got away.** I should have held on to her, and now I'm regretting it.*

2. Another expression with similar meaning to a ***fish story*** is a ***tall tale.***

Fishing expedition A search or investigation with the hope of discovering useful (and/or embarrassing or damaging) information but without any clear evidence or any indication of specific wrong-doing at hand when started

- *The president claimed that the Opposition Party went on a **fishing expedition** to smear good public servants.*
- *The police didn't really know who committed the crime. They were just mounting a **fishing expedition** in an attempt to get to a real suspect.*

Background: It is a metaphor that likens an investigation to an extended fishing trip. If one spends long enough time and casts a wide enough net, one is bound to score something. The information one finds may not be as significant as one has hoped, as when a fisherman comes up with an old boot or useless junk instead of catching a real fish.

Usage notes:
1. The term is often used in American legal and political circles.
2. It implies that the investigation is malicious, with improper ways of finding things out.
3. Often used in the expression ***go on a fishing expedition*** (sometimes, a ***fishing trip***)
4. ***Phishing***, on the other hand, is a term referring to online scams.

   You can become a victim of ***phishing*** when you are sent an e-mail or cell phone text message from someone falsely claiming to be an established legitimate enterprise that asks you to provide private information that will be used for identity theft.

Give a man a fish and you feed him for a day; teach a man to fish and you feed him for a lifetime. It's better to help people to stand on their own feet, instead of keeping them dependent on daily handouts; education is far more beneficial to the recipient than charity.

- *America's new approach to world food security: helping farmers around the world grow their own food, is much smarter than the decades-long policy of simply giving humanitarian aid and food to countries. As the old saying goes, 'give a man a fish and you feed him for a day; teach a man to fish and you feed him for a lifetime.'*

Background: This saying has been a slogan for all sorts of missions and social justice projects.

It is widely believed that it is originally Chinese. Specifically, it is attributed to Lao Tzu, a philosopher and the founder of Taoism (6th century B.C.).

Comment: From my personal experience, the Chinese, as hard-working as they are, are notorious for guarding their trade secrets; most don't like to share them with others outside their own families. My Chinese cousin once told me about this very common Chinese saying that he was taught when growing up: *"(It's OK to) teach a man how to eat, but don't teach him how to earn a living."* (i.e., something that will enable him to eat).

Could it be that Lao Tzu was well aware of this particular mindset of his countrymen when he came up with the 'fish' quote?

Hook, line and sinker Totally and undoubtedly

- *We fell for her story **hook, line and sinker**.*

Background: It's an American term. A sinker is a weight that is attached to a fishing line to keep it under the water.

Someone who is completely fooled is just like a hungry fish that gulps down not only the fisherman's baited hook, but the line and the sinker. In other words, he or she has been fooled beyond merely TAKING THE BAIT (also in this chapter).

Usage note: It's a hyperbolic expression since this practically never happens in real-life fishing, used to describe an extremely gullible person.

Hooked (on something) To be addicted to a drug; captivated by something or devoted to a habit

- *She has been **hooked on** cocaine for quite some time now. It's not going to be easy for her to get rid of this addiction.*
- *Once you start to read this novel, you'll be **hooked**.*
- *John is **hooked on** baseball; he never misses watching a game.*

Off the hook Free from blame; relieved of a worrisome obligation; no longer responsible for something

- *The suspect finally got **off the hook** because there was not enough evidence to convict him.*
- *Will you please let me **off the hook** for our dinner date tonight? I just found out I have to work late again.*
- *The boss got someone else to do the job, so Sue was **off the hook.***

Background: It alludes to a fish that is able to get off the fishing hook and swim away.

Usage notes:
1. The opposite term, **on the hook**, meaning to be responsible for (often in regards to finances), is not as commonly used.
2. **Off the hook** is also a hip hop expression meaning, awesome, really good:
   - *That new D.J. played music that was **off the hook**.*

Take the bait To react to something that someone has said or done exactly as he or she intended you to do

- *She just wanted to make you feel guilty. Don't **take the bait**!*

- *Our leaders carelessly* **took the bait** *of the Opposition Party and fell into their trap.*

<u>Background</u>: An obvious comparison of certain human responses to a fish seizing bait

<u>Usage note</u>: Also used, ***rise to the bait***

There are plenty of fish in the sea. There are many other choices available; there are other potential opportunities.

- *Cheer up! girl,* ***there are plenty of fish in the sea.*** *It just takes time to find the right guy.*
- *Too bad you lost out on that contract. But don't worry,* ***there are plenty of fish in the sea.*** *You may get a bigger contract next time.*

<u>Background</u>: The original version of this saying is quite old, dating from the late 16th century: *there are as good fish in the sea as ever came out of it.* The sentence structure is rather complicated, making it hard (even to native speakers, I suppose) to understand what it means. To paraphrase it, the fish in the sea right now are as good as the ones that have been caught earlier.

Figuratively, it means that you will find someone else (or get another opportunity at something) at least as good or even better and that you will have no trouble doing so at all.

The abundance of fish, and therefore the low cost, no doubt gave rise to this saying.

<u>Usage notes</u>:
1. This is a very common saying, most often used to comfort someone following a relationship breakup. Sometimes it is used when an opportunity of some sort has been lost.
2. Other variations:
   There are lots of (good/other) fish in the sea.
   There are plenty more fish in the sea.
   (He or she) is not the only fish in the sea.
3. Other expressions with the same idea:
   Not the only pebble on the beach
   Just because you missed the first bus doesn't mean there won't be another one coming along later/soon.

<u>Comment</u>: Someone even came up with a dating website called "plenty of fish."

• • • • •

FISH AND FOOD

"Little fish are sweet."
(An old saying meaning that even a small gift or small sum of money can be very welcome.)

As happy as a clam To be content with one's situation; feeling care-free
- *I don't need much - just a small house, a job, a TV and a computer and I'm **as happy as a clam.***
- *Under the covers, the little girl looked **as happy as a clam**.*

Background: This expression does not seem to make much sense unless one knows its original full version, *as happy as a clam at high tide* (or *high water*). Digging for clams has to be done at low tide in order to have any success. At high tide, the clams are nourished by particles of food floating in the water and they are safe from the attentions of gulls and human predators.

Usage notes:
1. Other 'as happy as...' expressions also used: ***as happy as a lark, as happy as can be, as happy as a bug in a rug, as happy as a dog with a bone***, AS HAPPY AS A PIG IN MUD (page 91)
2. According to Gary Martin at www.phrases.uk.org, the three most common 'as happy as...' similes are ***as happy as a clam; as happy as a sandboy*** (a Briticism; a sandboy was originally a boy offering boxes of sand for sale in the streets of London) and ***as happy as Larry*** (another Briticism; "Larry" is Australian slang for "hooligan")

Clam up To suddenly keep quiet or refuse to respond, often in regards to the divulging of information
- *The students **clammed up** when the principal walked in.*
- *As soon as the police took him in for questioning, he **clammed up**.*

Background: It likens closing one's mouth to the way a clam closes up its shell.

Usage note: Also, ***shut up like a clam***

Crabwise Sideways or in a cautious or roundabout manner
- *We had to edge **crabwise** along the crowded row of seats.*
- *He approaches life **crabwise** rather than head-on.*

Background: It alludes to the fact that when crabs scuttle along, they often move sideways.

Perhaps, the song *Crabs Walk Sideways* by the Smothers Brothers in the 1960s would help one remember what "crabwise" means:
"Crabs walk sideways and lobsters walk straight,
And we won't let you take her for your mate."

Usage note: There is a saying: **You can't make a crab walk straight** signifying attempting the impossible.

Fine/pretty/kettle of fish A mess; a sticky situation; an unpleasant predicament
- *Well, this is **fine kettle of fish** you've gotten us into! Well done, moron!"*

Background: A Briticism

"A fish kettle," used for cooking fish, is an oval-shaped pot or kettle which can hold more than one fish. The term derives from the Scottish riverside picnic where freshly caught salmon were boiled and eaten out of hand. Eating this way was quite messy.

A "fine or pretty kettle of fish" would be an awkward or perhaps hopeless situation (as it certainly would be to the fish simmering in the kettle or pot).

Usage notes:
1. Usually used as an exclamation
2. Another related term is a **different/another/kettle of fish** meaning a different scenario; another matter entirely.
   - *"I got a ticket for illegal parking this morning."*
     "Me too! I got one for speeding and driving without a license"
     *"Come on! That's a **different kettle of fish**."*

A more American term is *a horse of a different color.*

Like a fishwife Loud and foul-mouthed; crude and lacking social graces
- *Use your common sense, and don't shriek into my ear **like a fishwife**!*
- *She's got a mouth **like a fishwife**.*

Background: The original meaning of "wife" was simply "woman." So, a fishwife was a woman who sold fish. Since fish was highly perishable, the fishwives would yell loudly so as to attract attention to their wares and hopefully earn a living. Their association with the sailors on the dock also led to their unladylike speech and behavior.

Usage notes:
1. The term has derogatory connotations about women's temperaments, vocal characteristics and vocabulary.
2. Other verbs you can use:
   - s**wear/cuss/like a fishwife**
   (A female equivalent of *swear like a drunken sailor*)
   - *screech, scream, yell, holler, shout, squabble, snap, gossip*
3. Not always gender-specific:
   - *This guy harps on every missed opportunity and repeats it over and over. He whines and nags **like a fishwife**.*

Other fish to fry Other things to attend to and can't afford to give time and attention to this thing – whatever it is – that you have now presented me with
- *He didn't seem to be interested in the project I presented to him. He might have **other fish to fry**.*

Usage note: Also, **bigger fish to fry** (more important things to do)

Packed (in) like sardines Extremely crowded
- *Whenever I envision being **packed in like sardines**, as in a subway train, I often think of sweating armpits and unpleasant degrees of contact with strangers of all types.*

<u>Background</u>: It alludes to the way tiny sardines are tightly packed in cans.

<u>Usage note</u>: Also used, ***jammed like a canned sardine; jam-packed***

<u>Of interest</u>: The Japanese would say "packed in like sushi" (take-out sushi comes in a small box).

Red herring The deliberate diversion of attention from the real issue
- *Those were just **red herrings** the company showed to an auditor – some interesting but minor problems. But they did distract the auditor from the really serious issues that may be found elsewhere.*
- *The police followed all the leads but in the end they were all **red herrings**.*

<u>Background</u>: Fresh herrings are gray and hardly have any smell; smoked herrings are reddish brown and have a very strong smell.

In training hounds to hunt foxes, smoked herrings were dragged on a string through the woods to lay down a trail of scent for the hunting dogs to follow. Later in the training exercise, the herrings were sometimes dragged across the scent trail of a real fox to test the ability of the hounds to ignore a false trail and stick to the scent of the fox. From this practice comes our use of red herring to mean "a diversionary tactic."

• •

OTHER TERMS AND EXPRESSIONS OF INTEREST

A woman needs a man like a fish needs a bicycle. A feminist slogan, suggesting that men are superfluous to women's needs (i.e., women don't need men at all). It can also be used in other contexts.

All cats love fish but hate to get their paws wet. Sometimes we want things but we don't like to do the work that is necessary to get them.

Bait and switch An unethical, (and in many places illegal), tactic of attracting customers by advertising a really good bargain ("bait"), which is in very limited (if any) supply, then pitching some inferior but more expensive offer to them ("switch"). This practice was often resorted to by used car dealers at one time.

<u>Usage note</u>: The term is also used in political contexts.

Better than a slap in the face with a wet fish A humorous way of saying, "it's pretty good!"
- *"How was the food at the new restaurant you went to last night?"*
  "Better than a slap in the face with a wet fish!"

<u>Usage notes</u>:
1. It can also be used sarcastically to mean "it's not that bad; things could be worse," usually when someone is moaning about something.
2. Other similar expressions: ***better than a poke in the eye; better than a kick in the stomach***

Big fish eat little fish. The rich and powerful are likely to prey on those who are less strong. The term is used with the implication that each predator is in turn victim to someone who is stronger.

<u>Usage note</u>: Other terms also used are ***the food chain*** and ***the law of the jungle***.

Crabs in a barrel syndrome People who envy your success may go out of their way to do things to hold you back.

<u>Background</u>: You never need to put a lid on a basket of crabs to prevent their escape. No single crab can get out because the others are always hooking its legs with theirs and dragging it back.

Crooked as a barrel of fish hooks Very dishonest

<u>Usage note</u>: Also, ***crooked as a dog's hind leg***

Don't gut/count/your fish till you catch them. The *fish* version of the more well-known DON'T COUNT YOUR CHICKENS BEFORE THEY'RE HATCHED (page 86)

<u>Of interest</u>: Here's how this idea is expressed in other languages:
Dutch: *Don't cry herrings till they're in the net.*
Indian: *Don't bargain for fish which is still in the water.*
Italian: *Don't cry fried fish before they are caught.*

Fish eaters A reference to Catholics who used to be required to eat fish rather than meat on Fridays

<u>Usage note</u>: Also, ***mackerel snappers***, ("snapper" means a biter, an eater) used humorously or mildly derogatory; and ***mackerel snatchers***

Holy mackerel! An exclamation expressing astonishment

<u>Background</u>: It's a euphemism for the original sacrilegious exclamation "Holy Mary!" or "Holy Mother of God!"; also related to the term ***mackerel snappers.***

<u>Usage note</u>: There are a lot of "holy-" exclamations in English: ***Holy Moses! Holy moly! Holy smoke! Holy cats!*** HOLY COW! (See page 99).

Look like a boiled lobster To have a severe case of sunburn

<u>Usage note</u>: Also used, ***as red as a boiled lobster***

Mackerel sky Sky with extensive clouds that look like scales on a mackerel – usually signaling the coming of rain. A more common term is ***buttermilk sky.***

Neither fish nor fowl This is a very common phrase. It is said to be based on medieval class distinctions as indicated by diet: fish being eaten by the clergy, flesh or fowl by the rich and red herrings by the poor. This may be true, but it has little to do with the expression widely used in the U.S., *neither fish nor fowl*, which refers to someone or something that doesn't fit into either of two contrasting categories, having the defining characteristics of neither. An example would be: *The political commentator is **neither fish nor fowl** – he's not a liberal and he's not a conservative.*

Queer fish Someone with odd habits or whose personality you don't quite understand

Usage note: Also, *queer bird*, QUEER DUCK (page 100)

Shrimp Undersized child or person

Usage note: Often used in a derogatory way

Surf and turf A main course in some steak houses which combines seafood and meat; for example, lobster and steak. "Surf" refers to seafood; "turf" is beef fed on grass.

The world is my oyster. The world is full of opportunities ready to be taken, and therefore, I can get anything that I want.

- *I remember when I finally received my B.A. in English, I thought **the world was my oyster**. It wasn't; I ended up working as a restaurant cashier for three years after that.*

Background: Sometimes a bit of foreign material (grit) is trapped inside the shell of an oyster. The oyster responds to the irritation by coating the foreign object with a smooth surface of nacre (a combination of calcium and protein). It becomes a pearl.

This saying likens the world to an oyster – something from which a person may extract or derive advantage. Shakespeare uses it in his *The Merry Wives of Windsor* (Act 2, Scene 2).

Throw a sprat to catch a mackerel To gain a lot by paying a very small price or doing very little

Background: A sprat is a small herring-like fish found in Europe.

Of interest: Other cultures have a similar idea:

Thai: *To use shrimps to bait a perch*

Japanese: *To fish a snapper with a shrimp*

Warm the cockles of one's heart To make someone feel pleased and happy

- *This 'dog' movie will definitely **warm the cockles of anybody's heart**.*

<u>Background</u>: The origin is still unsettled. The shell of the cockle, a mollusk, is somewhat heart-shaped, and this may have given rise to "cockles of the heart."

A different theory is that it comes from the Latin name for the chambers of the heart "cochleae cordis."

<u>Usage note</u>: An old-fashioned term; a light, humorous way of saying, ***warm one's heart***

8
. . . . .
Spice It Up!

"He who has spice enough may season his meat as he pleases." English proverb

Strictly speaking, there is a distinction between <u>seasonings</u>, <u>spices</u> and <u>herbs</u>. *Seasonings* are what affect the basic tastes the tongue is capable of sensing - bitter, sour, sweet and salty. Examples of seasonings are *vinegar, salt,* SUGAR AND HONEY (See page 150).

Spices are from the bark, root, stem, seed or fruit of a plant (pepper, for instance, is a spice from the fruit of a vine) whereas *herbs* are from the leaves of a tree or plant. Spices seem to have a sharper flavor than herbs.

For many of us lay people, spices and herbs are just types of seasonings. It actually makes sense if one defines seasonings as *anything* that flavors food. It's easier to think of salt and pepper, for example, as seasonings rather than salt as being a seasoning and pepper a spice.

Season (verb) To add zest or interest to something
- *He knows how to **season** his speech with humor.*
- *His book is a lot like his newspaper columns: short, conversational essays, heavily **seasoned** with one-liners.*

<u>Usage note</u>: It can also mean to cause someone to gain experience and become more skilled; gain toughness and strength:
- *The governor needs a lot more **seasoning** before he gets a prime time slot.*
- *We obviously want the **seasoned** voices that viewers have come to know over the years on our show.*

Spice up To make something more interesting or exciting
- *Math can be boring, so I try to **spice up** my lectures by throwing in a few jokes.*
- *The basketball star's infamous real-life brawl will also be included in the movie to **spice it up** a bit.*
- *This article gives a lot of good advice on how to **spice up** your personal relationships and love life.*

<u>Usage notes</u>:
1. The basic meaning of both *season* and *spice up* is the same - to enliven something, making it more interesting; but *spice up* covers more ground, giving us the sense of either excitement or novelty, as well as adventurousness and eroticism.
2. **Variety is the spice of life** is a very old but still an often-quoted saying. It means that life would be dull if we were limited in our experiences.

A wide range of activities provide a full enjoyable life (spice).
- *He has always liked country music; now he is interested in opera, reggae, cajun, blues, you name it. As they say, **variety is the spice of life**.*

• •

COMMON EXPRESSIONS

MUSTARD

"It's like getting mustard after dinner." Polish saying (Too little, too late)

Doesn't cut the mustard Doesn't meet one's needs; doesn't perform satisfactorily
- *If this guy **doesn't cut the mustard**, we have to fire him and look for someone else.*

Background: The phrase is of U.S. origin and was first recorded in 1907 in a story by O. Henry called *The Heart of the West*: *"I looked around and found a proposition that exactly cut the mustard."*

Some say that it's a corruption of the military phrase, to *pass muster* (to pass inspection), indicating that military standards have been achieved. But why "cut" then? Others say that a cowboy expression *the proper mustard*, meaning the genuine thing, may be the origin – in the 19th century, the word "mustard" was used in the sense of "excellence."

I've also heard of another source for this phrase. On the old farmsteads of rural America, a man worked in the fields until he was too old for such heavy work. But, even then, he could still go out into the kitchen-garden and cut the mustard greens for the dinner table. However, inevitably, there would come a time when he wouldn't be able to do even that. He could no longer *cut the mustard.*

Usage notes:
1. It is often used in the negative.
2. Often shortened to **doesn't cut it** (meaning, not good enough) – a very common expression:
   - *Her explanation just **doesn't cut it**. It sounds more like an excuse to me.*
3. The expression **too old to cut the mustard** is always applied to men and conveys the idea of sexual inability.

• • • • •

PEPPER

"Throw salt in his eyes, pepper in his nose." Yiddish saying, used as an insult.

Pepper (verb) To sprinkle with pepper; to jab repeatedly or spray as with shotgun pellets
- *My mother was the queen of Thai idioms and sayings. Oftentimes they were **peppered** throughout any reprimands we children received from her.*

*- Angry stockholders **peppered** the chief executive with questions over the company's poor performance.*

Pep up To become energized

*- I feel really tired. I need a few cups of coffee to **pep me up**.*

<u>Background</u>: It is a shortened form of "to pepper" dating from the mid 19th century, used in the sense of "energy boost."

The name of the soft drink *Dr Pepper* has been explained as a play on the word "pep"– a "pepper" being something that peps you up.

<u>Usage note</u>: Other 'pep' phrases are:

Pep rally - A large gathering of people intended to arouse enthusiasm

*- The senator held a **pep rally** Wednesday to kick off his re-election campaign for next November's election.*

Pep talk - A brief, intense and emotional talk designed to increase confidence, enthusiasm or bolster morale

*- The coach's half-time **pep talk** really helped to turn the game around; they beat a much better team in spite of all odds.*

Full of pep - Full of energy and high spirits

Another common term often used is ***perky*** (easy and sprightly in manner)

• • • • •

SALT

"Salt is what makes things taste bad when it's not in them." Unknown

In these days of low-sodium diets, where salt is often considered an enemy, we tend to forget how precious salt has been to man throughout history – indispensable to life, vital to the preservation of food and a delicacy in cooking.

There are a number of expressions related to salt which reflect its value and importance, some of which are no longer current; for example:

True to one's salt Loyal to one's employer

Eat salt with someone Enjoy someone's hospitality

Salt of youth Amorous passion

It's the term coined by Shakespeare in *The Merry Wives of Windsor*, Act 2, Scene 3: *"We have some salt of our youth in us."*

Sit above the salt Be in a position of honor

Sit below the salt Have low social standing

These two expressions refer to the old custom of putting the salt cellar (or salt shaker) in the middle or some distance down a long table at a public or elaborate dinner. The guests of higher social status – royalty, nobility, the titled gentry, heroic generals, and so on – were seated "above the salt." Those of lower social standing were seated farther down the table and so found themselves "below the salt." In time, "below the salt" became a recognized phrase, often used whimsically or modestly, about one's own social status. The phrase, "above the salt" was not often used.

The following are in current use:

Back to the salt mines A return to hard and tedious work (after a relaxing break)

- *Lunch break is over. Time to get **back to the salt mines**!*
- *School starts tomorrow; **back to the salt mines** again - with all the homework and getting up early every morning.*

Background: It summons up an image of habitual confinement as well as drudgery - extremely hard, thankless physical labor.

The term originated in the mid-20th century. It was based on an idea, widespread in the West that Imperial Russia and later the communistic Soviet Union habitually sent prisoners, both criminal and political, to work in the salt mines of Siberia.

Usage note: Other expressions also used: ***back to the old grind; back to the mill***

Rub salt in someone's wound(s) To make someone's sorrow, regret, pain or bad experience worse, whether deliberately or with good intentions

- *He feels bad enough for losing that job. You don't have to **rub salt in his wound** by telling him how good his replacement is.*

Background: Salt used to be rubbed in wounds to help them heal and as a primitive antiseptic. This caused intense pain.

Usage notes:
1. Variant: ***rub/pour salt into the wound***
   Also, ***rub salt in an old wound***
2. It has been suggested that this is how the expression ***rub something in*** (to keep bringing up something unpleasant to make someone feel worse) originated:
   - *She always **rubs in the fact** that she went to college and I didn't.*
3. Another expression, ***add insult to injury*** is a little bit different from ***rub salt in someone's wound***. It means to make a hurtful situation even worse:
   - *It was bad enough we had to park so far away from the concert hall. To **add insult to injury**, it started to rain when we were trying to make our way back to the car.*

   Someone came up with this clever analogy: it's like when you punch someone's nose, breaking it, then say *"it was an ugly nose anyway!"* (www.everything2.com)

Salt and pepper (hair) Referring to hair that is partially black (or dark brown) and partially gray

- *Former President George W. Bush went from **salt and pepper** to just salt in what seemed like a blink of an eye.*
- *His hair was jet black at one time. Then came **salt and pepper**, and now he's running out of pepper.*

Background: From "salt and pepper" – a traditionally paired set of condiments on western dinner tables

Usage note: The term **salt and pepper** is also used in the entertainment business to refer to TV or movie pairing a white person and a black person. An example: Bill Cosby and Robert Culp were the first **salt and pepper** duo on an old American TV series *I Spy.*

Salt away To put aside, put in reserve

- *She makes a lot of money, but she's smart enough to **salt some away** each month rather than spending it all.*

Background: The term alludes to using salt as a food preservation. Meat and fish can be preserved for a long time if they are packed in salt because salt kills bacteria that would cause spoilage. If you "salt money away," you save it for future use.

Usage note: The phrase nearly always refers to money (usually with the understanding that only a little bit is put away each time).

Salt of the earth A person or people of great honesty, modesty, reliability

- *He's just a good, solid, decent person – **salt of the earth**, always lending a helping hand to friends who need help.*

Background: Salt preserves and purifies. According to one interpretation, Jesus uses the term to convey the idea that his disciples are responsible for preserving certain values and exerting a purifying influence on others (Matthew 5:13).

Usage notes:
1. The term denotes genuineness and positive ordinariness. Calling someone **salt of the earth** is a great or perhaps the highest compliment.
2. Sometimes used patronizingly by the rich and self-important to refer to those they would never actually come in contact with, i.e., it's an insincere way of elevating the hoi polloi (the common people); sometimes said with some condescension.

Salty Tasting like salt, having too much salt

- *This soup is too **salty** for me.*

Usage notes:
1. As slang, **salty** means angry, annoyed or having a bad attitude toward someone or something:
   - *"Don't get all **salty** with me just because your cat died!"*
2. **Salty** also refers to language that is "off color," lewd or risqué.
3. A **salty dog** is a well-seasoned sailor, rough and experienced. (Another term also used is an **old salt**, from the fact that sailors sail on the salty ocean.)
   Salty dog is also a drink of vodka and grapefruit juice with a salted rim.

Take something with a grain of salt To not entirely believe a story, or view it with a healthy degree of skepticism and reservation
- *Because she tends to exaggerate things, I often* **take what she says with a grain of salt.**
- *I can't verify all of these stories, so do* **take them with a grain of salt**.

Background: The term is a translation of an ancient Latin phrase, *cum grano salis*. The idea behind this expression is that the topic in question may be difficult to swallow and a little seasoning (i.e., by means of skepticism) might make that easier, just like a dash of salt can make bland food easier to eat.

Usage note: The British use is to **take something with a pinch of salt**.

A pinch is the amount you can pick up between the tips of your thumb and forefinger, a very small amount.

An interesting point about this version is that it allows you to place even more stress on your skepticism, *take it with a big pinch of salt*, for example, something that doesn't work with "grain."

Worth one's salt Efficient or capable; deserving of one's pay and respect
- *Anyone* **worth their salt** *will give 110% work each day.*
- *These CEO's are getting paid outrageously high salaries; most are not really* **worth their salt.**

Background: It was once believed that Roman soldiers were paid in salt, but most scholars now agree that they were given an allowance so that they could buy salt, a valuable commodity at that time. This allowance or payment was called a "salarium" and our word "salary" comes from it. When someone today says that a worker is "worth his salt," that someone is probably speaking truer than he or she knows – for "salt" and "salary" were once pretty much the same thing.

Usage note: It's now the term used to refer to a good worker.

• • • • •

VINEGAR

"When one always drinks vinegar, one doesn't know that anything sweeter exists." Yiddish saying

Full of piss and vinegar Full of youthful energy and vitality, extreme exuberance
- *I like him a lot; he's* **full of piss and vinegar** *– a real fighter, willing to make mistakes.*
- *Watch out! she's* **full of piss and vinegar** *today.*

Background: The first citation appears in John Steinbeck's *The Grapes of Wrath* (1938), but it was probably in colloquial use well before then.

Usage notes:
1. Some of the adjectives one can use to describe the idea of this expression are *feisty, ebullient, frisky, spunky, spirited and lively, ornery and mischievously playful.*
2. Often used as a compliment
3. Some dictionaries list FULL OF PEP (see earlier), *full of ginger* and FULL OF BEANS (Page 34) as its synonyms.
4. It is somewhat crude (i.e., the use of the word "piss"); many consider it vulgar and therefore never use it in polite conversation.

There are also some who try to be polite and use *full of pith and vinegar* instead of the original expression. ("Pith" is the soft sponge-like tissue in the core of the stem of certain plants; it can also mean "energy or concentrated force.")

You can catch more flies with honey than with vinegar. It's easier to get what you want if you do it in a nice, polite way than if you are confrontational, mean or rude.

- *You can catch more flies with honey than with vinegar is a good saying to live by. It doesn't always work, though. Sweetness alone is not enough sometimes. You also have to be assertive and respond to what works in the situation at hand.*

Background: The idea here is that if you are trying to catch and control a lot of annoying pesky flies, you'll catch more of them by using honey (which is sweeter and more attractive) than vinegar (which is sour and repulsive) in your trap.

Usage note: Another version of it that a lot of people also use is *you can catch more bees with honey than with vinegar.* Since flies are more likely to be attracted by honey whereas bees produce and store it, the 'flies' version does make more sense.

• • • • •

GRAVY

Gravy (Slang) An extra bonus; profit or unexpected reward

- *"To fulfill a dream, to be allowed to sweat over lonely labor, to be given a chance to create, is the meat and potatoes of life. The money is the gravy."* Bette Davis, American actress (1908-1989)

Background: The analogy is to the juices constituting gravy, which effortlessly and naturally drip from meat and vegetables during cooking.

Gravy is rich, decadent and fattening; the word is often used to describe luxuries or large amounts of money.

Usage notes:
1. A more-or-less synonymous expression is ICING ON THE CAKE (See page 153).

2. Used as an adjective to mean that something is cool, good, awesome:
   - *I love this new job. It's all* **gravy**.
3. Also used in the expressions: **everything else is gravy; the rest is gravy**:
   - *My mom taught me that as long as I have my health and my family,* **everything else is gravy.**
   - *If $1 covers the cost of this product,* **the rest is** *then* **gravy**. *At $2, I'm basically making a 100% profit.*

Ride the gravy train   To secure a position that provides good pay with little work involved
   - *The guy is making $5 million a year. He'll probably want to* **ride the gravy train** *for as long as he can.*

Background: The origin is not clear, except that it is related to the earlier slang *gravy*. Some say that it was railroad slang during the 1920s describing workers who got paid well for doing a relatively short or easy stretch of track. Others think the phrase originated among hobos and vagabonds around the same period, who hopped freight trains and whose life became easier because they now had shelter combined with transportation.

Usage notes:
1. Other expressions also used are **sitting pretty** and **living on Easy Street**.
2. There's also a newer term, **gravy time** which is defined as "a period of success, pleasure or good results" (www.doubletongued.org).

• • • • •

SAUCE

"Hunger is the best sauce in the world." Cervantes (1547-1616)

On the sauce   (Slang) Drunk
   - *He's going to feel really bad in the morning after being* **on the sauce** *all night.*
   Background: It refers to the runny texture of the liquor.
   Usage notes:
   1. "The sauce" is slang for hard liquor.
   2. Also, **off the sauce; back on the sauce**
   3. **To be sauced** means to be extremely drunk
      - *Man,* **I'm** *so* **sauced** *right now.*

What is sauce for the goose is sauce for the gander.   What applies to one person applies to another — they should be treated the same, not subject to different standards.
   - *If her husband can go out and have a good time with his friends, surely she can too with hers.* **What is sauce for the goose is sauce for the gander.**
   Background: The gander is a male goose, whereas the female is simply

called a goose. Once they are cooked, they both taste the same and for this reason, they are served with the same sauce.

The weight of this saying is on gender – the sexual difference.

Usage notes:

1. It is sometimes used in non-sexual contexts:
   - *If a child has to wear a seat belt for a safety reason, then the parents have to wear seat belts too.* **What is sauce for the goose is sauce for the gander.**

2. **What is sauce for the goose is sauce for the gander** is the original saying. However, the variant, **what's good for the goose is good for the gander** seems to be more common nowadays.

3. Another way to say this might be *two can play at that game*, used as a threat or retaliation.

• •

OTHER TERMS AND EXPRESSIONS OF INTEREST

As keen as mustard Very eager and interested in everything
   - *He's as keen as mustard. You can never say that he lacks enthusiasm. He's made it very clear that he is excited to become part of our team and help us win this year's championship.*

Background: "Keen" is a synonym for "sharp." It implies a tang, a sting and of course, an edge. (Most mustard today is rather bland, but presumably it was originally very pungent.) A lively and assertive person is said to be "full of mustard."

Usage note: This expression is quite archaic, dating from the mid 1600s. The usage is British and is listed "old-fashioned" in most dictionaries.

• • • • •

Condiments vs. Seasonings

The difference between **condiments** and **seasonings** is not always clear.

Most people, when talking about condiments, often think of something pungent like *onions* or something hot like *chili*.

Condiments can be in liquid form like *mustard* or *ketchup*, or in dry form like *salt* and *pepper*, which are found on most dining tables. And yet all of these can be considered to be seasonings as well as condiments. (Even *ketchup* is used in some recipes.)

There was a discussion on this topic on *http://separatedbyacommonlanguage. blogspot.com* which I found very interesting. And a good rule of thumb that I got from it is:

They are **seasonings** if they are in the kitchen where they are called for in the recipe.

They are **condiments** when they appear on the table, to be applied ad lib by the diners.

• • • • •

Ketchup vs. Catsup

Both spellings are correct. Since *ketchup/catsup* is not an English word, it is subject to spelling interpretation.

It's likely that *ketchup* is derived from the Chinese "ke-tsiap" which was a spicy pickled fish sauce popular in the 17th century (called "kecap" in Malay and "ketjap" in Indonesia – their version is a sweet soy sauce) imported into England through Malay (now Malaysia).

Ketchup may well be an attempt to 'naturalize' the foreign word by bringing it closer to sounds and words already existing in English. "Ketchup" reminds us of the small sailing boat called a 'ketch' (originally pronounced 'catch,' according to the *Oxford Encyclopedic English Dictionary*); to which is attached 'up,' so that it sounds like 'catch-up.'

Catsup sounds as if it means "cat's sup" – 'sup' meaning both 'to lap up with your tongue' and 'to have supper' – which evokes a rather distasteful image, since *catsup* and/or *ketchup*, made nowadays with tomatoes, looks very much like blood.

It was in the late 1700s that New Englanders (specifically, "the people in Maine" according to www.practicallyedible.com) began to add tomatoes to the blend and it became what we know as *ketchup*.

Heinz was the first company to successfully market ketchup and large and small manufacturers everywhere started producing their own version. By the 1950s, only three survived: *Heinz*, *Del Monte* and *Hunts*. All the big U.S. manufacturers now call their product *ketchup*.

Today, *ketchup* is the dominant term in most parts of the world, though *catsup* still has its strongholds, especially in the southern U.S.

• • • • •

"I'd rather be dead than red in the head." This is a saying used against kids with red hair, often as a taunt. When ginger is dry and in powder form, it sometimes looks pale reddish or sandy in color. Light red hair is often called ***ginger***.

- *Her hair is ginger.*
- *She's ginger. (having red hair)*
- *She's a ginger.*

The term is especially common in the U.K. According to statistics, there are more red-haired people in England, Scotland and Ireland than any place else.

Ginger has been a nickname for people with red hair for many centuries. Red hair is traditionally associated with fiery tempers and sharp tongues. Historically, there has been a suspicion that red-headed people had links with the devil. This explains why they are maliciously teased by people and often stereotyped as being eccentric and untrustworthy.

Prince Harry of England who has a reddish-blond hair was once quoted as saying that he was being bullied for being ginger.

Gingerism is the term used to describe prejudice against red-haired people. It has been compared to racism in the U.K. and there are actually support groups to help people cope with it.

The animated cartoon series *South Park* had an episode in which the demoniacal 8-year old, Eric, organized persecutions and physical attacks on "ginger-head" children. This seemed to have been the immediate inspiration for some attacks on red-headed children in U.S. schools.

See CARROT TOP on page 29.

• • • • •

Pronunciations of "herb" and "chamomile"

HERB

Americans pretty uniformly omit pronouncing the 'h' in "herb."

(Note: When **Herb** is the name of a person, the "h" <u>is</u> pronounced.)

All sources seem to agree that, historically, "herb" has been h-less, even in England, since the word was borrowed from France.

I say "even in England" because the British traditionally have regarded the dropping of the initial 'h' of a word ("It is 'and-made," "I am going 'ome") as characteristic of lower-class speech.

And, depending on the way you pronounce it, you would need to switch *an/a:*

- *Thyme is an herb* (pronounced *erb*).
- *Thyme is a herb* (pronounced *herb*).

CHAMOMILE

It's a daisy-like flower, dried and used as tea or in an extract, taken as a mild sedative.

Some dictionaries give two pronunciations, either as rhyming to 'meal' or 'mile.'

Just about everyone I asked said they pronounce it the first way, the same way you would pronounce *automobile.*

• • • • •

Spicy vs. Hot (when referring to food)

Some people use *spicy* as a synonym for *hot*.

Spicy means having pungent or zesty flavors of spices such as *ginger, garlic, cumin, mustard* or even *tomato sauce*.

Hot generally means plenty of *chili*, or occasionally, *pepper* (all one tastes is 'heat').

Indian food, for example, is usually spicy (it has a lot of spices) but not considered hot.

A lot of *Thai* dishes, on the other hand, are quite hot; the degree of 'heat' depends on how much Thai chili is used.

As a rule, I would view **spicy** as not being as hot as **hot**.

You can also use **hot and spicy** to describe a flavor along with a nice dose of 'heat' (i.e., there are multiple things going on in the taste.)

9
· · · · ·
Take a Sip!

"Eat, drink and be merry, for tomorrow we may die."
Ecclesiastes 8:15; Corinthians 15:32
(Modern-day versions would be: Live your life to the fullest;" "Live in the moment;" "Seize the day.")

ESPECIALLY FOR ENGLISH LEARNERS

THE MEANINGS OF "DRINK"

It can mean a few things depending on the context.

It refers to any kind of liquids:
- *I'm not a **coffee drinker**.*
- *Waitress: "Can I get you something **to drink**? Iced tea, soda, water?"*
  Customers: "One iced tea and two cokes, please."
  *Waitress: "I'll go get **the drinks** while you're looking at the menu."*

Drink can mean drinking alcohol:
- *"Would you like to go out for **a drink**?"*
  *" Sorry, but I **don't drink**."*
- *Don't **drink** and drive.* (It's against the law in the U.S.)
- *He's a **heavy drinker**.*
- HE DRINKS LIKE A FISH. (page 104)

DIFFERENT TERMS FOR "SOFT DRINKS"

Soft drinks are drinks without alcohol, as opposed to hard drinks; they are also carbonated (though we have "soft" drinks, like *Snapple* which are not carbonated).

There are several different regional names for soft-drinks, including soda and pop and soda pop, but these are now fast fading because of the influence of television, which is creating a nation-wide popular culture. Today it doesn't matter where you are in the U.S.: if you ask for "a coke" or "a soft drink," the waitress, the guy behind the counter or the store-clerk instantly understands you. Sometimes if you ask for "a coke," the guy behind the counter will say, "Sorry – we only have Pepsi;" for "coke" nearly always means "Coca Cola." ("Pepsi" is "Pepsi Cola.") Colas and other soft drinks (such as "Sprite") are now usually referred to by their brand-names.

On a personal note, my husband usually says *pop*, even though he was born and raised in California, where almost anyone else would say *soda* (though some might say *soda pop*). He tells me that when he was growing up, people would call any soft drink *coke*.

WHAT DOES "BREW" MEAN?

Generally, to **brew** means to boil things together for a period of time. It is the process used in making beer (boiling and fermentation):

- *"How long does it take to **brew beer**?"*
  "On average, probably a month."

When used in regards to tea, **brew** means to let the tea bag (or tea leaves) sit (or "steep") in very hot (close to boiling) water for a few minutes so as to extract the flavor, then remove it. No cooking is needed:

- *This article tells you step by step how to **brew** the perfect cup of tea.*

When it comes to coffee, **brew** means to make coffee using the roasted grounds of crushed seeds (coffee beans):

- *Can you get a pot **brewing**?* (Or, *Can you start/make a pot of coffee?*)
- *The pot is still **brewing**. It'll be ready in a few minutes.* (Or, *The coffee is still brewing.*)

Used figuratively, **brew** means to be imminent; something (usually bad) is beginning to happen:

- *The storm is **brewing** in the northern part of California; we in the Southland will probably get hit by tomorrow night.*
- *The crisis has been **brewing** since the beginning of the year.*
- *Let me know about what's **brewing** at your end.*

As slang, a **brew** means "a beer" in American English and "a cup of tea" (or any warm drink) in British English.

- *Give me a cold **brew**, will you?* (Another slang term is a **brewski** - just a fun way to say "brew")
- *Would you like to come in for a cup of **brew**?* (also, a **cuppa**)

• •

COMMON EXPRESSIONS

WATER, ETC.

He or she could sell a drowning man a glass of water. He or she is a highly persuasive person.

- *The coach is a great salesman for his team. He says things with such conviction you truly believe him. He **could** probably **sell a drowning man a glass of water**.*

Usage notes:

1. Often used humorously, referring to someone who is very good at what he or she does, whether a salesman, a persuasive speaker, or even a con artist
2. Other similar sayings:
   He could sell ice to an Eskimo; He could sell sand to an Arab; He is a very smooth talker.

3. *Like offering a drowning man a glass of water*, on the other hand, means to do something that you think is helpful but that only makes the situation worse:

  - *Giving money to these panhandlers is **like offering a drowning man a glass of water**; they would just use it to buy alcohol.*

I'll drink to that. I strongly agree with you; I completely support that opinion.

  - *Bob: "I think Prohibition should be restored."*
    *Mary: **"I'll drink to that!"***

Background: The term is believed to be of American origin. It was popularized in *Laugh-In*, an American sketch comedy in the 1960s, hosted by Dick Martin and Dan Rowan. Martin often responded with *Oh, I'll drink to that!* to something Rowan said that he liked.

Usage note: It is mainly used in the figurative sense and doesn't necessarily involve actual drinking.

Kool-Aid drinker Someone who accepts something fully and blindly

  - *They were **Kool-Aid drinkers**; they believed anything their religious leader told them.*
  - *Don't be a **Kool-Aid drinker**! Don't buy or sell stocks just because your broker tells you to.*

Background: *Kool-Aid* is General Foods' best-selling powdered drink mix. It comes in different flavors.

The term is a reference to the 1978 horrific cult mass-suicide in Jonestown, Guyana, South America. Jim Jones, the leader of the group, convinced his followers to move from the U.S. to Jonestown, where he established a commune. When the town came under investigation for various crimes, Jones ordered his people to commit suicide by drinking grape-flavored *Kool-Aid* (some sources say it was *Flavor-Aid*) laced with potassium cyanide. Over 900 people died, including Jones himself.

Usage notes:
1. It is a disparaging term -an inference that one can't think for oneself.
2. Also, **drink the Kool-Aid**:
   - *"We're not **drinking the Kool-Aid** here at our network,"* said the news anchor.
3. A very common expression, especially in political news commentaries
4. Some people consider it a cliché; others think it's a powerful metaphor for brainwashing.

My cup runneth over. I have more than enough for my needs.

  - *I consider myself quite lucky and have much to be thankful for, even though my house isn't big and I don't have a big bank account. **My cup runneth over.***

<u>Background</u>: It comes from the Bible, Psalm 23:5: David expresses his gratitude to God for providing for him:

"Thou preparest a table before me in the presence of mine enemies
Thou anointest my head with oil and my cup runneth over"

The "cup" is used literally and metaphorically - the speaker describes his life in terms of a cup that is full and continues to be filled with blessings and joys provided by God.

<u>Usage notes</u>:

1. Used to express gratitude and/or contentment - one has gotten more from life than one even had the right to expect
2. Another way of expressing this idea is *my life has been blessed* or *I've been blessed.*
3. "Runneth" is a very old form of "runs."
4. Sometimes used jokingly to refer to a full-breasted woman, with a low-cut top, who is wearing "C" cups (i.e., bra cups) when she should be wearing "D's" (i.e., too small a bra size):
   - *Look at the girl in this picture!- the one with a low-cut blouse.*
   Her cups really runneth over.

See/look at/the glass as half full To believe that the situation is more good than bad

   - *No doubt that it's a bad disease to have but you've got to **look at** this like **the glass is half full** and not half empty.*

<u>Background</u>: The question *"**Is the glass half full or half empty?**"* has been traditionally used to determine whether you are the type to see things in a positive or negative light. The typical answers are: *half full* (you are an optimist) or *half empty* (you are a pessimist).

<u>Comment</u>: This way of classifying people can be a bit too simplistic for the complexity of human personality types and moods. For example, if someone asks me this question, I'd say "it depends on whether the person is pouring or drinking. If I am drinking from the glass, it's *half empty*; if I am pouring, it's *half full*." Also, if I've had a good day, I'm more likely to say *"half full;"* a bad day, *"half empty."*

<u>Usage notes</u>:

1. A very common expression
2. Or, you can say, *look on the bright side*
3. Also used as an adjective:
   - *I'm **the glass-half-full** kind of person.*
4. This idea of "looking on the bright side" is also expressed in the following jingle about the doughnut:

   "As you go through life, brother,
   Whatever be your goal,

Keep your eye upon the doughnut
And not upon the hole."

I've heard that doughnut shops, at one time, often had this jingle framed and hung on their walls – usually, with the picture of a hobo (tramp) good-humoredly contemplating a doughnut.

It teaches us the virtue of contentment – we should focus on what we have, not on what we don't have, or wish we had.

Water-cooler talk Phrase used to describe office workers chit-chatting about the day's events or office gossip while standing around getting a drink from a water cooler

- *This scandal makes for great water-cooler talk.*

Usage note: Some offices may not have a water cooler, but the term still applies even if office workers drink water from bottles kept in the refrigerator or stand around the coffee pot talking and drinking coffee.

The term now extends to cover such online social-networking forms as blogs and twitter.

Water down (verb) To reduce the force or effectiveness of something
- *Lemon juice and cranberry juice are too strong and too bitter to drink straight, but they taste good when they are watered down and sweetened.*

Usage note: Also used as an adjective:
- *My cousin claimed that the drink 'Red Bull' originated in Thailand. To him, the U.S. version of Red Bull is not the true Thai drink -it's a watered-down version.*

Water, water everywhere, but/and/not a drop to drink It's not always possible to access or partake of what you see, feel, touch or desire in spite of its abundance.

- *New Orleans during the Katrina hurricane was a good example of water, water everywhere, but not a drop to drink.*
- *How ironic! I was the only girl surrounded by these very good-looking men. Too bad all of them were gay. It was just like water, water everywhere, but not a drop to drink.*

Background: It is a quote from *The Rime of the Ancient Mariner*, a very long poem written by Samuel Taylor Coleridge in 1797-1798: The Mariner, aboard a motionless ship - there has been no wind for weeks – has shot the only living thing in sight, an albatross, and so has been punished with a curse. He is stuck in the middle of the sea, surrounded by salt water which he cannot consume. Thus his lament.

The original version in the poem is *"Water, water everywhere, nor any drop to drink.* (Lines 121-22)

Usage note: Used to describe the irony of the situation

• • • • •

COFFEE AND TEA

"A true warrior, like tea, shows his strength in hot water." Chinese proverb

A tempest in a teapot A commotion raised about an unimportant matter

- *The whole issue was just **a tempest in a teapot**. Nobody really cared about the outcome.*

<u>Background</u>: "A tempest" can mean a severe storm with very high wind and often rain, hail or snow, (It is the background theme that Shakespeare uses in his play *The Tempest*.) or figuratively speaking, a violent emotional disturbance.

A tempest in a teapot is how the Americans would say it; the alliteration may be the main reason why it was chosen. The British version is *a storm in a teacup*.

<u>Usage note</u>: Another idiom used to express this idea is *to make a mountain out of a molehill.*

Coffeed out To have enough coffee for now

- *"Would you like more coffee?"*
  *"Oh, no! I'm **coffeed out** already.*

<u>Usage note</u>: A very common American expression

Some people also use it when they have had enough iced-tea (*I'm **teaed out**.*)

Fill to the brim To be as full as possible; to be completely satisfied

- *Customer to waitress: "Please don't **fill** my coffee cup **to the brim**. Leave some room for cream and sugar."* (Or, *Please don't fill it up **to the top**.*)
- *"**Fill** your bowl **to the brim** and it will spill. Keep sharpening your knife and it will blunt."* Lao Tzu, Chinese philosopher, 6th century BC
- *If you buy just a couple of items at the supermarket, you should not be expected to get in the same line to pay as those pushing carts **filled to the brim**.*

<u>Background</u>: It comes from the idea of a container filled to the very top.

Brim vs. Rim

The <u>brim</u> is the upper edge of a cup, dish or any hollow vessel/container used for holding anything; also the rim of a hat (though "brim of a hat" – the projecting edge, and "hat brim" is also commonly used).

Everything else is <u>rim</u> - the *rim* of the desk; the *rim* of the canyon or mountain. (In California, a community in the San Bernadino mountains is called *"The Rim of the World"* because it sits right on the upper edge of the mountains.)

In the 1980s, a coffee company took advantage of this confusion (some think it contributed more to the confusion) when it came up with a campaign ad, *"Fill it to the rim, with Brim"* - *Brim* being the name of the brand. Each ad always started with a hostess pouring coffee and a guest demurring with, *"No, only half a cup for me!"* Then someone will say, *"It's OK to fill it to the rim with Brim since Brim is decaffeinated and it doesn't keep you up all night."* (The ad should have been "Fill it to the brim, with Rim.")

Good to the last drop   Good to the end

- *Let me finish this iced-tea before we go. It tastes especially good today in this hot weather; **good to the last drop!***
- *This book is such a good read; it's **good to the last drop**.*

Background: *Good to the last drop* is the longtime slogan for *Maxwell House* coffee brand.

According to legend, when President Theodore Roosevelt was served *Maxwell House* coffee during a visit to the Hermitage, home of Andrew Jackson, in Nashville, Tennessee on October 22, 1907, he drained his cup then said *"It's good to the last drop."*

Whether there is any truth in this story or not, *good to the last drop* has helped build *Maxwell House* into one of America's leading brands.

Usage note: The expression usually refers to liquids, but it can serve as a metaphor for other things.

Not for all the tea in China   Not at any price

- *I would never invite this guy to my house again, **not for all the tea in China**.*

Background: It originated in the late 19th to the early 20th century.

Tea is the favored drink in China and the country has been for a long while one of the biggest exporters of tea. Since China is a very large country, the amount of all the tea grown there would be a tremendous fortune – which gives the expression its force.

Usage notes:
1. It's the phrase one uses to express the idea that nothing could persuade one to do something.

   Other variants include ***not for all the coffee in Brazil; not for all the oil in Iraq***.
2. Other ways of saying it:
   - *(There's) no way I would ever do it.*
   - *I wouldn't do it for all the money in the world.*
   - *You couldn't pay me to do it.*
   - *I wouldn't be caught dead doing it.*
   - *I'd rather die (than do it).*

Not one's cup of tea A person or thing that doesn't suit one's tastes or desires
- *"How do you like your new co-worker?"*
  *"Well, as you may have noticed, she's **not** exactly **my cup of tea.**"*
- *Soccer is **not my cup of tea**.*

Background: This expression is quite recent, probably from the mid 20th century. This is surprising, considering how far back the tradition of tea-drinking goes in English culture. No one knows for sure how it originated. One explanation I've read is that it is based on a matter of taste in tea-drinking. There are now available many kinds of tea and some persons will drink only the particular blend they like or are used to.

Usage notes:
1. It's a gentle way of saying that you don't really like someone or something without being that forceful about it.
2. Also used: ***It's not my bag; Different strokes for different folks.***
3. Its positive form, ***one's cup of tea*** is sometimes used, though not as common.

Read the tea leaves To try to predict the future
- *The Fed Chairman has proved to be particularly adept at **reading** economic **tea leaves.***

Background: If bulk tea leaves are used in making tea, the leaves will get into the cup. After the tea has been drunk, the leaves still remain at the bottom of your cup in various patterns. Some fortune-tellers claim to be able to predict your future by interpreting these patterns.

Usage notes:
1. Since most people don't really believe one can predict the future through tea leaves, the expression is used in the sense that it's just a best guess and that there is uncertainty involved.
2. Another expression used in this sense is ***look into one's/the/crystal ball.***

Talk/chat/over a cup of coffee To have a relaxed conversation while drinking coffee
- *I'd much rather sit down and **talk** with you **over a cup of coffee** than talk on the phone or by e-mails and text messages.*

Usage notes:
1. A very common expression; one can have more than one cup of coffee if one wants
2. Variations:
   - *(let's) discuss this over a beer*
   - *(let's) settle the matter/consider things over lunch/ a meal*

Wake up and smell the coffee!   Open your eyes, realize what's going on!
- *"**Wake up and smell the coffee!** Don't you have any idea he has been cheating on you?"*

Background: In America, coffee is the beverage of choice for most people in the morning.

According to www.barrypopik.com, the term was cited in print in the early 1940s.

From what I've heard, *wake up and smell the coffee* was at one time a campaign ad for *Nescafe'* instant coffee. I have not been able to verify this, however.

Ann Landers (1918-2002), an American advice columnist, was credited for popularizing it. She often told readers who are 'clueless' to *wake up and smell the coffee*, meaning to face facts. The phrase also became the title for one of her books of collected advice columns.

It was also used frequently on the TV sitcom *Mama's Family*, a spin-off of *The Carol Burnett Show*. "Mama" was played by Vickie Lawrence who said it to her (somewhat) dense son.

Usage notes:
1. Often shortened to ***wake up!***
2. Used as a rebuke to a person to become aware of the realities of a situation, usually an unpleasant one
3. Other similar expressions: ***get real!; wise up!***
4. A related term is a ***wake-up call*** (a reminder; a lesson) which is a very common expression:
   - *The 9-11 terror attacks were **a wake-up call** for the U. S. government to come up with better ways to protect the country.*

What's that got to do with the price of tea in China?   (Rhetorical question)
What you just said has nothing to do with what we're talking right now.
Bob: "The president hasn't done a good job so far."
Mary: "But his wife has such a great fashion sense!"
*Bob: "**What's that got to do with the price of tea in China?**"*
Background: It implies that "based on your reply, we might as well talk about the price of tea in China."

Considered American in origin, it may have been influenced by the expression NOT FOR ALL THE TEA IN CHINA, mentioned earlier.

Usage note: Used when someone makes a totally irrelevant comment

Variant: ***What's that got to do with the price of eggs/rice (in China)?***

• • • • •

ALCOHOLIC DRINKS

"Candy is dandy, but liquor is quicker." Ogden Nash, American light-verse poet (1902-1971) (The verse refers to seducing a woman.)

Belly up to the bar   To go up to the bar to order a drink

- *Let's **belly up to the bar** and order a few Margaritas before it gets too crowded.*

Background: It conjures an image of someone nudging one's way to the bar, leaning so close to it that one's belly presses against it.

In the play and the movie *The Unsinkable Molly Brown*, there is a song with the title *Belly Up To The Bar, Boys!*

Usage note: In another sense, it can mean to step forward assertively or get seriously involved:

- *The Senate majority leader said he would ask the lawmakers to **belly up to the bar** and state their views on the president's plan to increase troop level in Afghanistan.*

Champagne taste on a beer budget   Phrase used to describe someone who likes expensive things but can't possibly afford them

- *A lot of people in this country have a **champagne taste** while **on a beer budget**. That's exactly what has gotten us into this economic mess.*

Background: Champagne is the most prestigious of all the sparkling wines (wines that have bubbles or are carbonated), named after the place it is made and bottled – *Champagne*, in northern region of France.

The process of making champagne is long, involved and costly. This explains why champagne, like caviar, is associated with luxury, or anything very expensive.

Beer, on the other hand, is the least expensive of all the alcoholic drinks.

Cry in/into/one's beer   To try to treat one's sorrow with alcohol (usually without much success); to feel sorry for oneself; complain or lament in a maudlin manner

- *My friend called me up last night, whining and **crying in her beer**, and told me all her little problems one by one for the next four hours.*

Usage note: There is a slang term, **beer tears** - describing an unhappy drunk who, after a few drinks, begins to shed tears about anything remotely bothering him or her. (urbandictionry.com)

Drink someone under the table   To out-drink someone; stay reasonably sober while the other person is falling down drunk

- *She has always been a big drinker. In fact, she can **drink most guys under the table**.*

Background: "Under the table" here means being so completely drunk that one is literally lying on the floor beneath the table (i.e., possibly passed out).

Drive someone to drink To cause someone to turn to alcohol as an escape from frustration; make someone very upset or annoyed

- *This is exactly the type of news that will **drive him to drink**.*
- *"A woman **drove me to drink**...and I hadn't even the courtesy to thank her."* (This is humor.) W. C. Fields, American comic and actor (1880-1946)

Usage note: Often used in the pattern *is enough to drive someone to drink:*
- *The way the team has played the past few years **is enough to drive the fans to drink**.*

Fall off the wagon To resume a bad habit that one is trying to get rid of or control

- *Bill didn't have a drink in 20 years. He **fell off the wagon**, however, right after his wife left him.*

Background: The "wagon" here refers to horse-drawn water wagons (or water carts) that were used during the late 19th century to wet down dusty roads on hot summer days.

During that time, members of the temperance movement (i.e., total abstinence from alcoholic liquors) campaigned fervently for a government ban on alcohol in their attempt to reduce domestic abuse. Those who pledged to stop drinking were said to be "on the wagon" - they would rather climb aboard a water cart and drink water to quench their thirst than have a drink of liquor. The proposed ban on alcohol, known as Prohibition, eventually became law in 1919. It lasted until 1933.

Usage note: It denotes a failure to keep a vow to do something. Originally the term referred only to drinking (i.e., to start drinking again after one has stopped) but is now used for all sorts of situations - smoking, drug addictions, dieting, exercising, etc.:
- *The president-elect conceded he's **fallen off the wagon** at times, but pledges he won't light up.* (www.usatoday.com, 12-7-08)
- *The talk show queen confessed that she **had fallen off the weight-loss wagon**.*
- *My New Year's resolution is to start exercising again. But if I ever **fall off the wagon** this year, I resolve to not let a small failure get me down.*

New wine in old bottles Something new placed in an old or existing format or system; combining the new with the old

- *This is a different kind of war. Using old war tactics to fight this war is not going to work. That would be like putting **new wine in old bottles**.*

Background: The source of this expression is a parable mentioned in the gospels of Matthew, Mark and Luke.

Matthew 9:14-17, King James version:
Neither do men put new wine into old bottles; else the bottles break and the wine runneth out, and the bottle perish: but they put new wine into new bottles, and both are preserved.

The "bottles" were actually "wineskins" during the biblical times.

Old wineskins would have become dried and prone to crack, especially given the stresses caused by fermentation of new wine.

One interpretation of the parable is that one cannot live a new faith in a new way by continuing to behave as one formerly did; it requires a 'new man' to live the new faith correctly.

Usage notes:

1. In certain contexts, **new wine in old bottles** can imply deceptive practices - passing something new off as old.

   Some things become more valuable with age. Good examples are vintage wine, old coins and classic cars. If you dress up a new thing as an old thing and then sell it as an old thing then you are selling **new wine in old bottles.**

2. There is also an expression **old wine in new bottles/a new bottle:**
   - *What is so new about this CD? Just old Beatles songs. It is the same **old wine in a new bottle** with a different label.*

   This can also imply deception - people are packaging something old to make it look new.

One for the road Another drink before leaving the establishment (to sustain oneself during the drive home)

- *The bar is closing, so it's last call for anyone who wants **one for the road.***

Background: According to James Rogers (1985), this expression probably dates from the 1930s when long automobile trips had become fairly standard and Prohibition (of alcohol) in the U.S. had ended. The idea behind it is that "one could use (or need) another drink to fortify oneself for the journey ahead."

Wikipedia notes that *one for the road* has been very popular as a title. It has been used as a title for short stories, books, plays, songs and albums, and an episode of two different sit-coms.

Usage note: This expression can be used to refer to any kind of drink, not just alcoholic drinks:

- *Waitress: "Would you like more coffee?"*
  *Customer: "Yes, **one** more **for the road.**"*

Pop/crack/open the champagne To start celebrating

- *I force myself to write every day. If I can keep it up, I know good will come out of it. Maybe I'll even **pop open the champagne** some day.*

Background: While the wine is going through the second fermentation, the bottle is quickly corked to maintain the carbon dioxide inside. This leads to fizzy wine – the tiny bubbles remain in the champagne to enhance the drinking experience. It is the reason why champagne has been used for all kinds of celebration all over the world.

<u>Usage note</u>: Variations: *pop the cork; uncork the champagne*
It's time for a glass of champagne!; It's time for some bubbly!

Someone you want to have a beer with Phrase used to describe someone likable (especially one you can relate to) or fascinating

- *He may be **someone I want to have a beer with**, but voting for him to run the country is a different story.*

<u>Background</u>: Beer is considered to be the drink of an average guy. Having a beer with someone represents the idea of getting to know someone better. (An often-used question is *if you could have a beer with someone, who would it be?*)

This seems to be uniquely an American expression. It became very popular during the 2000 and 2004 presidential elections, used especially by the media to gauge the "likability" factor in each candidate. As it turned out, George W. Bush was the candidate that the average guy wanted to *sit down and have a beer with*. Some people think that this may have been one of the main reasons why Bush won the presidency both times.

THREE-MARTINI LUNCH See page 174.

Three sheets to/in/the wind To be staggering drunk

- *Susan was **three sheets to the wind** even before we got to the party, judging from the way she was staggering around, and speaking in a loud, slurred voice.*

<u>Background</u>: It's a sailor's expression. The sheets are the ropes holding the corners of the sails, used to adjust the sails making the most efficient use of the available wind. If they became loose, the sails would flap uncontrolled, making a lot of noise, going nowhere, thus causing the ship to wobble around and be out of control, much like a drunk person.

Three sheets <u>in</u> the wind was the original version. **Three sheets <u>to</u> the wind** came later and is now in common use perhaps more than the original one.

<u>Of interest</u>: To my knowledge, there are more words for drinking and getting drunk in the English language than on any other topics (though words and slang for "money" come pretty close).

The following is a scale (or rating) for drunkenness on a language forum (wordreference.com) that I stumbled upon while researching *three sheets to the wind*.

In order from least drunk:

to be tipsy
to be feelin' it
to be drunk
to be three sheets to the wind
to be blitzed (also being high from marijuana)

to get smashed (also from marijuana)
to be drunk as a skunk (the alliteration most likely accounts for the popularity of the phrase)
to be obliterated (also from marijuana)
to be gone (also from marijuana)
to be out (passed out after drinking too much)

I've also heard of a lot more, though I'm not sure where they would fit in the above scale:

to get wasted (also being high from marijuana)
in one's cups (a very old expression; often used in English literature of the 18th & 19th centuries and even – though with a humorous, archaic, literary intonation – in the 20th century. The cups are cups of wine and the expression is meant as an excuse: *"He is not fully responsible for what he did, for he was in his cups [drinking] at the time."*
to tie one on

TO BE STEWED (TO THE GILLS) See page 181.

to be trashed/stoned (also from marijuana)
to be seeing double
to be seeing pink elephants
to be feeling/ feel no pain

And there are hundreds and hundreds more.

Toast of the town A person or thing that is universally liked and admired or has earned the respect and praise of other people

- *Thanks to the rave reviews of her latest movie, the up-and-coming actress has now become the **toast of the town**.*
- *That restaurant has been the **toast of the town** since it opened two months ago.*

Background: Back in ancient Greece, people poisoned wine as a way to get rid of enemies and anyone else they didn't want around. So to show that wine had not been poisoned, the host would pour it from a common pitcher, toast his guests' health and then drink it before everyone. The Romans adopted the custom and began dipping burnt bread (toast) in the wine to reduce the acidity.

In the 1800s, a toast specifically meant to salute the health of a certain beautiful or popular woman who was admired but not present. Spiced toast was used to flavor the drinks of the time and the original toasters declared that the woman's charms spiced the drinks more than any piece of dried bread. Hence the term *toast of the town.*
Usage notes:
1. Used as a compliment
2. The expression ***talk of the town*** could also be used the same way; but it could also mean to be the subject of gossip or speculation:

- *The personal life of the media mogul has been the **talk of the town**. In a script worthy of a soap opera, his wife of 19 years has made a very public request for a divorce.*

Wet one's whistle To have a drink, usually alcoholic drink
- *This place is quite a popular spot to **wet your whistle** and at times can be filled to capacity.*

Background: A folk etymology that is fun to read is that English pub patrons used to drink their beer out of a ceramic mug with a whistle baked into their cup or handle. To order a refill, a patron blew the whistle to get the service, hence the term "wet one's whistle."

A more plausible explanation is that "whistle" was slang for mouth or throat; to **wet one's whistle** is merely a humorous reference to wetting one's mouth with a nice drink.

Usage note: It implies quenching a dry thirst; the expression is used to justify a drink:
- *I know it's early for a cocktail, but I could use one to **wet my whistle**.*

Wine and dine To entertain oneself or entertain someone lavishly
- *We **wined and dined** on our honeymoon, something I doubt we'll have a chance to do again.*
- *I don't mind **wining and dining** my clients. It gives me a chance to eat good meals and, besides, I often end up getting business deals from them.*

Background: Serving wine (or alcohol in general) is considered to be part of a lavish meal (though the individuals attending may choose not to drink). The alcohol served doesn't necessarily have to be wine; it can be any alcohol of choice. "Wine" is chosen in this expression simply because it rhymes with "dine."

What do you want? Egg in your beer? Why are you griping? Isn't that good enough?
- *It is a very decent HDTV at a rock-bottom price! **What do you want? Egg in your beer?***

Background: Some people put eggs in their beer. Some consider such a concoction an aphrodisiac; others think it is the best cure for a hangover.

According to word-detective.com, this was a catch phrase at the beginning of the 20th century. It gained popularity because the GI's used it during WWII. In wartime, both beer and eggs were hard to come by. So "wanting egg in one's beer" then was a good metaphor for wishing for more than what one could have.

Usage notes:
1. It's **Whadaya want?** in spoken form.
2. Used in response to someone's complaint for special treatment;

usually the person has already been given something, but is asking for something more to go with it.

• •

OTHER TERMS AND EXPRESSIONS OF INTEREST

Alky (Alkie) Short for an alcoholic

Usage note: Also, ***lives in the bottle; a rummy/ drunk/drunkard/lush/ boozer/wino*** (a drunk who drinks wine)

Aperitif A small drink of alcohol taken to stimulate the appetite before a meal

Barfly An alcoholic whose main interest in life is hanging around in bars

Beer belly A bulging stomach, seen mostly on men

Background: It is often said that beer belly is caused by drinking large quantities of beer. Some people argue that this is a myth; beer belly is only caused by eating too much. However, alcohol has been known to slow down the fat burning process. This would lead people to think alcohol is making them fatter.

Usage note: Other terms used are ***beer gut***, POT BELLY (See page 192.)

Beer goggles (Slang) The impaired judgment caused by excessive consumption of beer that makes an otherwise unappealing person seem attractive

- *John obviously had **beer goggles** on. He ended up taking the ugliest girl home last night, someone he wouldn't look at twice if he was sober.*

Bootlegging Making and distributing any product illegally and unauthorized (not paying taxes or royalties on it)

Background: Originally the term, in widespread use during the Prohibition era (1919-1933), referred to the sales of illegal whiskey (generally the MOONSHINE variety, to be discussed later). The name is said to have come from an early practice of hiding a contraband in the leg of one's boots (Cowboys in the Old West wore long leather boots.) to avoid detection. Now, it is being used in a general sense.

Usage note: In the music world, *bootlegging* is a recording of a performance by a band or artist, either live or in the studio that is not otherwise available to the general public. Many bands allow the taping of their shows for personal use and trading. But to do it as a business and make money from it is considered illegal.

Pirating, on the other hand, means illegally making copies of legitimate releases, then pressing them onto CD's and selling them as if they were legitimate.

Booze Slang for alcoholic beverage of any kind

Bottoms-up! A drinking toast

- *The host cries **"Bottoms- up!"** to his guests as an encouragement to drink.*

Background: The mentioned bottoms are the bottoms of glasses, which are of course tilted up as the host and his guests drink. Please note: this phrase is not used when drinking to the launching of new ships.

It has been reported that former Russian President Mikhail Gorbachev, raising his glass to an English-speaking audience, blurted out *"Up your bottoms!"*

Usage note: Also, **Cheers!; Here's (a toast) to you!; Here's looking at you!** (Humphrey Bogart made it famous in *Casablanca*: "Here's looking at you, kid!"- to Ingrid Bergman) **Down the hatch!** (like cargo/supplies being loaded into a ship via the hatch, a naval term for "door") and HERE'S MUD IN YOUR EYE! (see later).

BYOB An abbreviation for "bring your own (beer, bottle or booze)"

- *If you host a party, you should make it **BYOB**. It will ensure each guest is enjoying his or her drink of choice.*

Cheap drunk Usually used in reference to a female who gets drunk very quickly; it doesn't cost very much to get her drunk

Also a derogatory term for an alcoholic who buys cheap drink to feed his habit

Cup of joe Slang for a cup of coffee

Background: A prevalent folk etymology is that it is named after Admiral Josephus "Joe" Daniels, the Secretary of the Navy who banned alcohol aboard ships in 1914, making coffee the beverage of choice. Word experts think differently. Most suggest it could refer to the average American (as in ***an average Joe***) or it could have been a modification of "Java," another name for coffee (at one time much coffee came from Java, an Indonesian island).

Drink/get a drink/from a fire hose Used to describe a situation where the amount of information to be assimilated is overwhelming

- *We are blessed by many information tools and outlets, but it can be like trying to **get a drink from a fire hose**.*

Usage note: A recent term, a product of the information age, most often used in the business sector

DUI It is abbreviation for "Driving under the influence" of some intoxicating drug. This is almost always alcohol, but a DUI citation can be issued to anyone driving under the influence of any narcotic substance.

Dutch courage False courage or self-confidence induced by drinking alcohol

- *I'm really nervous about doing this. I need some **Dutch courage** to get me going.*

Background: Most sources interpret the phrase as a slur against the Dutch, deriving from the 17th and 18 century hostility between the Dutch and the British over control of the seas. It implies the Dutch's perceived cowardice - they have no real fighting spirit and have to get drunk to fight.

Hair of the dog (that bit me) A folk remedy for a hangover, based on the notion that the best thing for what ails you is more of it

Background: The ancient folk treatment for dog bite was to put a burnt hair of the dog on the wound.

Hangover The dry mouth, nausea, dizziness and headache that result from overindulging in alcohol

Happy hour A period of time in which a restaurant or bar offers discounts on alcoholic drinks. Typically, it is the late afternoon Monday through Thursday.

Here's mud in your eye! A drinking toast expressing good spirits and humor

- *"Bon appetit!. **Here's mud in your eye!***"

Background: There are a few theories as to the origin of this expression. The first one comes from horse-racing where the winning horse kicks mud into the eyes of the losing ones that follow; it's a back-handed toast among jockeys meaning, 'here's to you losing the race!'

Another theory is from farming. Farmers raise a glass to the success of a good harvest, with *"mud in your eye"* symbolizing a plentiful crop. Others say it started by the soldiers slogging through the muddy trenches of World War I.

Yet there are some who think it comes from the Bible (John 9:1-13): Jesus heals a blind man by spitting in the soil and rubbing the mixture on the man's eyes.

Usage note: A very old-fashioned expression; usually used as a humorous salute

Life is not all beer and skittles. Life is not always pleasant.

- *These immigrants soon found out that **life is not all beer and skittles** in their new country.*

Background: "Skittles" is a bowling-type game, a popular pub sport in certain regions of England and Wales.

Usage notes:
1. Quite an old expression; not commonly heard today
2. Other expressions also used: ***Life is not all fun and games; life is not always a walk in the park***; LIFE IS NOT A BOWL OF CHERRIES; LIFE IS NOT ALL PEACHES AND CREAM (See page 16).

Liquor before beer, never fear (or ***you are in the clear). Beer before liquor, never sicker***. A saying suggesting that if you are to drink two different kinds of alcohol, you should start with the stronger one and then go to the weaker one.

Background: **Liquor** (or **hard liquor**) is a distilled beverage such as whiskey, vodka, rum, brandy, gin, tequila and other spirits.

Both beer and wine are fermented beverages.

(A **liqueur**, on the other hand, is strong, sweet, highly flavored and aromatic. It is an elegant, expensive drink, and is usually drunk in small quantities.)

The saying is a common drinking advice shared but not scientifically proved yet to be true. There are people who believe that the order in which drinks are consumed makes no difference: that it is the amount consumed and the speed at which a person drinks that most affect the level of intoxication. Others feel that one should never mix one's drinks in any order. And there are yet others who think it's a question of psychology rather than chemistry.

Long drink of water Someone who is strikingly tall and usually lean (or thin), used for both a man or a woman

Moonshine Home-recipe illegal distilled alcohol (generally whiskey), concocted back in the woods at night, aided by the moonlight, hidden from government "revenuers" who want to tax their brew

The people who make it are called **moonshiners**.

The term originated in England, but is now thoroughly attached to the southern U.S.

Night cap A drink that contains alcohol which is supposed to help one go to sleep faster and better

Background: Literally, it means "a drink to cap off the night." It is in reference to the idea that it would keep you warm, much like stocking nightcaps were used to keep a sleeper's exposed head warm (this was before central heating).

Usage note: Fairly common

Small beer Persons or matters of little importance or weight

- *This is **small beer** compared to his usual work.*

Background: The expression is British and dates back to at least the 18th century. It refers to the way the beer was produced, as second or third runs of a batch of mash. It had far too little alcohol to be intoxicating and, therefore, was drunk in those times when drinking water was a health hazard.

Usage note: See also, SMALL POTATOES on page 37.

Teetotaler Someone who pledges total abstinence from all intoxicating drinks

Background: It is supposed to come from "total abstainer." At one time, it was common in slang to prefix a word with its own first letter to express emphasis, hence, a "t-total abstainer."

Turn water into wine To make something very ordinary into something exceptionally good

*- I can't remember where I got this from - they say that true love **turns water into wine**, while the best wine can't save a marriage lacking love.*

<u>Background</u>: From the Bible (John 2:1-11): Jesus performs his first miracle at a marriage, transforming water into wine.

Whiskey vs. Whisky

Individual manufacturers can use whatever spelling they want. As it stands, American and Irish liquor producers tend to favor the spelling *whiskey*, while Scottish, Canadian and Japanese producers tend to favor *whisky*.

A quick way to remember how some of the world's biggest producers spell their products is as follows:

Countries that have "e" in their names (The United States of America; Ireland) use *whiskey* (plural: *whiskeys*).

There are some exceptions:

George Dickel Tennessee Whisky
Maker's Mark Whisky (made in Kentucky)

Countries that don't have "e" in their names (Scotland; Canada; Japan) use *whisky* (plural: *whiskies*).

Wine snob One who possesses a supercilious (i.e., haughtily disdainful and/or contemptuous) air concerning wine and its appreciation, often looking down on any wine that is not sufficiently expensive or prestigious

10
· · · · ·
Save Room for Dessert

Americans love their desserts, sometimes with guilty pleasure. For many people, desserts are COMFORT FOOD (Page 207) or simply a *treat* (a reward). It's also a good ending to a meal.

ESPECIALLY FOR ENGLISH LEARNERS

Sweet is a common metaphor for women. It is also used as a term of endearment (also sweetie).

Sugar is often used as a term of endearment, usually to address a woman or a child.

Other food-related endearments include honey (-bunch); sugar-pie; sweetie-pie; cutie-pie; SWEET PEA (See page 31.); PUMPKIN (or PUNKIN) (See page 8-9.); pudding (or puddin)

Saccharine (adjective) means sugary. It is often used metaphorically, in a derogatory sense, to refer to someone who is over-polite or over-sweet.

- *Everybody at work likes him, but I find his behavior very* **saccharine**.
- *The movie is sweet without being overly* **saccharine**.
- *I don't trust her; she always gives me that* **saccharine** *smile*.

Saccharin (noun), on the other hand, is a sugar-substitute (e.g., a brand name *Sweet 'n Low*).

Syrupy is also used to show disapproval. It means overly sentimental.

- *Most of the songs from that era are full of* **syrupy** *lyrics*.

It can also mean too nice or kind in a way that seems insincere.

- *What a* **syrupy** *speech! I don't think he meant anything he said at all*.

Note: Most dictionaries list "saccharine" and "syrupy" as synonyms.

· ·

COMMON EXPRESSIONS

SWEETS FOR MY SWEET, SUGAR FOR MY HONEY

A spoonful of sugar helps the medicine go down. An otherwise unpleasant task can be more easily handled if something pleasant is mixed with it.

- *Try to put a little dab of humor into whatever you are doing;* **a spoonful of sugar helps the medicine go down**.

Background: This saying was popularized when it became part of the song *A Spoonful of Sugar* in the movie *Mary Poppins* (1964), starring Julie Andrews.

As slow as molasses Very slow

- *I try to write a little each day. It hasn't been easy, though. There are times that the ideas come **as slow as molasses**.*

Background: Molasses is a thick, brown syrup by-product from the process of converting sugar cane or sugar beet into sugar. It used to be the main sweetener in the U.S. before people switched to white sugar around World War I. Now it is used mainly in baking.

Due to the high viscosity (i.e., of a glutinous nature or consistency; sticky, thick) of molasses at room temperature, the liquid pours quite slowly. This is the idea behind this expression.

Usage notes:
1. Variation: *As slow as molasses (**in January flowing uphill**) (**in a blizzard**)*
2. Also used figuratively to refer to someone who is mentally slow
3. Some people might find it archaic.
4. Other expressions with the same meaning:
    - ***move at a snail's pace*** (or *as slow as a snail/ a tortoise*)
    - ***slow as dripping syrup; slow as a month of Sundays; slower than Christmas***

Have a sweet tooth To like foods with sugar in them (or other sweet taste)

- *My sister **has a sweet tooth**. Rarely will you see her end a meal without a dessert.*

Sugarcoat/candy coat To make something sound better or easier than it is

- *We have to make people understand that this is a difficult problem. No **sugarcoating**.*

Sugar daddy A rich and usually older man who buys lavish gifts for or gives money to a younger woman in order to spend time or have a sexual relationship with her

- *"That woman never has to worry about money. She has it made; she's got herself a **sugar daddy**!"*

Background: "Sugar" alludes to the sweetening role of gifts and "daddy" to the age difference between the two.

Sugar daddy is also a name of American chewy candy. There are also bite-sized pieces called *sugar babies*.

Usage notes:
1. It's the kind of term that you would generally use talking about a person, and not directly to the person.
2. Two other terms whose meanings come very close to ***sugar daddy*** are ***Santa Claus*** and A MEAL TICKET (See more on page 170.):
    - *He's her **Santa Claus**.* (implying an older man giving gifts)
    - *He's her **meal ticket**.* (implying that he supports her financially, though it doesn't necessarily imply that it's an older person who does it)

<u>Comment</u>: The question is what would you call the person on the receiving end? I've heard "sugar baby" and "gold digger," but the most common terms are "mistress" (especially in the U.K.) and "kept woman." But what about the female equivalent of ***sugar daddy***? Would that be "sugar mama?" Whatever she is called, her sex-partner would be a "kept man" or a <u>gigolo</u> (this last being a French word originally meaning "a paid male escort").

Sweet talk To talk to someone in a pleasing or clever way in order to persuade him or her to do or believe something
- *The salesman tried to **sweet talk** her into buying the latest model car.*

<u>Usage note</u>: Also as a noun:
- *She was the victim of her husband's **sweet talk** and lies.*

Sweetheart deal A deal so advantageous to at least one party that, ordinarily, it would be offered only to a family member, a close friend or a sweetheart and would never be offered to a stranger, a customer or a mere business associate
- *It has been confirmed that the senator received a **sweetheart deal** from this bank. The interest rates for the mortgage loans that he got were well below the market rates.*

<u>Background</u>: A sweetheart deal would probably be private and it might well be secretive, but it wouldn't necessarily involve anything illegal or dishonest – although it might: for the many laws and regulations involving stocks, bonds, interest rates and so on are there precisely to promote fairness and open dealing.

A "merger" may be a sweetheart deal for the top executives of the target firm because they get very attractive buyout packages. The term can also be used to describe a deal between an employer and trade union officials that benefits them both at the expense of employees.

• • • • •

CAKES AND ALE

(An old expression meaning, the good life (and all the fun); material pleasures)
Shakespeare uses it in his *Twelfth Night* (Act 2, Scene 3).
It is also the title of a novel by W. Somerset Maugham (1930).

Cakewalk An exceptionally easy task; a very easy victory against little or no real opposition
- *They thought beating this team would be a **cakewalk** for them, but they were wrong.*

<u>Background</u>: A *cakewalk* was a 19th century strutting dance – some say an exhibition of graceful walking – invented by African-American slaves in the southern U.S. states to satirize the stiff ballroom promenades of white

plantation owners. Unaware of this, the whites often invited their slaves to participate in contests, in which the man (or couple) with the most stylish steps would receive a cake as a prize.

After the American Civil War (1861-65), *cakewalk* came to mean "easy," hardly more than a walk; simple, easy to do with a sweet reward.

Icing/frosting/on the cake An additional benefit to something already good
- *I was so thrilled to finally get a promotion. Then my boss told me I would also get a big Christmas bonus. That was really the **icing on the cake.***

Usage notes:
1. Other synonyms are a *bonus* and a slang expression GRAVY (See page 125).
2. It can be used to show sarcasm:
   - *At the end of his term in office, he issued close to 200 presidential pardons, but the **icing on the cake** was that he pardoned just about any member of his administration who was in trouble with the law.*

(If the people have no bread,) let them eat cake. A flippant remark showing ignorance and indifference for others less fortunate implying, "that's their problem"
- *These lawmakers seem to have "a '**let them eat cake**' mentality." They are totally insensitive about the lack of health care and the outrageous cost of prescription drugs for the average American.*

Background: The quote is often attributed to Marie Antoinette (1755-1793), the wife of Louis XVI of France, although there is no evidence that she actually said it. According to legend, when the notoriously extravagant queen was told her subjects had no bread to eat, she replied, *"Qu'ils mangent de la brioche!" ("Let them eat cake!")*

Usage note: Often shortened to *let them eat cake*, the quote has repeatedly been used to refer to the rich, privileged or empowered being so out of touch with the common man that they would utter something totally insensitive in the face of other people's plight.

Piece of cake Something that can be done easily and pleasurably, like eating a piece of cake, which most people enjoy (though not the making of it)
- *When you know what you're doing, it's a **piece of cake**.*
- *"No problem! **Piece of cake!**"*

Usage note: You can also use it sarcastically, with the right tone of voice and the appropriate body language.

Take the cake To outdo others in absurdity; to be the winner in a bad way
- *I've known some jerks, but you **take the cake**.*

Background: Most people think that this phrase originated from the dance CAKEWALK (see earlier). However, Michael Quinion, of www.worldwidewords.org argues that the first known examples of *cakewalk* appeared some 30 years after *take the cake*. He thinks that the origin of *take the cake* may go back to the ancient Greeks, when they awarded cakes as prizes to the winner in a drinking contest. Also, according to Quinion, the variant, *take the biscuit*, is originally American, not British, as most people have thought.

Americans do eat biscuits. A British biscuit is unleavened, flat, brittle and sweet – it is eaten as a dessert or a treat (although there's also a savory kind, the equivalent of the American CRACKERS; see page 60). An American biscuit is the opposite: it is yeasty, puffy, soft, usually bland but sometimes sour, and is eaten as a bread, often with gravy or beans.

Usage note: There are other ways to express this idea, for example:
- *Well, if that doesn't beat all!*
- *That's unbelievable!* (expressed with shock, anger, disgust, etc.)
- *That's the most outrageous thing I've ever seen/heard!*

You can't have your cake and eat it too. Sometimes one must make a choice because one can't have it all.

- *If you use all your savings to buy this new car that you really want, you won't have any money left. Are you OK with that? After all, **you can't have your cake and eat it too.***

Usage notes:
1. Another way of saying it is **you can't have it both ways.**
2. Even some native speakers find this saying difficult to understand. This is because they confusingly think that "have" means "eat" (as in, "here, *have this piece of cake*!") when it simply means "possess" in this context. It would be more logical to say "You can't eat your cake and (still) have it too."

• • • • •

FRUITCAKE

Fruitcakes are made with plenty of nuts and spices. The two main ingredients, candied fruits and liqueur, act as preservatives, giving rise to its legendary ability to remain edible for months or years!

Fruitcake is the most-derided confection and the butt of holiday jokes because of its hefty weight (it has a reputation as the food equivalent of a brick!) and its dense texture (there's very little cake; the ingredients are held together by the sticky dough).

The reason fruitcake is so popular as a Christmas gift is because it can be shipped or mailed and will arrive at its destination intact.

One of the most famous jokes was made by the late Johnny Carson. He said this in the early 1990s on his *The Tonight Show*; *"There is only one fruitcake in the entire world, and people keep sending it to each other."* It's a nod to fruitcake's inability to go bad and the fact that no one actually eats it or likes it.

(As) *nutty as a fruitcake* Mentally unstable or strange in behavior; highly eccentric

- *She's **nutty as a fruitcake**, but harmless. She's actually fun to talk to.*

Background: It contains two words implying eccentricity or craziness: 'nutty' and 'fruitcake.'

Usage notes:
1. Often simplied to a *fruitcake*
2. Depending on how you say it or who you say it to, it can be a fun jab, or a bit of an insult.
3. Also, ***nuttier than a fruitcake***
4. See also FRUIT (slang) on page 6.

• • • • •

PIE

A *piece/a slice/of the pie* A share in something
- *According to the L.A. Times survey, the CEOs at 100 big CA companies are getting handed a **bigger slice of the pie**.*
- *I want my **piece of the pie**.*

Usage note: A very common expression

As *American as apple pie* Uniquely American
- *Levi's, Mickey Mouse and McDonalds are **as American as apple pie**.*

Background: Judging from the way it is used in this expression, one would think that the Americans invented apple pie. They didn't; they imported it from European countries. But they liked it so much they adopted it as their own.

Apple pie, together with motherhood, often represents American values like "wholesomeness," "honesty" and "simplicity." As a matter of fact, the full form of this expression is *as American as motherhood and apple pie*.

English learners are often confused by this. Why is it unique only to Americans?

Somehow thinking of motherhood and apple pie together is just heart-warming and comforting to most Americans. This could have come from the fond memories of growing up in a house (***the good old days!***) where your mom made hot home-cooked meals and your favorite pie FROM SCRATCH (See page 209). (And this gives us another expression ***the way Mom used to make*** or ***just like Mom used to make***; one that is used a lot in the food commercial world).

Some even go further and call apple pie "an American (cultural and/or patriotic) icon."

It's no wonder that U.S. advertisers would exploit this patriotic pride. In the mid 1970s, for example, Chevrolet came up with this commercial jingle:

"Baseball, hot dogs, apple pie and Chevrolet
They go together in the good 'old U.S.A"

There were also claims, according to Wikipedia, that the Apple Marketing Board of New York used *as American as apple pie* (along with AN APPLE A DAY KEEPS THE DOCTOR AWAY; see page 10) in their slogans to successfully 'rehabilitate' the popularity of apples after the Prohibition that outlawed the production of cider.

Still, with this much information out there, I could not find out how and when the phrase *as American as apple pie* exactly got started. Some speculate that it was rather new, though the sentiment seems to go back to the 19th century.

<u>Usage notes</u>:
1. I've noticed that it is often used more nowadays in a sarcastic, dismissive way:
   - *The practice of using steroids in our society in order to get bigger, faster and stronger is nothing new. In fact, it is **as American as apple pie**.*
2. Some even came up with a newer version: ***more American than apple pie***:
   - *Competition is **more American than apple pie**. It is why we love our sports and our sports heroes so much.*

Easy as pie Effortless, straightforward

- *This assignment is **easy as pie**.*

<u>Background</u>: As in the case of PIECE OF CAKE (see earlier), the reference here is more to the eating of a pie than to the making of it.

<u>Usage notes</u>:
1. It has the same idea as PIECE OF CAKE. People tend to use them interchangeably.
2. Also, ***simple as pie***

Have one's finger in every pie To be involved in lots of different things

- *He **has his finger in every pie**; he's basically running the place.*

<u>Background</u>: This old expression presumably originated with kitchen visitors who couldn't resist testing the food by sticking a finger in it and then licking their finger.

<u>Usage notes</u>:
1. Often with the implication that the person is overactive to the point of being a busy body
2. "Finger" in this expression is used in the singular form.
3. Other related-expressions are:
   - ***Keep one's finger out of the pie*** (mind one's own business)
   - ***Too many fingers spoil the pie*** (or TOO MANY COOKS SPOIL THE BROTH; see page 75)

No matter how/anyway/you slice it No matter how you look at it
- *No matter how you slice it, the first half of the game was ugly.*

• • • • •

CANDY

Arm candy An extremely beautiful person (usually female) who accompanies a member of the opposite sex to a party but is not necessarily romantically involved with that person; someone or something that is used just for show

- *The actress didn't want to play just 'the girl' roles – the **arm candy** – because she wanted to be taken seriously.*

Background: According to www.phrases.uk.com and www.wordspy.com, Marcia F. Coburn at the *Chicago Tribune* first used this term in 1990s when she wrote about Marilyn Monroe and the movie *All about Eve* (1950):

- *She'd already had mini-roles in eight movies when she turned up as George Sander's **arm candy** in the party scene in this film.*

Ear candy Music that is pleasant but not very satisfying (i.e., with very little substance)

- *It's nice **ear candy**, but it didn't move me that much.*

Background: The term was used as a title for the singer Helen Reddy's LP in 1977. Reddy was, at the time, criticized for her easy-listening, pleasant voice without much depth to it. (www.phrases.uk.com)

Eye candy Someone who is attractive but not intelligent or not particularly useful; something which looks good but serves little or no purpose

- *This anchorwoman is **eye candy**, but I don't see any wit in her.*

Background: The *Oakland Tribune* first used the term *eye candy* in its review of the then new TV sitcom *Three's Company* about three roommates - one man and two women.

Of interest: According to http://fenglish.wordpress.com, the Chinese equivalent for *eye candy* is "ice cream for the eyes." Interesting! They must really like ice cream.

If 'ifs' and 'buts' were candy and nuts, wouldn't it be a merry Christmas (every day)?
If all these reasons (why we can't do something) were party goodies instead of just words, we could have a really great party.

Background: The quote is attributed to Don Meredith (1938-2010), a football player and commentator. It seems to be patterned after an old nursery rhyme:

"*If wishes were horses, beggars would ride
If turnips were swords, I'd wear one by my side
If ifs and ands were pots and pans
There'd be no need for tinkers' hands*"

It means that if wishing could make things happen, then even the poorest of people would have everything that they wanted.

Sometimes people simply say *"If wishes were horses."*

The implication of both the saying and the rhyme are rather alike: that it is useless to make excuses and useless to idly wish for something.

Like/as happy as/a kid in a candy store Overwhelmed; filled with childlike excitement (with many good or tempting things all around you)
- *If you like working with computers, you will feel **like a kid in a candy store** with this company.*

Like/as easy as/taking candy from a baby It's too easy to do.
- *Some say identity theft can be done easily, just **like taking candy from a baby**.*

<u>Usage note</u>: Same idea as LIKE SHOOTING FISH IN A BARREL (See page 105.)

• • • • •

COOKIES

For the British, it's <u>biscuits</u>.

Caught with one's hand in the cookie jar To be caught in the act of doing something one is not supposed to or something dishonest
- *I was **caught with my hand in the cookie jar** eating ice cream when I was supposed to be on a strict diet.*
- *The cashier was finally **caught with her hand in the cookie jar** and was immediately fired.* (Or, ***caught with her hand in the till***)

<u>Background</u>: Most American homes traditionally have a jar of cookies in the kitchen area. Children are not supposed to touch it without permission. Sometimes they just can't resist the temptation.

In the second sentence, *the till* is a money box or a drawer.

Cookie-cutter Term used to describe merchandise that is mass-produced quickly and cheaply and which nearly always lacks originality and durability
- *Contractors like **cookie-cutter** houses because they are cheaper to build; buyers don't like them because they lack uniqueness.*
- *This is not just another **cookie-cutter** horror movie; it has some originality and creativity that sets it apart.*

<u>Background</u>: The term comes from a *cookie cutter* – a kitchen utensil that can stamp out any number of identical cookies from a given amount of cookie dough.

(One) tough cookie strong, durable, unyielding person
- *He has the reputation of being a **tough cookie** – the enforcer.*
- *She's **one tough cookie**. She's done a good job defending herself.*

<u>Usage notes</u>:
1. The peculiarity of this phrase consists of the combination of "tough" and "cookie." The first is usually a negative word, as in "a tough" (a hoodlum) or "tough guy" (often a gangster), but the word "cookie" removes the menace from "tough" – it is forgiving, slightly humorous and cautiously affectionate. The phrase is often used as a compliment, sometimes grudgingly:

it implies that the person described is capable of defending him- or herself; capable of holding his or her own ground.

2. The term a **smart cookie** is also used as a compliment and not limited to just women.
3. **Smart cookies don't crumble** is a rather newer saying – a combination of *smart cookies* and *that's the way the cookie crumbles*.

That's the way the cookie crumbles. That's the way things are and there's nothing you can do about it.

- *"I'm so disappointed I didn't get that job."*
*"**That's the way the cookie crumbles**. Maybe you will have better luck next time."*

Usage notes:
1. Often said of unpleasant things or said to someone who might have suffered a recent misfortune
2. Another expression used in this sense is **That's the way the ball bounces**.

• • • • •

"A FAMILY IS LIKE FUDGE — MOSTLY SWEET, BUT WITH A FEW NUTS!"

Fudge is a type of very sweet, semi-soft confection, often used in the U.S. synonymously with *chocolate fudge*. It was invented by accident in the late 19th century when a batch of candy (most likely chocolate caramels) didn't turn out quite right, and the main ingredient -sugar- recrystallized into a semi-soft mass.

Fudge To patch something together (especially in a sneaky manner) to disguise its faults

- *Corporations always **fudge** the numbers when trying to convince the political powers to do what they want.*
- *The governor may have **fudged** the facts in his Katrina boat story.*

Fudge! An exclamation of surprise or disbelief (like when you've messed up) - a replacement for the F-word

Background: Whether the verb *fudge* and the exclamation *fudge!* are related or not is often disputed.

The verb came into the language either in the middle of the 16th century (Mark Morton, 2000) or in the late 17th century (www.worldwidewords.org); the exclamation started to be used around the middle of the 18th century (Mark Morton 2000).

The failed batch of candy might have caused someone to use this exclamation; hence the name *fudge* for the candy. Or, since to *fudge* means to pull together various pieces and that's what it takes to make *fudge*, someone may have thought that *fudge* was an obvious name for the new candy (Mark Morton 2000).

• • • • •

PUDDING

For the Americans, *pudding* is mainly a soft, usually sweet dessert (such as rice pudding; bread pudding or chocolate pudding).

The British pudding is more of a basic dish than it is for the Americans; it means any food, sweet or savory (a salty dish, with cheese, for example) inside a crust.

The proof of the pudding is in the eating. The true value or quality of something can only be judged when it is put to use.

- *We'll find out soon whether your ad will help us sell our product or not. After all, **the proof of the pudding is in the eating**.*

Background: "Proof" here does not mean "conclusive evidence" in the scientific sense, but in a personal and pragmatic sense. If you don't know whether the pudding on the table before you is good or not, you taste it. If you like it, the question has been solved.

Usage note: Even some native speakers are confused by this saying. They say *the proof of the pudding* or *the proof is in the pudding*, not realizing that they have omitted the essential part - the testing of the pudding by eating it. These corrupted versions are now widely used.

You can't have your pudding if you don't finish your meat. You must finish your meal if you expect dessert.

Background: It comes from Pink Floyd's song *Another Brick in the Wall*.

Although Pink Floyd is a British rock band, they use "pudding" here in the American sense, i.e., a dessert. They might have gotten the idea from this often-cited line that most American children heard growing up: ***You can't have any dessert if you don't clean your plate.***

Usage notes:

1. Variations:
   If you don't eat your meat, you can't have any pudding.
   How can you have any pudding if you don't eat your meat?
2. It can also be used in a figurative sense:
   - *I won't let my kids watch TV until they finish with their homework.*
   How can they have any pudding if they don't finish their meat?

• •

OTHER TERMS AND EXPRESSIONS OF INTEREST

Ambrosia Anything imparting the sense of divinity; also something especially delicious to the sense of taste and smell

- *That first cup of coffee on a freezing morning like this was pure **ambrosia**.*

Background: In Greek mythology, *ambrosia* is the food of the gods, whereas nectar is their drink. Both ensure their immortality.

There is a dessert called *ambrosia*. It is made mostly of oranges and coconut, but some people add pineapple, marshmallow, whipped cream and different kinds of nuts in it.

Cheesecake Provocative pictures of attractive women with very little clothing
- *As a woman customer, I don't really like to see all the **cheesecake** on the walls in this place.*

Background: *Cheesecake* is a rich dessert made of cream cheese, butter and sugar, in the form of a shallow cake. The slang term dates from the early 1930s, at the height of the Great Depression. Cheesecake, a new delicacy at that time, was an unattainable luxury to many. So, it's not surprising that the women on the covers of risqué magazines, also unattainable to the average guy, would have become known as "cheesecake."

Usage notes:
1. A derogatory term with sexist overtones
2. There's also **beefcake**, a display of male physique, such as in photographs or calendars.
3. Both terms are considered old-fashioned nowadays.

Cracker Jack vs. crackerjack

Cracker Jack is a snack food of caramel-coated popcorn and peanuts.

In lower case, *crackerjack* was originally a noun appearing in the U.S. around 1875 describing a person of excellence and superior knowledge. It was later, and still is, used as an adjective meaning someone or something very pleasant, splendid or excellent. Capitalizing on this, the German immigrant entrepreneurs Frederick William Rueckheim and his brother Louis adopted it as the trade name for their confection in 1896. Their "Cracker Jack" (no –s) was immortalized in 1908 in the lyrics of *Take Me out to the Ball Game*, written by Jack Norworth and Albert Von Tilzer composed the music:

"Buy me some peanuts and Cracker Jack
 I don't care if I never get back…"

According to www.word-detective.com, *crackerjack* is most often heard today in the U.K or the British Commonwealth countries.

In his *The New Dickson Baseball Dictionary* (2009), Paul Dickson defines *crackerjack* as first–rate or spectacular player or team.

Cracker Jack is well-known for being packaged with a "toy surprise inside" (later replaced with paper prizes displaying riddles and jokes). This leads to an expression **come in/get something in/a Cracker Jack box**, referring to an object of no real value or something that is useless, cheap, fake and is not very recognized.

- *Where **did you get your driver's license, in a Cracker Jack box**?*
  (A very common phrase used by some angry drivers to bad drivers they encounter)

Cream puff As a slang term, it can mean:
1. A used vehicle in excellent condition; the opposite of LEMON (See page 6.) (Also used, *in mint condition*)
2. A person who is weak, ineffectual, lacking physical strength; other terms with similar meaning are a *wimp* or a *sissy.*
3. **Light as a cream puff** Someone/ something that weighs very little.

Background: A *cream puff* is a small, light puff pastry shell filled with whipped cream or custard.

Do donuts (Slang) To rotate the rear of the car around the front wheels continuously, thereby creating skid marks in the shape of a donut and causing lots of tire smoke. It's a skilled maneuver done mainly to show-off.
- *Witnesses claimed two cigar-chomping cops in a squad car nearly hit two little kids while **doing donuts**.*

Usage notes:
1. It's the term also used by some commentators in car-racing events.
2. It's either **dough**nut (because it is made of "dough") or **do**nut (probably due to the influence of *Dunkin Donuts*, a chain of donut shops).

   Doughnut is the original spelling. The simplified spelling, **do**nut, only came into use during the last 60 years and was meant to be mildly and pleasantly comic.

   I use both spellings here, depending on what the context is.

Dollars to doughnuts Phrase used to affirm that one is sure of one's assertion
- *I'll bet (you) **dollars to doughnuts** our team will make it to the playoffs.*

Background: According to www.randomhouse/wotd.com, this is an American phrase from the late 19th century. It alludes to odds in a bet and dates to when doughnuts were far less than a dollar. Being willing to bet real money to win doughnuts (which are often viewed as worthless or worth very little) means that one is absolutely confident that one is right.

Usage note: I was told that it is still in fairly common usage. It probably makes less sense now because doughnuts are more expensive than they used to be. Nowadays, you probably would have to settle for something like *I'll bet you the hole of a donut.*

Flavor of the month A person or thing that is currently but only temporarily popular or of interest
- *They are calling the candidate the **flavor of the month**. He's on everyone's radar now – the candidate most appealing at the moment, but it may not last.*

Background: According to www.phrases.uk.com, the phrase originated in the U.S. in the 1930s when ice-cream companies used it in their advertising slogans. No one knows for sure which company started it first.

Usage notes:
1. The term is often used ironically for things or people that fall out of fashion or favor quickly.
2. A more modern-day variant is *flavor du jour.* Now they give you even less time, a day instead of a month ("Le jour" is "the day" in French.)

Give me some sugar (Southern expression) An old-fashioned way of saying, "give me a kiss, a hug"

Usage notes:
1. Used especially to a child
2. When used by lovers, it means something like "do that thing you know I like" (often said in a sexually toned kind of way).
3. Although this expression is common in the south, it may be misunderstood in other parts of the country.

Gotta make the donuts Got to work to earn a living

Background: A catch phrase from the 1980s, it comes from a commercial about this old *Dunkin Donuts* man who was always shuffling around early in the morning before the sun came up mumbling *"time to make the donuts; gotta make the donuts."*

Usage note: The expression is not in common usage nowadays.

Jello Soft and wiggly – like jelly

- *"My knees turned to jello when I heard that siren."*

Background: *Jello* is actually a trade-marked dessert (as Jell-O). It is made of gelatin (a colorless, tasteless, transparent water-soluble protein), boiled sugar and various fruit flavors. It is soft and quivering, but cohesive enough to be molded into various shapes. It is very popular in the U.S. In the U.K. it is usually called jelly. Americans also eat what they call jelly and which comes in various fruit flavors. It is firmer and less-transparent than Jello and is usually spread on toast, bagels and so on. (See page 211.)

Life is like a box of chocolates - you never know what you're going to get.
It's hard to predict where your next step in life will lead you - just as you can never know what kind of chocolate you'll get on your next pick.

Background: It's a catch phrase from the movie *Forrest Gump* (1994). Usually, the wording on the covers of the boxes from *See's*, *Whitman's* and *Stover's* is "Assorted Chocolates" meaning, with different fillings.

I don't think this catch phrase really caught on. I remember hearing people use it right after the movie came out, but mostly in a humorous way.

Like trying to nail jello to a tree/a wall/the wall Referring to a difficult or impossible task

- *Raising teenagers is like trying to nail jello to a tree.*

Nose candy Slang for powdered cocaine or heroin that can be inhaled (and/ or snorted)

Usage note:

Candy is slang for illegal drugs.

Needle candy is liquid drugs that can be injected into a vein.

Rock candy is crystallized cocaine or heroin that can be smoked in a pipe.

Candy store is where you buy these drugs.

Candy man is the drug dealer. (Palmatier, 2000)

Over-egg the pudding (British) To spoil something by trying too hard to improve it

Background: The eggs add a richness to the pudding, but too much egg would make the pudding rubbery.

Usage note: Reminiscent of TOO MANY COOKS SPOIL THE BROTH (page 75) but mostly used when it's the content at issue and not the process

Pie hole An old-fashioned slang term for the mouth

- *Shut your pie hole!*

Usage notes:

1. Still common today especially on talk in sports shows
2. Also, **cake hole**; but *pie hole* is much more commonly used and sounds more brutal

Pie in the sky An unrealistic prospect of future happiness after present suffering

- *My nephew's hope to get a big break in show business proved to be **pie in the sky**.*

Background: This American term was coined by Joe Hill in 1911 for the labor organization he belonged to, in reference to Christian evangelists' promise of life in Heaven after death. The phrase was used to criticize their concentration on the salvation of souls rather than the feeding of the hungry.

Comment: This is the kind of expression that, unless you know its background, is hard to understand. I've asked a few of my American friends (those of a younger generation) about it; most didn't know what it means. One friend told me she would use **pipe dream** instead.

I've read that the British version is **jam tomorrow** though **pie in the sky** is also used there.

Plain vanilla/vanilla Bland, dull, boring (not considered adventurous or unusual)

Background: As a noun, vanilla is a basic flavor of ice cream and an essential flavoring for many types of desserts.

Usage note: Often used pejoratively

Many things come in *plain vanilla* versions, such as super-simple cell phones. Even the plain-looking Camilla (wife of Prince Charles of England) has been called by some British newspapers "plain vanilla Camilla."

Play patty cake To play nice; pretend to be friends

- *Both countries **play patty cake** with America while covering for the terrorists.*
Background: It comes from a traditional English nursery rhyme, a children's game called *Pat-a-cake, pat-a-cake, baker's man*, used as an exercise in rhythm and coordination. It is often accompanied by hand-clapping between two people sitting face-to-face.

Pop tart Young female performer who depends as much (or more) on her sex appeal as on her talent to be able to make it in show business
Background: *Pop tart* is a flat, rectangular, pre-baked toaster pastry made by Kellogg's, eaten as a quick breakfast. It has a sugary filling, resembling a dessert with no nutritional value.

Pudding head A dim-witted but amiable person (i.e., "soft in the head" like soft pudding)
Background: The term came from the belief that if children learning to walk fell frequently and hit their heads, they could scramble their brains, making them like the consistency of pudding.

Mark Twain uses the term as the title for one of his novels, *Pudd'nhead Wilson* (1893). The title character, lawyer David Wilson is so named by the locals who have a low opinion of his intelligence and common sense.

Sitting around eating bonbons Living a life of leisure and excess, doing nothing
Background: A *bonbon* comes from a French word, "bon" meaning "good."

According to www.wisegeek.com, a bonbon, the kind known in France and other European countries, is a chocolate-covered candy or truffle, often with a butter cream center. Sometimes it refers mainly to any fancy and round candy, not necessarily covered. This is the kind of bonbons that the supposedly 'idle' housewives in this expression eat.

In the U.S., a bonbon is a frozen confection, consisting of vanilla ice cream dipped in chocolate. It is also a trademarked name of Hershey Co.
Usage notes:
1. Other spellings are "bon bon" and "bon-bon." "Bonbon" seems to be the most common one.
2. The term can be offensive to some people because it stereotypes housewives and stay-at-home mothers as never having to work, but instead spending endless leisure hours eating sweets, watching daytime television, reading trashy novels and gossiping.
3. Variations: - *lying in bed eating bonbons/sitting around eating cupcakes and watching Oprah*

Take the gilt off the gingerbread To take away or spoil the attractiveness of a plan or a situation
- *"It seemed like a dream job to me, but finding out that I had to work six days a week really **took the gilt off the gingerbread**."*

<u>Background</u>: This is a rather old expression. *Gilt* is a thin layer of gold or gold paint. *Gingerbread* is a cake spiced with ginger. In Britain, up until the middle of the 19th century, it was often baked in fancy shapes or as toys ("gingerbread men"), decorated with imitation gold-leaf, and sold at fairs. In time, "gingerbread" became a metaphor for anything showy but insubstantial.

Tart Figuratively, a promiscuous young woman who dresses provocatively
- *"She is a brainless **tart**."*

<u>Background</u>: *Tart* is a small pie or pastry, e.g., fruit tart, cream tart.

<u>Usage note</u>: To **tart up** means to dress up in a sleazy, cheap or provocative way; to modify or repackage a product, service or idea to make it more attractive or easier to sell (often with the result that it comes out worse):
- *He likes his wife to wear short, tight, sexy dresses when they go out. He likes her to **tart up**!*
- *The ex-anchorman bashed his successor for dumbing down and **tarting up** a serious news program in hopes of attracting a younger audience.*

Twinkie Figuratively, someone (male or female) who is attractive, but not very smart and lacks substance

<u>Background</u>: *Twinkies* are cream-filled, yellow sponge cakes made by *Hostess*, widely considered to be a junk food snack. (They "stay fresh forever" because they contain only chemicals and no actual dairy-based products that could quickly go bad.)

The term likens a person to a Twinkie cake that's too airy, full of empty calories and doesn't have enough nutritional value to satisfy one.

There was a famed courtroom defense in the 1979 trial of former San Francisco Supervisor Dan White, accused of shooting San Francisco city mayor, George Moscone and another Supervisor, Harvey Milk. His attorneys argued that he suffered from severe depression that had been exacerbated by junk food bingeing. Although Twinkies were only mentioned in passing, the term **Twinkie Defense** was quickly coined by journalists to explain the legal strategy that led to White's conviction on a lesser charge.

<u>Usage notes</u>:
1. It is also used as a racial slur to refer to an Asian who has lost or renounced one's roots (yellow on the outside, but white inside).
2. An *Oreo* is a popular snack consisting of two chocolate cookies pasted together with a white cream-like filling. It is often used as a derogatory term for a black person of suspect ethnic loyalty – meaning that he is black on the outside but white inside.

11
· · · · ·
Meals of the Day

"Sing before breakfast, cry before supper (or night)." Proverbial saying
(A warning against overconfidence in early happiness; there could be a reversal of good fortune)

ESPECIALLY FOR ENGLISH LEARNERS

TERMINOLOGY

Breakfast is the first meal of the day, usually in the morning.

Breakfast, in the U.S. at least, consists of such dishes as *pancakes*, *hot* and *cold cereals*, *French toast*, *ham*, *bacon*, *sausage* and *eggs* and the like. If you have pancakes later in the day, you can still say you are having a breakfast.
  - *Customer to waitress: "I know it's lunchtime, but can I still order breakfast? I was so busy the whole morning I haven't had my breakfast yet."*
  - *My husband is a breakfast person; he can have pancakes at 10 o'clock at night!*

Note: This may be confusing to English learners with different eating habits. Some cultures define daily meals simply by when one eats, and not necessarily by what one eats. Thai people, for example, can have a bowl of beef noodle soup three different times in one day and consider themselves as having breakfast, lunch and dinner. It's not surprising that some, when eating at an American restaurant, would attempt to order soup during breakfast hours.

Brunch (from breakfast + lunch) Usually on Sundays; almost always eaten "out" in a restaurant, served usually from 10 a.m.– 2 p.m.. Some are quite fancy (like *champagne brunch*).

Lunch is the midday meal, usually light (sandwiches, soup & salad, etc.).

Lunch vs. Luncheon

A lunch – usually going out with just a few friends (Also, "to lunch")

A luncheon is a more formal event with more people. It may involve an invitation that needs to be responded to, as well as specific table settings. It is usually held in connection with a meeting or some other special occasion.

Dinner is the biggest meal of the day, usually eaten in the early evening.

Sunday dinner – Many people (regardless of whether they go to church or not) have Sunday dinner earlier than on other days, usually in the early afternoon and so there is no need for lunch that day.

People in rural communities often call their midday meal "dinner."

One usually says *going out to dinner* when going to a restaurant (or, *going out to eat*).

<u>Supper</u> generally means "a light dinner," especially when eaten informally and at home. It is defined as the evening meal when dinner is eaten at midday. Some people use "dinner" and "supper" interchangeably to refer to the evening meal.

Note: The terms described here are how they are used in the American context. The British often use the term <u>tea</u> to refer to an afternoon snack and <u>high tea</u> or <u>meat tea</u> to refer to "dinner."

GRAMMATICAL POINTS

We say, have *breakfast*; have *lunch*; have *dinner*.

Have *a breakfast meeting; a lunch break; a dinner date* (*breakfast*, etc., used as adjective).

Have a *big breakfast; a quick lunch; an expensive dinner* (when *breakfast, lunch, dinner* have a qualifier, an article is needed).

• •

COMMON EXPRESSIONS

As flat as a pancake Extremely flat

- *"Don't get near that bulletin board. If it fell on you, you'd be squashed* ***as flat as a pancake!****"*

Background: A pancake is a thin flat cake of batter, cooked on both sides until brown, served with butter and syrup. People often eat a few of them at a time, one stacked on top of the other, hence the name *a stack (of pancakes)* used on restaurant menus. Other names also used are *hot cakes* (See SELL LIKE HOT CAKES later.); *griddle cakes* and *flap jacks*.

Usage notes:
1. It can be used figuratively:
   - *The coach admitted that his team's performance last night was **as flat as a pancake**.*
2. It's also slang for a flat-chested woman. Another expression is ***pancake flat***.
   - *She is **as flat as a pancake**, but she's also as cute as a button.*
3. To ***pancake*** means to flatten; reduce to a flat state:
   - *Both cars got **pancaked** in the collision.*

Brown-bag it (verb) To bring one's own homemade lunch (in a brown bag or otherwise) to eat at one's work or school, rather than buying it and paying more

- *"Mike and I are going out for lunch. Do you want to come with us?"*
  *"No, I'm **brown-bagging it** today."*

Usage notes:
1. A ***brown-bag event/seminar/meeting*** is a lunchtime event at work or in academic setting where a professional of some kind gives a presentation in his or her area of expertise. Each participant is expected to bring his or her

own food to be eaten during the presentation. It's very common in the U.S., especially in academia.

2. To **brown-bag** can mean to drink alcohol from a bottle that is wrapped in a paper bag, a way around the general prohibition on street drinking in the U.S.

It can also mean to bring one's own liquor in a brown paper bag to a public place or restaurant not licensed to sell it.

3. In the U.K, the term to **brown bag** may refer to what responsible dog owners do – cleaning up after their pets.

Eat someone's lunch To completely dominate or defeat someone

- *It was a decisive victory. We **ate their lunch**.*

Background: It is a reference to school bullies who take away other kids' lunches and eat them.

Usage notes:

1. Also, *We **had them for lunch**.*

2. It means the same as to *eat someone alive*.

Have/get/your lunch handed to you To be easily and embarrassingly outperformed

- *This guy is a pro. If you think you can go head-to-head against him, then you are about to **get your lunch handed to you.***

Background: Being handed your lunch and sent off to eat signals your exit since the competition is over. It could be based on the same idea as *to have your hat handed to you* (from the days that men wore hats as part of their clothing and took them off indoors) meaning that you are being kicked out of a place.

Usage note: Used when one goes up against a stronger and more experienced opponent

It's a meal in itself. Used to describe a side dish whose portion is big and filling

- *This salad is huge! **It's a meal in itself**. I don't think I can eat anything more after this.*

Usage note: A very common expression

Let's do lunch. Let's meet for lunch sometime soon (to continue our conversation).

- *John: "Nice hearing from you. **Let's do lunch** sometime."*
  Bill: "Good idea. Call me."

Background: This was popularized, if not also coined, in the 1980s in entertainment circles, as well as among yuppies (young urban professionals), influenced by fast-paced lifestyles.

The use of "do" instead of "have" seems to be the 80's jargon.

Usage note: A phrase most associated with people in business, it is often used in the context of "I don't have time to talk right now. Let's meet later when it's convenient for both of us."

Depending on the people involved, such a vague statement can be sincere – some might actually call each other to set a lunch date. Others say those words without really meaning it (i.e., you never hear from them again) – for them, it's more like a polite brush-off to end a conversation than anything else.

Lunch is on me. Phrase used to mean one will pay for the other person's meal when eating out

- *"Don't worry about it. **Lunch is on me** today."*

Usage notes:

1. A very common expression
   Also, ***breakfast/dinner/is on me*** (no article is needed)
2. Other expressions also used: ***I'm buying it; it's my treat; it's on me; let me get the check; It's my turn; I'll pick up the check this time;*** (to a server) ***put his/ her order on my tab/check.***
3. To ***go Dutch***, on the other hand, means that each pays his own bill.
4. One can also ***split the bill*** with the other person or ask for ***separate checks.***

Make a meal of something To exaggerate the significance or amount of effort one has had to put into something

- *"He really **made a meal of** organizing his desk. It took him most of the day!"*

Meal ticket A person or thing depended on as a source of financial support; ability possessed by a person that is necessary to that person's livelihood or successful quest for something

- *I think he really loved her, but he also needed a **meal ticket**.*
- *His basketball skill was his **meal ticket** when he applied to that college; he got accepted right away on a full scholarship.*

Background: The term is known more for its figurative than its literal meaning. Meal tickets were a way of life in America at the end of the 19th and the beginning of the 20th century, especially for working people who lived alone in single rooms with no kitchen. They had to rely on eating out and often bought meal tickets that were good for a week at discounted prices.

Not know where one's next meal is coming from To be very poor; destitute (have nothing)

- *It's hard to believe, but there are millions and millions of people in the U.S. who **don't know where their next meal is coming from**.*

Usage note: Other idioms also used are to **live from hand to mouth** and **live from day to day.**

Power breakfast A meeting of influential or business people to conduct business while eating breakfast

- *This restaurant is a powerhouse for the **power breakfast**. Every weekday morning, the city's lawyers, important business people, media moguls and politicians meet and eat here.*

Background: It is difficult to pinpoint when the term originated; the practice, however, had been around long before it was assigned the prefix 'power.'

According to www.barrypopik.com, Washington D.C. during the 1960s was the home of both *power breakfast* and *power lunch.*

Some suggest that the term was born in the 1980s when Ronald Reagan began assembling his KITCHEN CABINET (page 192) in the White House dining room each morning.

Usage notes:
1. "Power" is used here to enhance the word "breakfast" – to charge it with added importance.
2. Other terms also used, ***working breakfast; business breakfast***
3. Nutritionists sometimes use the term ***power breakfast*** to advocate the importance of breakfast. For them, breakfast is the most important meal of the day. Their mantra is probably this old saying: ***Eat breakfast like a king, lunch like a prince and dinner like a pauper.***

Power lunch A meeting over lunch that gives the opportunity to network or discuss high-level business (or political) matters
- *The **power lunch** has been a casualty of the economic crash. Business, for a lot of people, is now done early from 7 to 9 a.m.*

Background: It was Lee Eisenberg, writing in *Esquire* magazine in the late 1970s, who is thought to have coined the term "power lunch" in a reference to the noon meal at the *Four Seasons Restaurant* in New York.

Usage note: Not everyone who practices it likes the term; some prefer ***business*** or ***working lunch***.

Out to lunch Not attentive, not mentally there; crazy
- *He didn't hear a word you said; he was completely **out to lunch**.*
- *If you believe in such a theory, then you really are **out to lunch**.*

Background: From the literal meaning of ***out to lunch***, to be away to eat one's lunch.

Usage note: For the first meaning, you can also say, (be) ***in another world*** or (be) ***daydreaming.***

Sell like hotcakes To sell fast and in large quantities
- *This new version of Windows isn't just getting good reviews; it's also **selling like hotcakes**.*

Background: Back in the 19th century, before the appearances of the hot dog, ice cream cone, pizza and other tasty items, hotcakes were the best selling hot food at carnivals, fairs and church benefits. They sold so fast that they became the basis for the metaphor of a (new) product that goes over big.

Usage note: Very common

Other expressions also used are *fly off the shelf*; (*it*) *caught on fire* and *become a hit product*.

Sing for one's supper To work for one's pay or reward; earn a favor by providing a service in return

- *His wife wouldn't cook dinner for him unless he helped her clean the house first. She really made him* **sing for his supper!**
- *We all have to* **sing for our supper** *in this world, one way or another.*

Background: In bygone days, wandering minstrels traveled around entertaining people and were given food and lodgings in return. The term was popularized in a nursery rhyme *Little Tommy Tucker*:

Little Tommy Tucker, sang for his supper
What shall we give him, white bread and butter

There is also a saying **whose bread I eat, his song I sing** – I'm loyal to whoever feeds me.

Usage note: A modern version would be **wash the dishes** - to pay for a meal at a restaurant; used jokingly when one thinks one might not have enough money to cover the check.

There's no such thing as a free lunch. You cannot get something for nothing.

- **There's no such thing as a free lunch**. *In return for your help, what do you ask?*

Background: The saying is closely associated with the economist Milton Friedman (1912-2006), who popularized it and used it as the title of his 1975 book, but it is much older. The acronym TANSTAAFL (for *There ain't no such thing as a free lunch*) appears in Robert Heinlein's 1966 sci-fi novel *The Moon Is a Harsh Mistress*. Heinlein was undoubtedly quoting an expression that predated him.

The origin of this saying is believed to have come from the widespread practice of saloon keepers of the 19th and early 20th century offering a "free lunch" (usually a cold buffet) to anyone who purchased a drink. Those who stayed sober soon figured out that they were paying for their "free" lunch with what they were being charged for their drinks.

Usage note: This saying is the most basic principle of economics – a warning against the hidden costs of anything seemingly free. It is also in general use.

Three-course meal A meal which consists of a soup or salad, an entree (a main course) and a dessert

- *"We are offering a* **three-course meal** *for two for $20. Diners share one salad and one dessert."*

Background: *Entree* is a word often used on restaurant menus in the U.S. to indicate the main dinner dishes.

In France, it originally referred to what was called, rather magnificently, "the grand entrance of the signature course." The word itself was coined in the 18th century, following the adoption by the French Court of the habit of presenting a dinner "a la Russe" – in the Russian style – which meant that the dishes were served in order, rather than, as before, having all the dishes on the table at once, from the beginning.

From what I've read, many British speakers equate *entreé* with *starter*, which Americans would call the *appetizer*.

According to the *Oxford Encyclopedic Dictionary*, in Britain the *entreé* is "a dish served between the fish and meat courses," but in the U.S. it is "the main dish of a meal."

The order of the courses is natural – at least to Western eyes. Dessert is a luxury, a special treat, usually sweet, not a dish of substance and sustenance, and so comes last. Many, perhaps most, Americans feel – and often say – that if they should eat the dessert first, it would "spoil" their dinner – that is leave them with no appetite for the meat and potatoes.

Usage notes:
1. Depending on various configurations, one can also have a *four-course meal* or more (an appetizer, a soup and salad, an entree and a dessert).
2. A *three-course meal*, when used figuratively, means "satisfying" and "complete."
   - *This Festival was a **three-course meal** of the arts, offering audiences a multimedia experience of performances that fused film, live theater and music.*
3. *Appetizer* and *main course* can also be used figuratively.
   - *According to the president, the reforms he has initiated so far are just **appetizers**; the **main course** is still coming.*
4. *Dessert* is a metaphor for pleasures, indulgence.
   *"Life is uncertain, eat **dessert** first."* Ernestine Ulmer, American writer (1925-   )

• •

OTHER TERMS AND EXPRESSIONS OF INTEREST

Bed and breakfast An accommodation offered by a private residence, consisting of a room for the night and breakfast the next morning for one inclusive price

Bon appetit! (pronounced "bon appe-tee") literally means "Good Appetite." There are similar phrases in other languages; but, curiously enough, "Good appetite!" doesn't sound quite right to American and British ears, and so the French phrase is used. "***Bon appetit!***," composed of soft vowels, sounds gracious and cordial. (But it's not really much used.)

Dog's breakfast/dinner British slang for a mess
- *He made **a** complete **dog's dinner** of that display.*
Usage note: The British expression **dressed up like a dog's dinner** means to be dressed in a way that shows you are trying to impress people but is unsuitable for the occasion.

Early bird dinners/specials Restaurant dinners served earlier than traditional dinner hours with a reduced price and often more limited in selection than the standard dinner menu (and also smaller portions). The term is often stereotypically associated with the elderly.

Ladies who lunch Women with both means and time who meet each other socially for lunch at expensive restaurants. The term is used in a semi-derogatory sense.
Background: The phrase was popularized by a song in Stephen Sondheim's musical *Company*.

Lose your lunch A euphemism for "to vomit"

Lunch lady American slang for a woman who works and serves food in a school cafeteria; often caricatured as overweight, uncaring, wearing hairnets and gloves. The British term is **dinner lady**.

Scattered from hell/here/to breakfast Spread out over a wide area
- *There's dust and dried leaves **scattered from here to breakfast**.*
Background: It's an old expression alluding to cattle that are scattered so far that it will take all night and until breakfast the next day to round them up.

Square meal A satisfying, wholesome and balanced meal
Usage note: The meal is 'square' in the sense of 'proper' (as in **square deals** and **fair and square**).

Three-martini lunch A derisive term for lavish business lunches involving heavy drinking and claimed as tax-deductible business expenses. The practice is not as common as it once was.

TV dinner Any pre-packaged frozen dinner bought in a supermarket and reheated at home and eaten while watching TV, hence the name *TV dinner*. (Nowadays watching TV isn't necessarily a part of eating a TV dinner.) The first company to successfully market the product was Swanson.
There are also **TV breakfast, TV lunch** and all kinds of **TV snacks**.

You can call me anything you want, just don't call me late for dinner. This is a funny saying, playing on the double-meaning of the word "call"-- the first to name someone ("Call me George.") and the second to summon someone in to dinner with a raised voice (a call or yell, "It's dinner time!"), or possibly, nowadays, by telephone.

See also COME AND GET IT! (Page 207).

12
. . . . .
Cooking Terms and Kitchenware

The English language uses many cooking methods to describe different kinds of activities.

COOKING TERMS

COOKING IN GENERAL

Cook one's goose To ruin one's chances, hopes or plans; destroy one's good name
- *Her goose was cooked when they found out she lied in her resumé.*
- *The treasurer cooked his own goose when he was caught stealing the company's money.*

Background: Why geese? Supposedly they used to be more common food than they are now.

Usage notes:
1. It is used in the sense of sealing one's doom.
2. There's an old saying: *If you cook your own goose, you will have to eat it.*

Cook the books To deliberately distort a company's financial records, to avoid paying taxes or to impress investors
- *They'll find ways to cook their books just to impress their stockholders, so that these people will stay with the company.*

Background: The allusion could be the changing of one thing into another, as in the conversion of food ingredients into meals.

Usage note: Another term often used is *doctor the books*, meaning to tamper with, to patch and mend. *Cook the books* is more often used probably because of the rhyme.

Cook up Literally, to make a meal; figuratively, to set up a plan
- *We will have only a few guests and none of them is a big eater, so we are not planning on cooking up a lot of food.*
- *"Hey, good- lookin', whatcha got cookin'?*
  How's about cookin' somethin' up with me?"
  (a classic country song by Hank Williams Sr.)
- *She cooked up yet another excuse for not paying her rent on time.*

Usage note: Depending on the context, the figurative *cook up* can be used either in a positive or negative sense.

Cook up a storm To do something with a lot of energy and skill; cause a big fuss or generate a lot of talk about something

- *This is the season to spread a little holiday food cheer and many people are* **cooking up a storm.**
- *Experts* **cook up a storm** *urging pregnant women to eat fish.*

Cooked (Slang) In big trouble

- *The guy is* **cooked**, *completely cooked.*

Usage note: Other slang terms used in this sense are TOAST (Page 62) and DEAD MEAT (Page 78).

Now we're cooking with gas. Now we're doing something in an effective way.

- *We just had the latest updated software installed in our computer at work, so* **now we're cooking with gas.** *Hopefully we'll finish our project a lot sooner now.*

Background: The term is said to have come from an early advertising slogan from the time when cooking with gas was the height of innovation – the suggestion was that stoves using natural gas as a fuel cook better, faster and more effective than wood burning stoves.

Usage notes:
1. Used whenever something really gets rolling, as when a big project or a long-held dream finally moves toward reality
2. Often shortened to **now we're cooking**
3. You can also combine the two together:
   - **Now we're cooking, let's turn up the gas**. (Things are working out, let's go for it.)

The fat is in the fire. Something that is likely to lead to trouble has started and looks like it can't be stopped.

- *Because of the mayor's offensive joke, now* **the fat is in the fire**. *Not much one can do except wait for the situation to unfold.*

Usage note: A related expression, ***pull the fat out of the fire*** is rather new. It means to do something to avoid further trouble; to save a situation from getting worse.

It's simply a mix-up between these two expressions: ***the fat is in the fire*** and PULL CHESTNUTS OUT OF THE FIRE (FOR SOMEONE) (page 17):

- *The corn industry hopes Congress will* **pull its fat out of the fire**. (www.grist.org, 12-1-07)

This expression can be used only in a figurative sense. Literally, it's impossible to do. Once the fat (e.g., grease, oil, lard) is well melted in the fire, it's already too late to save anything.

What's cooking? What's happening? What's going on?

- *"Too many people work up a head of steam before they find out* **what's cooking**." Unknown

Usage note: Other slang expressions with the same meaning: ***What's up?/What's new?/What's the haps?/What's shakin'?/What's coming down the pike?***

• • • • •

BAKING AND ROASTING

TERMINOLOGY

<u>Roasting</u> is similar to <u>baking</u> (both are done in the oven) but roasting implies cooking at a higher temperature, at least at the beginning to get the surface of the food to brown. <u>Roasting</u> can also refer to cooking food in dry heat either in the oven or over an open flame.

<u>Baking</u> is done at a lower temperature with the heat all around.

Half-baked (Ideas, plans, solutions or philosophies that are) not completely planned or thought out
- *The name of the blog is "muddled ramblings and **half-baked** ideas"; I find many of the blogger's ideas, however, really thought-provoking.*

<u>Background</u>: Food that is half-baked is obviously insufficiently cooked.

<u>Usage note</u>: The opposite is **done (roasted) to a turn** meaning, to be cooked just right. Like **half-baked**, it can be used figuratively:
- *The governor, the guest of honor at last night's roast, was **done to a turn**.*

<u>Background</u>: '**Done to a turn**' was originally referred to meat that was roasted on a spit over an open fire.

The first spits were simply pointed sticks used to hold meat close to or over a fire; but in time metal spits (also called skewers) were devised. These were supported by metal legs over an open fire or in a fireplace, and the meat, skewered on a spit, could be rotated (turned) over the fire by means of a handle at one end. To say that a piece of meat was done to a turn meant that it had been turned the exact number of times to be cooked to perfection.

Roast (someone) (verb) To criticize someone or something severely or mercilessly; poke fun at someone, especially one who is being honored at a special event
- *The movie was **roasted** by the critics.*
- *The class clown was just **roasted** by his classmates.*
- *We are here at this special occasion to **roast** him, not to give him compliments.*

<u>Background</u>: Regarding the second meaning of the term: The idea is that the roast is done good-naturedly, affectionately and in a spirit of fun. The challenge to the speakers (the **roasters**) is to come as close as possible to insulting the guest of honor without offending him or her. It is a peculiarly American institution, popularized by the so-called *Rat Pack*: Frank Sinatra, Dean Martin (who hosted *the Dean Martin's Celebrity Roasts* from 1973-1984 on NBC), Sammy Davis Jr., Joey Bishop and others.

• • • • •

BOILING

People often use the word **boiling** to describe their troubled emotions. **Boiling mad, boiling with rage, reach the boiling point** and **make one's blood boil**, for example, are used hyperbolically (i.e., obvious and intentional exaggeration) to describe a person's extreme degree of anger.

- *He's not just slightly mad; he's **boiling mad**.*
- *They obviously feel betrayed and are **boiling with rage**.*
- *The mayor has **reached the boiling point**. He has been struggling to contain his anger and frustration over the constant barrage of questions about his character and judgment.*
- *Seeing how badly he treated his own mother **made my blood boil**.*

Other related terms also used:

An extremely upset person is said **to be steamed**. A workplace can be described as a **pressure cooker**. When a person doesn't want to do anything, the co-workers may say, "*Somebody ought to **light a fire** under him*." On the other hand, someone who is energized, eager to get things done is said **to be fired up**.

Boil down to something To be the main reason, the essence

- *His speech **boiled down to** this – a plea for more contributions.*

Usage note: Used about a situation or a problem

Boil something down/boil down something To make something short or simple by getting rid of the parts that are not important or necessary

- *I don't think people want to buy an 800-page novel. Somehow you're going to have to **boil it down** to at least half of that size.*

Boil up To feel negative emotion strongly; to grow toward a dangerous level

- *I could feel anger, frustration and fear **boiling up** inside of me not knowing when this financial meltdown is going to end.*

Usage note: **Boil over** is one step further from **boil up**; the difficult situation or negative emotion cannot be controlled anymore:

- *Anger over budget cuts **boils over** at L.A. schools.*

Come to a boil To reach the point of greatest activity; no turning back

- *A simmering debate that was underway since last week in the Senate over new energy legislation finally **came to a boil** this week.*

Usage notes:
1. The implication is that this is the climax of the activity, when most things will be resolved.
2. Also used, **hit (a) full boil**
3. The opposite: **come off the boil**, to cool down (after having been so 'hot' that it was boiling):
   - *His political career **came off the boil** after losing his reelection bid for the Senate seat.*

He or she can't even boil water! He or she doesn't know how to cook, period! (Can't even do the most simple thing)

• • • • •

BROILING AND GRILLING

TERMINOLOGY

<u>Grilling</u> refers to cooking food quickly over high heat, with the food sitting on a metal grate that leaves "grill marks." This direct heat sears the food, giving it a flavorful charred texture. It can be done outdoors on charcoal grills, gas grills or using stove-up "grill pans" which have raised metal ridges for the food to sit on, or even on an indoor electric grill.

<u>Barbecuing</u>, on the other hand, refers to cooking with low temperatures using indirect heat from smoke. Usually some sort of marinade or sauce is brushed on the food before or during cooking.

<u>Broiling</u> is similar to grilling except that the heat comes from the top (usually a gas flame or an electric coil) whereas in grilling, the heat comes from the bottom. This is based on my experience living in the U.S. The terms might mean different things in other countries.

I've also noticed that the meanings of *grilling* and *broiling* have changed somewhat in recent years. An example of this is in restaurant lingo. Most restaurants have flat, heavy grills. If you ask for your meat to be grilled, it will be cooked on this flat grill. If you want a charred flavor (with all the grill marks) you have to ask for it to be "(char-) broiled."

Broil To become very hot, especially from the sun; be in a rowdy controversy, dispute or argument

- *Triple-digit temperatures **broiled** Southeast U.S. over the weekend.*
- *The controversy over this issue has been **broiling** for quite some time.*

<u>Usage note</u>: Adrian Room in his *Dictionary of Confusable Words* (2000) points out that figuratively, **boil** and **broil** are closer in meaning than when they are used literally:

- *It was **boiling** in the sun.* (It was very hot.)
- *We were **broiling** in the sun.* (We were very hot and cooking in it.)

<u>Comment</u>: I would also say, we were ***baking/roasting/*** in the sun.

Grill To give someone an intense interrogation

- *This guy is tough; he **grills** every politician that has shown up on his show.*

<u>Usage notes</u>:

1. This is a very common term that is used quite a lot in the news.
2. Also, ***give someone a grilling; get a grilling; get grilled; face/endure (tough/light) grilling:***
   - *The lawmakers are to **get a grilling** from local students on a range of issues.*

3. The opposite is *give someone a pass* and *get a pass*; also, *get an easy ride*:
   - *There are perceptions that this president **has gotten an easy ride** from the press.*

• • • • •

HEATING

In cooking terms, heat refers to the temperature:
   - *Do you want me to cook the meat on a high or low **heat**?*
   (At a high or low temperature?)

It can also be used as a verb and adjective:
   - *to **heat up** the soup for lunch*
   - *a **heated** swimming pool*

Heat Metaphor for criticism, blame or pressure
   - *To make it in politics, politicians have to learn to **take the heat**.*
   (To endure heavy criticism)
   - ***The heat is on** as soon as someone announces his candidacy to run against the incumbent.* (The pressure has begun.)
   - *Once the political race **heats up**, we will hear all kinds of **heated** campaign rhetoric.* (Once the race gets intense, we will hear all kinds of angry comments.)
   - *And, **in the heat of the moment**, either side may say things that they'll later regret.* (At the time when one is very angry)
   - *They will try to **turn up the heat** on the other side whenever they can.* (To increase the pressure)
   - *Smart politicians know how to **take the heat off** themselves, however.* (To reduce the amount of criticism)

If you can't stand the heat, stay out of the kitchen. If the pressure of the task is too much for you, just quit and leave it to someone who can handle it.
   - *"I had no idea that being in charge of this project would be such a stressful job."*
   *"Well, **if you can't stand the heat, stay out of the kitchen**."*

Background: It was supposed to have been coined by Harry S. Truman (1884-1972), the 33rd U.S. President (1945-1953), who was famous for folksy sayings (including *the buck stops here*).

However, Ralph Keyes in his *The Quote Verifier* notes that Truman biographer, Robert Ferrell, gives the credit to Eugene I. "Buck" Purcell, someone Truman used to work with before he became president. To his credit, Truman did help popularize the saying.

Usage notes:
1. A very common expression; used in every kind of situation
2. It could be somewhat insulting to the person addressed to, since it implies he or she can't handle the pressure.

• • • • •

STEWING

TERMINOLOGY

Stewing is the process of cooking by slowly simmering ingredients (vegetables and/or meats) in a little liquid until all the ingredients are tender.

In a stew Worried or upset
- *She was in a stew over the lost keys.*

Usage notes:
1. An old-fashioned term
2. **To be stewed**, on the other hand, is slang for being drunk, possibly alluding to the idea that is what the alcohol is doing to one's internal organ.
To be **stewed to the gills** means to be extremely drunk.

Comment: Some people got creative and came up with to **get (someone) out of a/the/ stew**. I've seen it used in advertising and newspaper headlines.

Let someone stew Keep a person in a state of uneasy anticipation or suspense
- *"You should take a break from your boyfriend, don't answer his calls and **let him stew** for a while without any contact with you."*

Usage notes:
1. Also, **leave someone to stew**
2. To **stew in one's own juice** means to sit in a mess of one's own making
Let him stew in his own juice! He created the problem, so let him suffer for it. (This sounds rather inept to me. I would think that food stewing in its own juice is a good thing since it brings out the flavor that way.)

Simmer down To become calm or quiet, especially after a state of agitation, anger or excitement
- ***Simmer down!** I don't think ranting will help you solve the problem.*

Of interest: There was a skit on *Saturday Night Live* some years ago with a character named Nadeen (played by Cheri Oteri), a testy employee at *Burger Castle* who constantly ordered everyone to *"simmer down, now!"*

Stew (over, about) To brood, hold simmering anger over an extended time
- *Sometimes, you make things worse when you **stew over** someone's words.*

Usage notes:
1. Other terms also used are to **bear a grudge; harbor ill-feeling/resentment.**
2. It can also mean to think things over, waiting for an idea to emerge.

• •

KITCHENWARE

Everything but the kitchen sink Including just almost anything
- *He just bought the latest model of Jaguar. It's got **everything but the kitchen sink.***

Usage note: The implication is that the kitchen sink would have been included too, but that was impossible because it is heavy, connected to pipes and usually bolted down.

Kitchen sink is sometimes used as a visual gag in visual media to denote a level of excess.

(Put something) on the back burner To put off or postpone doing something; the opposite is **(remain/is/is back) on the front burner**

- *Thousands of career women nationwide opt to **put their careers on the back burner** to stay home to care for their children.*
- *After all these years, immigration issues still **remain on the front burner** in this country.*

Background: Both terms come from the setup of a cooking range. Most stoves, in American kitchens at least, have two front burners and two back burners. The back burners are used for simmering while the front ones are more for fast cooking. The metaphor has been extended to all kinds of activities.

Put food on the table To provide for one's family

- *There are a lot of people out there struggling to **put food on their table** and to make sure their children have a better life.*

Usage notes:
1. A very common expression
2. Another related-term is **the kitchen-table issues**, everyday concerns that confront ordinary people on a daily basis, things like mortgages, health care and wages:
   - *The most important thing for our candidate to do is find a way to show concern with the **kitchen-table issues**.*

Some people use **pocket-book issues** in this sense.

• • • • •

POTS AND PANS

A watched pot never boils. Watching something not only doesn't make it happen faster, it makes the time seem longer.

- *Just as **a watched pot never boils**, so too does a watched clock seemingly never move.*
- ***A watched pot never boils**. So maybe that's why my hair is not growing fast enough for me.*

Usage note: It warns against impatience.

Bang (on) pots and pans To get one's message out; raise consciousness about something or protest against something

- *Let us **bang pots and pans** about sending these people back to where they belong.*
- *They simply use the media to **bang pots and pans** when they want attention.*

<u>Background</u>: The term may have come from the ritual in the old days in many cultures of literally banging on pots and pans to scare away evil spirits.

<u>Usage note</u>: Other expressions also used are to **make a noise** and to **take to the streets**:

- *The governor asked citizens to **make a noise** about proposed tax cuts.*
- *We might have to **take to the streets** to stop our country's slide into socialism.*

Jump out of the frying pan (and) into the fire To get out of a bad situation and end up in one that is even worse

- *He soon realized that quitting his old job and coming to work here was **jumping out of the frying pan into the fire.***

<u>Usage notes</u>:

1. Sometimes shortened to **out of the frying pan**
2. There are also some new twists to this old expression:
   - *We've just come out of the frying pan, let's not jump into the fire yet.*
   - *Into the frying pan or the fire – which way should we jump?*

<u>Of interest</u>: Many languages have a phrase to express this concept:
Arabic: *To get out of the hole and fall down the slope*
German: *Out of the rain into the gutter*
Malay: *To escape from the tiger's mouth into the crocodile's mouth*
Russian: *Out of fire, and into flame*

The pot calling the kettle black A criticism a person is making of another could equally apply to himself or herself.

- *If I were you, I wouldn't call him lazy. That would be like **the pot calling the kettle black.***

<u>Background</u>: It refers to the fact that both pots and kettles (or any other cookware) would turn black when put over a fire. This expression probably originated when people still used coal and wood to cook.

<u>Usage notes</u>:

1. Used to accuse the speaker of hypocrisy
2. Other expressions with the same meaning: **Look who's talking!** and **It takes one to know one.**

<u>Of interest</u>: Wikipedia provides a long list of similar expressions in other languages. Some of the interesting ones are:
Arabic: *The camel cannot see the crookedness of its own neck.*
Chinese: *A soldier retreating 50 steps laughing at a soldier retreating 100 steps*
German: *One donkey chides the other for being long-eared.*
Russian: *To see a little straw in another's eye, and not to notice a log in his own*
Spanish: *As the frying pan said to the sauce pan: "Get away from me, you're smudging me!"*

Keep the pot boiling To keep something going

- *The parents have tried to do as many interviews as possible to **keep the pot of public interest in their daughter's disappearance case boiling.***
- *The governor has **kept the pot boiling** to further his self-interest.*

Background: It comes from the concept of always having food in the pot in the old days, which was kept boiling over the fire. You didn't make it new everyday; you just added more food to it and kept it going.

Usage note: A related term with a derogatory connotation is ***potboiler***, which refers to any book, screenplay or other work an author writes solely to keep the pot boiling – that is, he does it for the money and not from some creative (artistic) motive. Such a work is likely to be written rapidly, using recycled situations and characters, to make a quick buck and probably will be poorly done.

Authors of potboiler novels or screenplays are often called ***hack writers***.

Such works are sometimes called ***pulp fiction*** – in reference to the many fiction magazines printed on the cheapest grade of pulp paper that flourished during the first half of the 20th century (before television) – or ***page turners*** (because the reader keeps turning to the next page to find out what happens next).

Potboiler films are sometimes called ***popcorn movies*** because they are most enjoyable (or only enjoyable) if you're eating popcorn while watching them.

Stir the pot To bring forgotten issues for which there was disagreement to the surface in order to create awareness or to affect change

- *Scientists **stir the pot** for right to grow marijuana.*
  (Headline, www.nature.com, 6-29-07)

Usage note: The term can have a negative connotation because some people who do so are only trying to cause trouble by rehashing issues that have already been settled. Some do it for personal gain; others more for the thrill of confrontation:

- *Mary is an instigator, always **stirring the pot**.*

Take a pot shot To criticize an easy target in an unfair way

- *"It's easy to **take a pot shot** like that. But how about coming up with a useful suggestion?"*

Background: It comes from the idea of shooting animals solely for the purpose of having food to go in the dinner pot (as opposed to hunting by the rules of sport). The implication is that it's an easy shot, with the animal having no chance of escape or self-defense.

Take pot luck To eat whatever happens to be available without special preparation

- *It's getting late. You can stay for dinner if you want to. But you'll have to **take pot luck**.*

Background: It probably comes from the traditional practice of never throwing anything away (which is also the basic idea of the origin of KEEP THE POT BOILING; see earlier). Meal leftovers would be put into a pot and kept warm and could be used to feed people on short notice. So, when people showed up for a meal, they took the "luck of the pot."

Usage notes:
1. The term is also used figuratively – to take whatever is available or comes one's way (and hope that it is good):
   - *We didn't make definite plans. So we'll have to **take pot luck**.*
2. **Potlucks** are common practices in an American setting. If a party is described as a potluck, it means that each guest is expected to bring at least one dish of his or her choice to be shared. The idea behind it is probably to help alleviate the workload and the expense for the host.

There is a lid for every pot. There's always a certain special someone out there for everyone, no matter how seemingly hopeless it is or how seemingly outlandish he or she may be.

   - *"**There's a lid for every pot**. At least I hope so. Right now, all I have is the pot."*
   "That's OK. After all, you can still cook without a lid."

Usage notes:
1. It's a very common saying about marriage, more like a consolation for people who are looking for a mate.
2. Variations:
   - *Every pot has its lid.*
   - *A pot is never so crooked that you can't find a lid to fit it.*
   - *There's not a man or dog alive that some woman won't love.*

• • • • •

PLATES AND DISHES

"Everybody wants to eat off a clean plate, but nobody wants to do the dishes."
Mike Huckabee (1955-   ), former Arkansas governor, TV talk show host

Eat off a clean plate means using a clean plate when eating.

Clean one's plate, on the other hand, is to eat everything on the plate and **do the dishes** refers to the act of washing the dishes.

Being told to **clean your plate** (or to **finish what's on your plate**) has been a familiar rite of American childhood for decades. Parents often say to their kids:
   - *"Clean your plate! There are starving children in Africa who would love to eat that."*
   - *"Finish what's on your plate! When I was your age, I didn't let food go to waste."*

Comment: This may sound funny, but both **clean one's plate** and **do the dishes** would literally mean "wash the dishes" in Thai.

This story from my husband's side of the family is also true. His step-father, a

French-Canadian who was born and raised in the state of Maine but spoke French at home, often told the children to 'eat their plates' when he meant for them to clean their plates. I'd bet that's how the French people say it and he simply translated it into English.

See also CLEAN YOUR PLATE CLUB, later in this chapter.

Have a lot on one's plate/have a full plate To be very busy; have a lot to do
- *We shouldn't give this task to Linda. She already **has a lot on her plate**.*
Background: It transfers the idea of a plate full of food to a full agenda.
Usage notes:
1. A very common expression
2. Also, ***have enough on one's plate (at the moment)***
 One's plate is full/a little full/too full/is overflowing.

 "The cow jumped over the moon
 And the dish ran away with the spoon" Lines from an English nursery rhyme
 In English, "dish" has a few figurative meanings:
 It can mean the contents of the dish rather than the dish itself:
 - *We just added a few new **dishes** to the menu.*
 Or a particular type of food:
 - *Sushi is a Japanese **dish**.*
 Or a course of a meal:
 - *the main **dish**; side **dishes***

According to Robert Palmatier (2000), "dish" came to mean "whore" during the Elizabethan times. It has since acquired the much pleasanter meaning of "pretty woman," although even that is offensive to some people.

In the 1970s, the word "dish" was first applied to a satellite antenna, as it has a dish-like shape. It is now common usage.

Dish (verb) To gossip about
- *The women stayed up all night, **dishing** their former husbands.*
- *The former coach **dishes** on steroids and the media.*
Usage notes:
1. Many newspapers use the term ***dish*** for their gossip columns, for example:
 The New York Daily News has a section called *"Daily Dish & Gossip."*
 The Toronto Sun calls theirs *"Entertainment/Daily Dish."*
2. The person who writes this kind of column is a ***disher:***
 - *The **disher** was fired after posting a review of a pirated version of the network's movie before its official release.*

Dish out/up Literally, to serve food from a serving dish; figuratively, to dispense freely
 - *The super rich are still willing to **dish out** the dough for elaborate parties.*

- *She likes to **dish out** advice without being asked.*
- *He's very keen to **dish out** criticism.*

Usage notes:
1. Also, **dish it out**, to administer punishment, praise, criticism or abuse
   - *When it comes to flattery, he can really **dish it out**.*
2. **He or she can dish it out but can't take it.** This is a very common expression. It means that he or she (let us say 'he' in this instance) is quick to disparage or ridicule others, but if anyone replies in kind, he is deeply and/or loudly wounded and unforgiving.

Dish out the dirt To maliciously spread gossip or scandal
- *She was notorious for **dishing out the dirt**.*

• • • • •

KNIVES, FORKS AND SPOONS

"A knife wound heals; a wound caused by words does not." Turkish proverb

Go under the knife To have surgery
- *More kids are altering the body parts that give them angst by **going under the knife** or laser or lipo tube to get the look they want.*
  (www.usatoday.com, 6-25-09)
  (Angst is a German word meaning <u>anxiety</u> or <u>fear</u>.)

Like a (hot/sharp) knife through butter Describing something that can be done very easily and quickly
- *This cutter cuts through styrofoam **like a knife through butter**.*
- *I guarantee this bill will pass the Senate **like a hot knife through butter**.*

Usage note: The term implies swiftness and without any difficulty and/or resistance.

Some think it's a great simile (maybe that's why it is used quite a lot in advertisements for such things as saws, knives, cutters and pruning shears); for others, it's just a cliché.

Not the sharpest knife in the drawer Not very smart
- *"This girl is **not the sharpest knife in the drawer**, if you ask me."*
Usage notes:
1. It uses the word "sharp" as a synonym of "intelligent."
2. Same idea as A FEW SANDWICHES SHORT OF A PICNIC (page 63)

Fork over/out/up (Slang) To hand over, to pay or give up
- *Want Super Bowl Tickets? **Fork Over** $4,300.*
  (Headline, www.foxnews.com, 1-28-08)
- *A gift is much less charming if the recipient has to **fork over** part of the cost in order to use it.*

<u>Background</u>: As one can easily see, there are similarities between a fork (a solid handle with prongs) and a human hand (with fingers). The displacement from a living hand to a metal object suggests mechanical compliance – in other words, reluctance.

<u>Usage notes</u>:
1. It usually refers to money.
2. It almost always means that the person is forced to pay an amount of money he thinks is excessive.

Speak with a forked tongue   To deceive or mislead

- *People who **speak with a forked tongue** will eventually lose the trust of others.*

<u>Background</u>: The term is probably in reference to the snake (the Serpent in the Garden of Eden, for example), considered the symbol of evil. Snakes actually have forked tongues.

Speak with a forked tongue suggests *equivocation* – a double or doubtful meaning – since the tips of the snake's flickering tongue are pointing in different directions. But, no matter: the phrase is always taken to mean "lying."

Someone who ***speaks with a forked tongue*** never does what he says he is going to do and nothing he says is true.

A classic line in old cowboy-and-Indian westerns is *White man speak with forked tongue.*

Stick a fork in something/someone   (Slang) To be done, finished or over, or even completely destroyed or defeated

- *School is done, **stick a fork in it.***
- ***Stick a fork in this candidate.** He's finished.*

<u>Background</u>: You stick a fork into meat to see if it's done – or to show that it's done.

<u>Usage note</u>: Very common

"A spoon does not know the taste of soup, nor a learned fool the taste of wisdom."
Welsh proverb

Born with a silver spoon in one's mouth   To be born into wealth, comfort or privilege

- *Most people would agree that this hotel heiress was **born with a silver spoon in her mouth.** She probably hasn't had to work a day in her life.*

<u>Background</u>: At one time, it was customary for wealthy godparents to give their godchildren silver spoons as gifts during their christening ceremonies. Because only the rich could afford such an item, a silver spoon became a symbol of the affluent; it also came to represent the child's good fortune.

The term was used by Cervantes (1547-1616) in the early 1600s in *Don Quixote de la Mancha.*

Spoon-feed To provide help, information or instruction to someone without requiring any effort on the recipient's part

- *You will not be **spoon-fed**. You have to start your own investigation and gather your own evidence.*

<u>Background</u>: A mother spoon-feeds her baby, because the infant or toddler is as yet too young to handle a spoon.

See CUP/GLASS-RELATED EXPRESSIONS in Chapter 9.

• •

OTHER TERMS AND EXPRESSIONS OF INTEREST

A dish fit for the gods Phrase used to describe lavish and delicious food

<u>Background</u>: It came from Shakespeare's *Julius Caesar*. When planning to assassinate Caesar, Brutus says:

"Let's carve him as a dish fit for the gods
Not hew him as a carcass fit for hounds" (Act 2, Scene 1)

The essence of this remark, which is not at all appetizing, is that Caesar should be killed in a reverent, ceremonious way and his body should be left in a suitable state for the gods to view.

All hands and the cook All able-bodied men are needed to respond to an emergency

American vs. British

We say ***silverware***; they say ***cutlery.***

In restaurants in the U.S., you ask for ***silverware***, even if it is made of stainless steels (or plastic, as in for take-out orders or in fast-food places). You can also ask for (***eating***) ***utensils***.

There are also ***cooking utensils*** such as *soup ladles*, *spatulas* and *tongs*.

In the U.S., the term ***cutlery*** only describes different kinds of knives for cooking, not to use at the dining table. You would only ask for that in a kitchen supply shop, not at a restaurant.

Blue plate special A set meal sold at an especially low price in cheap diners and cafes

<u>Background</u>: The term was very common in the U.S. from the 1920s through the 1950s. The plates, usually blue or blue-patterned, were divided into sections to separate various kinds of food (meat or fish, vegetables and potatoes), thus helping to cut down serving sizes, as well the servers' time and dishwashing.

The divided plates are no longer used in most places but the 'special low price' they encourage still goes by the adjective ***blue plate***. There are names like "***blue plate*** catering"; "***blue plate*** café."

And it doesn't apply only to food, there are websites by the name of "***blue plate*** fashion"; "***blue plate*** books" and "***blue plate*** digital," for example.

Boil the ocean To try to do something on a scale beyond human capacity

- *You try to **boil the ocean** and odds are it's not going to work.*

Background: Boiling a pot of water is easy, but anybody would agree that it's practically impossible to boil the ocean. Besides, the time and effort spent will not justify the return (all you get is just a handful of salt).

Will Rogers, an American humorist and entertainer (1879-1935) was credited with coining the term. He was once asked how the Allies should deal with the German U-boats during World War I. His answer:

"You just boil the ocean. The U-boats will turn pink and pop to surface. Then you just pick them off."

When asked how he would boil the ocean, he responded,

"I'm the idea man here. Get someone else to work out the details."

Usage notes:
1. ***Don't boil the ocean***, on the other hand, means don't try to achieve the impossible. You need to be selective and figure out what your priorities are and identify the most efficient way to meet them. In other words, you need to learn to work smarter, not harder.
2. Both terms are popularly used in the computer and business world. Some think they are overused.

Chief cook and bottle washer A person who does a wide range of duties, from being in charge to doing the most menial work

Clean your plate club The term helps signifying the uniquely American compulsion to finish everything on the plate.

- *Do you push your plate away if you've had enough, or are you a member of the **clean your plate club?***

Background: During World War I, the U.S. Food Administration created an advertising division which used the "clean plate" as a slogan to conserve food.

When the U.S. launched the Marshall Plan to help rebuild Europe after World War II, President Truman called upon the country to eat less poultry to conserve food for the Europeans. The "clean plate" then became the "clean plate club." The campaign encouraged school children to pledge to eat everything on their plates at mealtime. The clean plate clubs were formed in a large number of elementary schools.

Do it up brown To do something carefully and thoroughly

- *They really **did it up brown** for their Christmas party.*

Background: The term probably has to do with baking bread or browning meat. When the surface of the bread or meat starts to turn brown, it's a good indication that it's being cooked right.

Don't dig your grave with a knife and fork. (Old saying) Don't overeat to the point of gluttony.

Fingers were made before forks (and hands before knives). It's all right to eat using one's fingers.

It is sometimes said by children when they are told to use a fork instead of eating with their fingers as they often do. Some adults may say it light-heartedly as an excuse to eat with their hands.

Fork in the road Literally, a single road splitting into two roads; figuratively, a time in one's life where one has to make an important but difficult life-changing decision

- *Life is a series of **forks in the road**. At each junction, you have to take one path or the other, and the whole rest of your life can be permanently altered by this choice.*

<u>Background</u>: To *fork* is to split or divide into two, like the forked branch of a tree. Similarly, a road forks when it divides; so that, looking down from above, you have three roads coming together; and a traveler, coming to that juncture, must make a decision.

Johnny Carson had a favorite joke, which he repeatedly used in skits on *The Tonight Show*. Playing an unscrupulous traveling salesman he would come to a kitchen fork lying on the floor and exclaim, *"There's a fork in the road!"* The dumbness of this joke always got a laugh.

Greasy spoon A small, inexpensive eating place

<u>Background</u>: The term refers to both the kind of food served (mostly fried, greasy) and the unsanitary aspect of the place and its utensils (though not always the case nowadays, especially with the health laws governing food in the U.S.). It is not known for its quality but its relatively cheap cost and large portion sizes.

<u>Usage notes</u>:
1. It is an Americanism, but I've read that it is used in the UK and Canada as well.
2. In the U.S., it is sometimes synonymous with the term ***truck stop***.
3. The term can also be used as an adjective:
   - *The menu is pretty basic, consisting of all your typical **greasy-spoon** items.*

He who gives fair words feeds you with an empty spoon. We gain nothing from being flattered nor do we profit from other people's promises.

See also FINE WORDS BUTTER NO PARSNIPS (Page 40).

He who sups with the Devil should have a long spoon. (Old saying) One should be extremely careful when dealing with someone with a dubious reputation.

<u>Usage note</u>: A recent slight variation: ***If you sup with the devil you need a long spoon.***

It's so tender you can cut it with a fork. It's very tender indeed, so much so you don't need to use the knife to cut it.

Usage note: Another expression also used: ***It's so tender it melts in your mouth.***

Kitchen Cabinet (Political term) It was first used by the opponents of President Andrew Jackson (1767-1845) to describe his 'unofficial' advisers – his inner circles of trusted friends and allies -whom he consulted after expelling six members of his official Cabinet. They reportedly met in the White House kitchen, hence the name of the term.

The term has also been used in England as well, starting when Harold Wilson was the prime minister (1964-1970; 1974-1976).

Panhandle A geographic term used mainly in the U.S. to refer to a narrower strip of land projecting from a larger area in shape of a pan handle. Unlike a peninsula, a panhandle usually doesn't border the ocean. It's usually inland and its boundaries are state lines.

Some of the states that have panhandles are Texas, Florida, Oklahoma and West Virginia (called the Panhandle state).

Usage note: To ***panhandle*** means to approach people and beg for money. It is so called because of the resemblance of the extended arm (thrusting out a tin pan) to a pan handle:
- *Get Ready to **Panhandle**: Unemployment Checks Running Out.*
  (www.gothamist.com, 01-19-09)

Most dictionaries say that it is an Americanism- a back formation of the noun a ***panhandler*** (i.e., someone who handles the pan).

Pot belly A large round stomach that sticks out

Usage notes:
1. It has quite a number of synonyms, some of which are ***paunch, the middle-age spread***, BEER BELLY (Page 145).
2. There are also ***potbellied stoves*** and ***potbellied pigs***.

Recipe for disaster A mixture of people and events that could possibly result in trouble
- *The president's position on the issue is a **recipe for** national **disaster.***

Usage note: The opposite term is ***recipe for success*** – a formula for a desired result.
- *Let the true experts – ordinary people who have lost weight and kept it off – share their **recipe for success**.*

Revenge is a dish best served cold. To be successful, revenge should be planned and executed when the time is right, rather than done hastily which will increase the chance of failure. Also, you will be calmer after some time has passed and will enjoy your enemy's suffering more.

Background: It's a rough translation from the French *"la vengeance est un plat qui se mange froid"* ("Revenge is a dish one eats cold.") used by Pierre Ambroise Francois Choderios de La Clos (1741-1803) in his 1782 novel *Les Liaisons Dangereuses.*

Teflon Politicians or public figures who seem immune to accusations of misconduct, i.e., negative stories about them never seem to stick. Some that have been often mentioned are Bill Clinton, Tony Blair and the Mafia boss, John Gotti.

Background: *Teflon* is a coating on cooking utensils to prevent food from sticking to them.

The figurative use of *Teflon* entered the American political lexicon in 1983 when Patricia Schroeder (1940-   ), then a Democratic congresswoman from Colorado, said this about then-President Ronald Reagan, the Republican:

"I was cooking breakfast this morning for my kids, and I thought,
"He's just like a Teflon frying pan: Nothing sticks to him."

Since then, Reagan has been nicknamed *the Teflon President.*

Usage note: We now talk about *(having) a Teflon coating/coat; Teflon character/quality; to be Teflon-coated* or simply *to be Teflon.*

The melting pot Term used to refer to the U.S. Its basic idea presents the whole nation as one large pot of soup. Anyone who enters the U.S. is automatically thrown into this 'pot' and gets blended together as one to form a new culture described as characteristically American.

Some think this is an outdated metaphor since it's noticeable that there are differences in cultures in this country. For them, *the salad bowl* is a better metaphor. It is based on the idea that each culture is part of an American system but that each retains its own identity, just as different ingredients (such as lettuce, carrots, etc.), are all mixed together to make a salad, yet each ingredient also maintains its original shape and characteristics.

Tote one's own skillet To make one's way by one's own effort

Usage notes:
1. The term is no longer in common use.
2. Other similar expressions are *paddle one's own canoe; saddle one's own horse.*

13
. . . . . .
Talking About "Eating"

"You are what you eat." (You are as healthy as the food you eat.)
"Eating is a big deal; dying is not." Thai saying

Where I came from, *"Have you eaten?"* is the predominant method of greeting, especially when someone comes to your home. The same is true with the Chinese. My late mother, who lived in the U.S. for almost 20 years, would greet people that way, even to my American friends. No matter how much I tried to explain to her that it was not how the Americans greeted each other, I could never change her mind.

Greetings aside, it's safe to say that eating-related words play a big role in the lexicon of just any language. And in English, there are plenty of these words to talk about.

ESPECIALLY FOR ENGLISH LEARNERS

(SLANG) TERMS FOR "EAT"

EATING LIGHT

Snack To eat something small between regular meals
- *It's OK to **snack**; but don't **snack** too much on sugary foods.*

Usage notes:
1. A **snack** (or snack food) is what you eat to fend off hunger between meals.
   - *Not all **snacks** are bad; some can be really healthy.*
2. The Yiddish slang for **snack** is **nosh**; the term is used quite generally.
   - *We just **noshed** while having a cocktail. Now, let's go get a real meal.*

Munch To snack on a hard fruit or vegetable, or chips
- *I need something to **munch** on while waiting for dinner.*
- *John is **munching** on carrot sticks with obvious enjoyment.*

Usage notes:
1. Usually signifying eating audibly (and often with pleasure)
   Strictly speaking, to **munch** is to eat steadily with the front teeth and a pronounced action of the jaw. A squirrel *munches*; a dog *gobbles* his food down. Apples, carrots and potato chips are ideally suited for munching.
2. **Munchies** are food meant for snacking:
   - *There were all kinds of **munchies** served at the party.*
3. **The munchies** is a term referring to the craving for sweets and snacks

during the pregnancy, the premenstrual period and marijuana use.
- *I've got **the munchies** so bad; I'm going to run to the market right now to get some chips and ice cream.*

EATING A MEAL

Chow down (on something) To eat, especially quickly or enthusiastically, often without good manners
- *They **chowed down** on pizza after the game.*

<u>Background</u>: It was originally military slang around World War II but is now more widely used.

The noun **chow**, meaning food, originated from either Chinese or pidgin English in the 18th century. It also appears in such terms as **chow time** (meal time) and **chow line** (line of people waiting for food).

<u>Usage notes</u>:
1. To **chow down** is similar to the British **tuck in**.
2. Another newer slang term is a **chowhound**, someone with a big appetite and loves to eat. A **foodie**, on the other hand, is someone who is knowledgeable and particular about food, perhaps a gourmet.

Grab/have/get/ a bite to eat To eat a quick, small meal (small nosh)
- *We'll **grab a bite to eat** and come back to finish the work within an hour.*
- *Don't leave just yet; stay and **have a bite to eat** first.*

<u>Usage note</u>: Also, **grab some grub** (*Grub* is slang for food.)

LET'S DO LUNCH See page 169.

EATING IN A HURRIED MANNER

Bolt down To swallow food hastily, greedily, without proper chewing (See **Inhale**.)

Garbage down To devour hungrily and greedily
- *The poor kid **garbaged down** his dinner the minute it was served.*

Gorge on To feast; to eat a large amount of food, usually of one kind, such as turkey, cake or candy. (*"He **gorged on** popcorn."*) As a noun, **gorge** refers to the contents of the stomach: that which has been swallowed.

Guzzle Used mostly for drinking, but sometimes for eating (greedily, frequently and plentifully, just like a big car guzzling all the gasoline)

Put it away rather quickly

Scarf down (British: *scoff*)

Shovel in

Stuff/feed/one's face To eat an inordinate amount of food with great vigor and speed

Stuff oneself

Wolf down
- *Boy! You sure **wolfed that down** fast!* (i.e., in the manner of a wolf)

Gobble (up/down) To eat very fast
Usage notes:
1. It can also mean to make the sound of a turkey (onomatopoetic).
2. A **gobbler** can refer to a person who eats too fast or the turkey:
- *Don't be such a **gobbler**! Don't **gobble** that **gobbler** just yet. Wait until everybody is ready.*

Inhale Implying that someone has ingested the food so quickly that it looks as if he or she hasn't bothered to chew or swallow
- *He didn't really have time to enjoy his meal; he just **inhaled** it and left.*

Devour To eat ravenously and quickly
- *I was so hungry I **devoured** everything instantly.*

Usage note: ***Devour*** can be used figuratively; to ***devour a book***, for example, means to read rapidly (as though hungry or greedy) and with great pleasure (as if one couldn't get enough).

USEFUL PHRASES
WHEN YOU NEED SOMETHING TO EAT
Starving Extremely hungry
- *"Are you hungry?"*
 "Starving!"

So hungry one could eat a horse

To be **starved** (**to death**) (or to be **famished**)
 Both are used as humorous exaggeration:
- *I haven't had time to eat all day. I'm **so hungry I could eat a horse**.*
- *Is there any way you can rush the order for us? We **are starved to death**.* (Or, we **are starving**.)

WHEN YOU'VE HAD ENOUGH
That hits the spot. That was just what I needed. A very common expression

To be **full**

To be **stuffed** To be extremely full

My eyes were bigger than my stomach. My desire for the food was greater than what I could comfortably eat. (A discovery nearly always made <u>after</u> one has eaten.)
- *What a meal! **That** really **hits the spot**. Now, **I'm** so **full**; really **stuffed**, actually. I couldn't even finish what I'd ordered. I guess **my eyes were bigger than my stomach**.*

GENERAL

Eat out To eat at a restaurant; the opposite is to **eat at home** (some people may say, **eat in**)

On a (strict, special) diet

Watch what one eats To be more careful about eating healthy foods and not eating too much

Eat light To eat foods that will not cause you to gain weight

Have a craving for something (or to **crave something**) To strongly desire to eat a certain food

Give oneself a treat To reward oneself or indulge oneself with something pleasurable

Splurge To spend money freely and extravagantly

- *It's too expensive to **eat out** all the time. We **eat at home** more now trying to save some money. Besides, my husband is **on a strict diet**. His doctor told him he needs to lose some weight, so he has to **watch what he eats**. He has been trying to **eat light** and exercise more. Today, we decided to eat out because I really **had a craving for** a steak. And since we both just got our pay checks, it's a perfect time to **give ourselves a treat**. I think I'll **splurge** and have a piece of pie too after I'm finished with the steak.*

• •

COMMON EXPRESSIONS

THE UNCONSUMABLES

Eat crow To be forced to admit that one's previously (and often strongly) stated opinion was wrong

- *When you blow smoke about your football team and your team lays an egg, you really deserve to **eat crow**.* (To blow smoke is to make exaggerated claims; see LAY AN EGG on page 54.)
- *"The easy way to **eat crow** is while it's still warm. The colder it gets, the harder it is to swallow."* Unknown

Background: Crows are scavengers, not suitable for eating; they are very distasteful. Apologizing also 'tastes' bad because it hurts one's pride.

How bad does a crow taste? There's a joke that if you get stuck out in the wilderness and you happen to catch a crow, you should boil the crow for a week with one of your boots and then eat the boot.

Eat crow is an American phrase from the mid 19th century. The origin is uncertain, although a (rather colorful) story relates that it involved an encounter between a British officer and an American soldier at the end of the 1812 war. The officer made the soldier eat part of a crow he had shot in British territory. Once the soldier got his gun back, however, he turned around and made the officer eat the rest of the crow.

A related expression is the British **eat humble pie**, which is also used in the U.S. During medieval times, "humble pie" (or "umble pie") was an actual dish made out of entrails of an animal -heart, liver, intestine and the like- served to the servants and lower classes.

Usage note: To **eat crow** and **eat humble pie** are slightly different. The former is more severe and more humiliating than the latter. To eat humble pie simply means to recognize that one was wrong (or in the wrong).

To **eat crow** is also more emphatic and more expressive than to EAT ONE'S WORDS (also in this chapter) because it involves imagery.

Eat dirt To accept blame, insult, criticism or bad treatment without response or complaint
- *I had to **eat dirt** from that customer just because he is a friend of my manager's.*
- *The school bullies made other kids **eat dirt**.*

Usage notes:
1. One can also use it sarcastically in a literal sense:
   - *I'd rather **eat dirt** than eat this food.*
2. There is a saying, **you have to eat a peck of dirt before you die.**
   Literally, it's not always possible to avoid eating a certain amount of dirt on one's food. Figuratively, everybody must endure a number of unpleasant things in his or her lifetime.
   - *"You should have washed that apple before you ate it!"*
     *"Oh, well, **you have to eat a peck of dirt before you die.**"*
     "You're probably right. I'd bet I've eaten more than a peck so far, with all these problems in my life."
   A peck is two pounds (a dry measure).

Of interest: The habit of eating clay, mud or dirt is known as *geophagia*. It's not far-fetched for some women to crave dirt when they are pregnant. In fact, research has shown that dirt has the binding effect which makes it an effective antidiarrheal. However, there is also a negative social stereotype associated with anyone who would consume dirt right off the ground. Dirt-eaters are often considered poor, ignorant and malnourished.

Eat/chew/nails To do something extreme in extreme anger
- *He was so mad he could **eat nails** and spit tacks.*

Background: The above sentence refers to carpenter's nails, but it can be taken to mean finger nails in a different context as well.

Usage note: To **eat nails** (or **bullets**) **for breakfast** is a phrase used to describe a "tough" person, i.e., someone who is physically strong and intimidating. It can also mean someone who thrives on danger and taking risks.

Eat one's words To take back what one said, admitting one was wrong
- *"I'll make you **eat your words** for calling me lazy."*
- *"It's better to swallow **words** than to have to **eat them** later."*
  Franklin D. Roosevelt (1882-1945), the 32nd U.S. President

Eat your heart out! Get ready to be jealous! A taunt, often exaggerated, joking or boastful of being better than another person or of having something that person greatly desires
- *"**Eat your heart out!** Kobe Bryant," said the high school basketball player after he made 10 free throws in a row.*
- *"This is a very good painting. **Eat your heart out!** Picasso!"*
- *"**Eat your heart out!** I'm dating Paul now. You had your chance."*

Background: It refers to a state of envy, which corrodes or eats at the heart of a person, destroying him or her completely.

Usage notes:
1. It's similar to the playground taunting, insulting gibe of children, *nyah, nyah, nyah.*
2. When not used to gloat, it can mean to be consumed with envy; to grieve or brood about something that makes one unhappy:
   - *She's still **eating her heart out** whenever she sees him with a new girlfriend.*
   - *The children **ate their hearts out** over a lost cat.*
   - *It's better to talk about your problems than to let them **eat your heart out**.*

I'll eat my hat. Used to express complete confidence about something or in the outcome of something
- *There's no doubt in my mind he's having an affair. If that's not true, **I'll eat my hat**.*
- *If the newlyweds are not happy with this very generous gift certificate, **I'll eat my hat**.*

Background: One of the early examples of this phrase is from Charles Dickens' *The Pickwick Papers* (1837): "*If I knew as little of life as that, I'd eat my hat and swallow the buckle whole.*"

This expression may sound strange to the hatless generation of today; one has to keep in mind that it was coined at the time when hats were an important headgear for men. To promise to eat something a person could not part with reinforces the idea how certain he or she is about a particular outcome.

Usage note: It almost always follows an -if clause.

• • • • •

THE HYPERBOLES & SIMILES

Eat like a bird To eat very little

- *She **eats like a bird**; how does she survive on that little food? I'd pass out.*
- *You **ate like a bird** at the party; what was wrong?*

Background: It alludes to the mistaken impression that birds don't eat much. They do, relative to their size. Many birds eat as much as 50 percent of their weight in a day. Although birds do eat tiny mouthfuls of food, they do so hundreds and hundreds of time each day. They have to eat a lot just to keep their energetic little bodies moving.

Of interest: *"Eat like a bird, poop like an elephant"* is a quote from *Rules for Revolutionaries*, a book by Guy Kawasaki. In essence, his guide to success in business is this: one has to consume as much information (just like the way a bird actually eats) and spread the knowledge as much as one can (much like the way an elephant poops - about 160 pounds per day!).

Eat like a horse To eat a lot

- *"Boy! Your son has grown so much since the last time I saw him."*
  *"I know, he **eats like a horse**."*
- *"I'm sure glad your husband really enjoyed the meal I cooked."*
  *"I noticed that too. He **ate like a horse** the whole time we were at the table."*

Background: It alludes to the tendency of horses to eat whatever food is available. They also seem to be able to eat all day long. In fact, left to graze freely, the average horse eats approximately one to two percent of its own body weight daily. A horse weighing 1000 is likely to consume 15-20 pounds of hay in one day.

Pigs eat a lot too; but unlike horses, pigs eat messily and nosily.

Usage notes:

1. Other related-phrases are **big eater**; a **bottomless pit; have a big/huge/ appetite; have a hollow leg:**
   - *My husband is a **big eater** – a **bottomless pit**! He usually eats three times as much as I do. The only time he **doesn't have much of an appetite** is when he's really, really sick. Come to think of it, all his brothers seem to **have a hollow leg** when it comes to food.*
2. See the figurative sense of HAVE AN APPETITE later in the chapter.

EAT LIKE A PIG See page 91.

EAT SOMEONE ALIVE See page 169.

Eat someone out of house and home To strain someone's resources by relying on them for food, shelter and other necessities – the resources usually being those of a relative, an in-law or a friend

- *"My old college room-mate came for a visit – and stayed and stayed and stayed. She is **eating me out of house and home**."*

Usage note: Often used humorously and hyperbolically, but sometimes desperately. The expression is not necessarily confined to food and shelter only. The complainer may also be providing clothing, transportation and entertainment.

• • • • •

THE OTHER FIGURATIVE ONES

A tough/bitter/hard/pill to swallow Something that must be accepted, even though it is painful or difficult to do so
- *The loss was **a tough pill to swallow** because I thought we had an unbelievable tournament and we really had a good chance of winning the game up until the final minutes.*

Usage note: Also, *His idea/argument/message, is **tough/hard/to swallow***

Bite off more than one can chew To take on more than one can handle
- *The president **bit off more than he could chew**. He made a lot of changes before he was ready to replace what was there before.*
- *The owners of this new restaurant are playing it safe; they are being careful not to **bite off more than they can chew**.*

Background: The image here is of someone taking such a big bite of something – a sandwich, say – that he is unable to chew it. It completely fills the mouth, not leaving enough room for the action of the teeth, and he is in some danger of choking on it. The only thing he can do is to disgorge the chunk of food and try again with a smaller amount of it.

Chew the cud To think something over deliberately; ponder on something done, said or experienced
- *She tends to **chew the cud** before she answers.*
- *My cousin constantly **chews the cud** of old hurt feelings and anger, which is not really good for his mental health.*

Background: Among ruminating animals such as cows, goats, deer and sheep, cud is the food brought up into the mouth from the first stomach and chewed again.

Usage note: Also, to **ruminate** (to ponder, reflect)

Comment: From what I've read and heard, a lot of people use **chew the cud** in the same sense as CHEW THE FAT (see below). It could be that the word "chew" conjures an image of the use of the mouth, making people immediately thinking of "talking or chatting."

Chew the fat To chat and gossip to pass the time
- *They don't get to see each other that often; so whenever they do, they'll spend the whole afternoon **chewing the fat**.*

Background: It likens using one's mouth for a long period to chewing the fat of meat. Both take a lot of effort (i.e., a lot of jaw work) for not much reward.

The origin is uncertain. Up until 1880s, the phrase meant "to grumble."
Most sources think it's a reference to salt pork or similarly tough dried meat, common among military people and sailors in the 1800s. Sailors working their jaws on the tough salt pork rationed out when supplies ran low constantly grumbled about it while literally chewing the fat.

Some think that *chew the fat* may have derived from **chew the rag** ("rag," among many speculations, referring to either a chewing tobacco substitute or slang for the tongue) which was first recorded around 1885.

Usage notes:
1. *Chew the fat* is a very common idiom. When you *chew the fat*, you do it in an unhurried manner over a long period of time, usually about nothing important. *Chew the rag* is not as common but is not completely antiquated either.
2. Another expression with similar meaning is **shoot the breeze**.
3. Also, other slang terms: to **jaw, chitchat, powwow** and (*have*) **a rap session**

Digest (verb) To break something down into more understandable parts, or until it becomes a part of one's thoughts

- *When giving a speech, you should pause after every major point you make. This will allow your audience to **digest** and process your message.*

Dine out on something To keep using a story that one knows or has experienced in order to entertain people, usually as a subject for dining table conversation

- *My husband's friend used to live next door to Richard Nixon (before he became President). He **dined out on** that for years. People would stop and listen whenever he talked about it.*

Usage note: The idea behind it is that it's something one uses to gain social success; one is admired and made the center of attention because of it. And it can be anything intangible as in:

- *Some people can **dine out on** personal charisma and charm for a long time. But once that fades, they become ordinary and boring again.*

Eat into/away To gradually destroy, or take away something

- *A new poll showed her opponent **eating** slightly **into** her lead as he drew more support from men and young voters.*
- *The mildew began to **eat away** at the window frame.*

Eat out of someone's hand To be manipulated or dominated by someone; to be submissive

- *He was such a charismatic politician that he could soon get the media to **eat out of his hand**.*

Background: It alludes to the way an animal (such as a squirrel or a bird) that is tame enough will eat food from your hand.

Usage notes:
1. It emphasizes one's ability to control others.

2. Other expressions with the same idea: (*have someone*) **in the palm of one's hand** or, **in one's back pocket**

Eat up To use up (time or resources, etc.)
- *Most people's savings have been **eaten up** by inflation.*
Usage notes:
1. One can also be eaten up with/by envy or bitterness:
   - *She was **eaten up** with envy at her brother's success.*
   It has similar meaning to EAT ONE'S HEART OUT (see earlier).
2. To **eat something up** means to enjoy it greatly:
   - *I thought the speech was too long and boring, but the audience **ate it up**.*

Glutton for punishment Someone who willingly does something painful or difficult again and again, or who habitually takes on disagreeable tasks even if the cost is painful and unpleasant to him- or herself
- *Sue went back to that no-good boyfriend of hers again. She must be a **glutton for punishment**.*
- *I should have quit this job long time ago. I guess I'm a **glutton for punishment** to still stay here.*
Background: A **glutton** is someone who is greedy and habitually overeats. There's a French proverb that says, "*Glutton: one who digs his grave with his teeth.*".

Gluttony is overeating. It is one of the seven deadly sins. The others are **pride, covetousness, lust, anger, envy, sloth.**

To be a **glutton for punishment** is different than being gluttonous, however, since it's more about wanting to please others, not about self-motivation.
Usage note: Often used wryly and humorously

Have an appetite for something To have a strong desire or wish for something
- *She loves to read and **has an** insatiable **appetite** for books.*
- *We Americans **have always had an appetite** for celebrity gossip.*
- *When hard times come, people **have little appetite for** celebrations.*

Leave a bad taste in someone's mouth To make a lingering negative impression on someone
- *That argument **left a bad taste in my mouth**, so much so that I refused to discuss politics with her again.*
Background: It transfers the feeling one has after eating something distasteful to other kinds of experience.

Sink/get/one's teeth into something To tackle something enthusiastically; become fully and eagerly engaged in something
- *I can't wait to **sink my teeth into** this new project.*
- *This had turned into a topic he could really **sink his teeth into**.*

<u>Background</u>: It transfers the literal sense of enjoying what one is eating to the figurative sense of eagerly devoting one's full attention to doing something.

What's eating you? What's bothering you?

- *You're in such a bad mood today.* ***What's eating you?***

<u>Background</u>: "Eat" here is used in the sense of "to be consumed by."

There was a movie (from a novel by Peter Hedges) in the early 1990s with the title *What's eating Gilbert Grape?* starring Johnny Depp and Leonardo di Capprio.

<u>Usage notes</u>:

1. Also, ***what's bugging you?***
2. ***I won't eat you*** (or ***I won't bite***) means you don't have to be afraid of me:
   - *"If you have any problems, you can come talk to me anytime.* ***I won't eat you***,*"* said the new owner.*

Whet one's appetite To sharpen one's desire for something; to stimulate, arouse one's interest

- *This is the kind of TV program that will* ***whet people's appetite*** *for travel.*

<u>Background</u>: *Whet* is an old-fashioned word which no longer exists in the language except in this idiom. "To whet" originally meant to sharpen. The allusion is to the sharpening of knives and razors on a whetstone.

<u>Usage note</u>: This is another example of EGGCORN (page 39); some people mistakenly use "wet" instead of the correct version "whet" in this expression.

(A whetstone is nearly always wetted with water before the knife or razor is sharpened on it. This may have contributed to the confusion between 'whet' and 'wet.')

• •

OTHER TERMS AND EXPRESSIONS OF INTEREST

All-you-can-eat buffet A type of eating place where you pay a fixed price and can eat all you want. Usually, there's a salad bar (with soup, salad, entrees and desserts) to which you can return as often as you wish. An older name for it is a ***smorgasbord*** (Swedish in origin)

Betcha can't eat just one! Once you start it, you'll like it so much you can't stop eating.

<u>Background</u>: Now quite a common catch phrase, it started as a *Lay's* potato chips advertising slogan in the early 1960s.

Don't know whether to eat it or rub it on Don't know what to do with something (used humorously with regards to food)

- *What kind of sauce is this? I* ***don't know whether to eat it or rub it on***.

Eating disorder A medical condition in which one does not eat normally, such as anorexia (an obsessive fear of gaining weight, resulting in extreme thinness and a distorted "body image") and bulimia (frequent binge-eating, followed by vomiting, fasting, excessive use of laxatives and compulsive exercising)

Full as a tick The state of having eaten so much that one feels as full as a tick that has just gorged itself on blood

Look good enough to eat A humorously appreciative statement
- *"This appetizer **looks good enough to eat**."*
  "And it really is."

Usage note: It is not limited to talking about food:
- *"Honey, you look lovely today. You **look good enough to eat**."*

It may relate to the idea of calling an attractive woman A DISH (page 186):
- *That's one hot little **dish**!*

A general observation: There are two main bodily appetites: gustatory and sexual. It is tempting and easy to transfer the language of the first to the second.

Off one's feed To have lost one's appetite; not eating as much as one usually does
- *I've noticed Dad has been **off his feed** the last few days; maybe he's not feeling well.*

Background: It originated in the 1800s and was first used only for animals. Later it was applied to humans as well.

A ***good feed*** means a large and tasty meal.

Real men don't eat quiche. The stereotypical man does not do certain things that are considered effeminate (such as eating quiche); doing so would imply that he is less a man.

Background: A quiche (pronounced "keesh") is a French pie-like dish with an unsweetened pastry shell filled with milk, eggs and usually flavored with cheese, onions, bacon, etc., eaten as breakfast or otherwise.

The term comes from Bruce Feirstein's 1982 tongue-in-cheek book that discusses stereotypes about masculinity.

A ***quiche-eater*** comes to mean a man who is effeminate or lacks masculine virtues. Because of the success of the book, both terms became popular catch phrases in the 1980s.

Table manners The rules of etiquettes used while eating
- *"Don't talk with your mouth full" and "keep your elbows off the table" are some of the basic good **table manners** everyone should be aware of.*
- *Different cultures observe different rules for **table manners**. The Chinese, for example, have a lot of rules about how to use chopsticks.*

You want me to eat it for you too? (Sarcasm) Phrase used when someone asks to have part of what you are eating and expects you to also do the cutting, unwrapping, etc. for him or her
- *"Can I have one of your candy bars?"*
  "Sure, go right ahead."
  "Do you mind taking it out of the wrapper for me? My hands are busy at the moment."
  "You want me to eat it for you too?"

14
· · · · ·
A Potpourri of Other Expressions

"Don't yuck my yum!"

("Do not say that my food tastes bad." In other words, one should learn to tolerate other people's enjoyment of something one finds gross.)

Yuck and **yum** are examples of words in English that are used onomatopoetically to describe one's dislikes or likes of something, often as interjections:

- **Yuck!** *I could never eat that.*
- **Yum, yum!** *That cake is good!* (Often used by and to children)
  Mmmm! is also generally used, and by people of any age.

Also as adjectives:
- *That looks* **yucky***!*
- *The cake looks* **yummy***!*

A la carte (Restaurant term) Just ordering a food item by itself, for example, meat or fish, not the whole set meal (with vegetable and potato, and sometimes with soup or salad)

Customer: *"Can I just order the steak* **a la carte***? I don't really need potato and vegetable."*
Waitress: *"You can, but it would cost you more for what you get."*

Background: *A la carte* is French for "according to the card (menu) with a stated price."

Usage note: Some people may simply say, *"Can I just order it by itself?"*

A la mode (Restaurant term) With ice cream

- *I splurged on apple pie* **a la mode** *today - first time in five years!*
- *All we want is two slices of carrot cake. Can we please have them* **a la mode***?*

Background: *A la mode* in French means "according to the prevailing style or fashion."

Among attempts to explain the origin of the "with ice cream" meaning, one plausible theory is that the person who first used the term probably thought eating pie with ice cream was a good new idea (since it had never been done before) and doing so was "a la mode" i.e., fashionable.

Acquired taste You may not like some strongly-flavored or fancy exotic food at first, but, after trying it a few times, you find that you have come to like it.

- *My husband got me into the habit of eating sardines, anchovies and herring; they are somewhat of an* **acquired taste***, but very good once given a chance.*

- *Venison can become an **acquired taste** – if you cook it right.*

Usage notes:
1. Sometimes the term simply means that it is food not everyone likes at first and some will never like. And some people use it as a polite way of saying they think a certain food is awful, but recognize that others may like it.
2. It can be used in reference to art, literature, music – to just about anything where taste varies.
3. It is also used to describe a person; *I'm an **acquired taste*** means that people normally don't like me at first, but they'll like me once they get to know me better. In other words, *I'll grow on them*.

After the feast comes the reckoning. A period of indulgence has to be paid for
- *John never realized the truth in the saying **'after the feast comes the reckoning'** until he woke up one morning with the worst hangover of his life.*
- *You may enjoy charging everything on your credit card right now, but you have to pay high price for it when the bill comes. Remember the saying, **"after the feast comes the reckoning."**?*

Cheap as chips (British) Very cheap; a bargain
Usage note: The British "chips" (as in *fish and chips*) is what the Americans call "french fries."

Come and get it! The food is ready! Come and eat!
A typical call (by parents or the person who does the cooking) for family members to come eat

Comfort food Typically food with a high sugar or carbohydrate content that calms one down or reminds one of pleasant times (i.e., childhood or home-cooking)
- *People often resort to **comfort food** when they are sick.*
- *Noodle dishes are my favorite **comfort food**. I can have them anytime of the day, even breakfast.*

Cuisine (pronounced "kwee-zeen") In French, it means kitchen, cooking (as a noun), cookery and food. Carried over into English, it refers to a style of cooking or choice of food peculiar to some country, so that we have Mexican cuisine, Italian cuisine, and so on.

Doggie (doggy) bags/boxes Containers provided by a restaurant for customers to put the uneaten part of their meal in to take home. In theory, they are supposed to be for the dog. But usually, they are for people to eat as leftovers later. Asking for doggie bags is a common practice in the U.S. when eating out.

Eighty-six To be out of something; to get rid of someone or something
- *Manager to wait staff: "**Eighty-six** salmon!" ("We're out of salmon.")*
- *"I thought that customer was **eighty-sixed** yesterday. How come he's here again?"*

- *The city just **eighty-sixed** over 400 attorneys because it couldn't afford to pay them.*
- *You can't fix it; just **86** it.*

<u>Background</u>: It first appeared as restaurant-worker slang in the 1930s in the U.S., meaning to be out of a certain food item, or, stop serving a certain customer. It later entered popular speech as a general term for dismissal or termination.

There are all kinds of theories about the origin of *eighty-six*. Some are far-fetched and there is no definite proof of any theory. The most popular one refers to *Chumley's Bar* at 86 Bedford Street in New York City. The place, a Prohibition speak-easy (i.e., an establishment that illegally sold alcoholic beverages) had at least five or six hidden passageways that led to exits. To "86-it" meant to simply vanish from a "dining" establishment. This theory, however, is now discredited, for there is evidence that the term was being used before *Chumley's Bar* came into existence.

Enough is as good as a feast.   Just the right amount is as good as more than enough; having more of something is not necessarily better.

- *It's OK to have sweets and salty snacks for special occasions even when you are on a diet, if you have just a small portion. You may be surprised to find that a small taste satisfies your craving. **Enough is as good as a feast**, as the saying goes.*

<u>Background</u>: This is an old proverb, from the late 15th century. It was popularized in the movie *Mary Poppins* (1964), starring Julie Andrews.

Most people would agree that this is a sensible approach to life (i.e., to know when enough is enough) though they don't always live by it.

<u>Usage note</u>: Another proverb with a similar idea is: ***There is virtue in moderation***.

<u>Of interest</u>: The Swedish have a similar expression: *lagom är bäst*
(just enough is best).

Feast for the eyes   Phrase often used when one is delighted to see someone or something (a landscape, a painting or a parade, etc.)

- *This documentary on animal behavior was quite a **feast for the eyes**.*

<u>Usage note</u>: An often-used variation on this is a *feast for sore eyes*, a humorous way to state how happy/glad one is to see someone:

- *After all these years, seeing her again was a **feast for sore eyes**.*

Feast or famine   Signifying two extremes, where things are either wonderful or they're really bad; either nothing is happening or everything is happening all at once

- *Our sales were so strong during the holidays that we just had to hire extra help around the clock. Then they fell so sharply we had to lay off half of our employees. It's **feast or famine**!*

Usage note: A related expression is **feast today, famine/fast/tomorrow** referring to how things can change suddenly.

Feel one's oats To feel particularly frisky, energetic
- *The old man was dancing, laughing, **feeling his oats**.*

Background: It's an allusion to the liveliness of a horse that has just been fed on oats.

Usage notes:
1. In the U.S., it can also mean to act in a self-important manner:
   - *All of a sudden, Bill was **feeling his oats** and started bossing people around, much to everyone's surprise.*
2. It can mean to feel sexually charged; feel horny, lustful.
3. To **sow one's (wild) oats** means to do foolish things in one's youth (often assumed to have some sort of sexual meaning):
   - *Some people have an urgent need to **sow their oats** and others don't.*
4. To **get one's oats** is a very informal British expression meaning, to have sex regularly:
   - *Tom has been in a good mood lately; he must be **getting his oats**.*

Food for thought Something that is worth thinking about or considering seriously
- *"Your comments and suggestions have given us good **food for thought**."*
- ***Food for thought** for people who are thinking about dating co-workers:*
   "Don't get your honey where you get your money."
   "Don't fish off the company's pier."
   "Don't get your meat and your taters at the same store."
   "Don't get your butter where you get your bread."

Background: A classic metaphor, it transfers the idea of digesting from the stomach to ruminating something over in the mind.

From scratch Starting from the individual basic ingredients and not from a packaged mix; starting with nothing
- *A pumpkin pie made **from scratch** - from a real pumpkin, tastes much better than the one made with canned pumpkin.*
- *It's nerve-racking to lose all the records you've saved on the computer and have to start everything **from scratch**.*
- *John built his business **from scratch**, with hardly any money or help from family or friends.*

Background: The phrase has been used since the 19th century as a sporting term referring to the "scratch" drawn in the ground which served (and often still does) as a starting point (for example, in a foot race).

(*Give*) *my compliments to the chef* Please let the chef know that I enjoyed the food that he or she cooked.

- *My dinner was simply delicious - **my compliments to the chef.***

Usage notes:
1. It's an expression often used by customers when they truly enjoy their meal(s) at a restaurant - a thank-you gesture to the chef (who is not in the presence of the speaker) via the server.
2. It's also common for customers to say to their server, ***you're a good cook!***, usually in a joking manner, even though the server is not the one who does the cooking.
3. Both expressions can also be used when one is invited as a guest and served a meal at someone's house.

Good for what ails you Able to cure any problem or illness

Usage notes:
1. Often said in jest
2. Usually used to describe food or liquor

Have seconds/go for seconds To have a second serving of the food

- *"This pot roast is good; I definitely will **have seconds."***
- *In Thailand, the portions of food served are traditionally small; so small that it's a very common practice for people to **go for seconds** or thirds, even when they eat out.*

Usage notes:
1. Also used, ***have a second serving***
2. Used with regards to food; with drinks, one would say, *(**to have**) a refill/refills*:
   - *Customer to server: "Are there **refills** on drinks?"*
   Also, to ***top it off***, if the cup is partially empty

Home-made Anything (food-related or not) that you make yourself; not buying it ready-made

- *Customer to server: "Is your soup **home-made?"***
   (Is the soup made by your cook or does it come out of a can?)

Usage notes:
1. Also spelled, ***homemade***
2. It is the term most restaurant patrons use to determine the food's freshness (and how good the food is).

It's all grist for the mill. It all helps or can become useful; it can all be turned to profit.

- *I'd welcome any kind of exposure and publicity for the book. **It's all grist for the mill.***
- *Might as well learn Spanish. **It's all grist for the mill**, especially when you live in California.*

Background: "Grist" is grain taken to a mill to be ground.

It must be jelly, cause jam don't shake like that! It must be fat because muscle isn't that soft.

Background: It's the title and the first two lines of a famous blues-song from 1942 that was co-written by Chummy MacGregor and George 'The Silver Fox' Williams (lyrics by Sunny Skylar). The song was played by Big Band musician Glenn Miller (1904-1944).

It's also a provocative line used to flatter the moves of a dancing lady, common in juke joints and honky tonks.

Musical anecdotes aside, the comparison mentioned in the song is a good way of contrasting *jelly* and *jam*.

Jelly is clear, made of fruit juice and with pectin added to thicken it.

Jam is made with whole fruit that is cooked down and crushed to release the pectin; it has a lot of fruit bits. (*Preserve* is similar to *jam*, but the whole fruit is used without breaking it up.)

In the UK, *jelly* can mean a dessert (called *Jell-O* in the U.S.) or it can be a spread for bread or a relish for meat.

Live out of cans To eat only canned food for lack of other foods or time to prepare them

- *We never have time to cook; we always end up **living out of cans** or eating TV dinners.*

On the house At the expense of the establishment

- *Since it's your birthday, this cake will be **on the house**.*

Usage notes:
1. A very common expression
2. Not limited to restaurant use; it can be used in any kind of commercial establishment that caters to customer satisfaction

Separate the wheat from the chaff To find things of value and separate them from things of no value

- *The preview of the auto auction is a good way for the public to **separate the wheat from the chaff**.*
- *There are all kinds of reference books and dictionaries out there, and it's very difficult to **separate the wheat from the chaff**.*
- *"An editor is someone who **separates the wheat from the chaff** and then uses the chaff."* (a sarcastic quote by Adlai Stevenson, American politician, 1900-1965)

Background: The chaff is inedible. It is the dry husk surrounding the wheat berry that is the actual grain used for food. To separate the chaff from the good grains (the agricultural term is *winnowing*), farmers at one time would expose wheat to the wind, so that the light chaff blew away and the heavier wheat grains remained.

It is the phrase from the Bible (Matthew 3:12). According to one interpretation, "the wheat" refers to those who belong to Christ and are judged worthy; "the chaff" are those who have rejected him and remain unrepentant and therefore, have no place in his kingdom.

Waffle To waver; vacillate; equivocate; keep changing one's mind
- *It's obvious that she **waffles on** this issue. What she said today was different from what she said last week.*
- *John **waffled** so long between choosing a stack of pancakes or a waffle that the waitress lost her patience and just walked away.*

Background: Most etymologists agree that the verb *waffle* and the noun *waffle* come from different sources.

The verb was a derivative of the 17th century *waff*, the sound a dog made (it's *woof* to our modern-day ears). Apparently the notion here is that a waffler's words have as much meaning as a dog barking.

Waffle, the food (a crisp batter-cake, baked in a waffle-iron that gives it the crosshatched surfaces) is based on the Dutch word "wafel."

Usage notes:
1. The term has become part of the U.S. political jargon. Politicians like to accuse opponents of "waffling" on certain issues – although this sometimes means that the opponent is taking a nuanced position on a complex subject and not simply assuming an ideological stance.
2. The British use it to mean to talk or write using a lot of words but without saying anything important:
   - *Why don't you stop **waffling** and get to the point?*

(With all) the works With all the condiments that are typically served with a particular dish at that establishment
- *Customer: "I'd like a cheeseburger and french fries."*
  Waitress: "With tomato, lettuce, pickles, thousand island dressing and onion?"
  *Customer: "Yes, **with all the works**."*

Usage notes:
1. Also used, **with all the trimmings**:
   - *It was a typical Thanksgiving dinner, a turkey **with all the trimmings**. I personally preferred the trimmings to the turkey – especially the stuffing and the cranberry sauce.*
2. If you don't want everything that goes with a particular dish, you can say
   - **Hold** (or **skip** or **minus** or **without**) *the onion.*
   Also,
   - *Can I have the onion **on the side**?*

You want (some) fries with that? A sarcastic comment when someone asks you to get or buy him or her a lot of things

- *John:* *"Hey, can you buy me a soda, a hot fudge sundae, apple pie..."*
         (and on and on)?

  Mary: *"(Sarcastically)* **You want some fries with that?***"*

Background: In the U.S, order-takers at a fast -food place (and sometimes a restaurant) have usually been trained to suggest a side-dish if the customer doesn't mention it first.

Usage note: If you want to suggest to someone that he or she will never amount to anything, you might say, *"Hey, maybe you should start practicing the line '***would you like fries with that?***'"* — the implication being that your friend will end up working at a fast-food place.

Bibliography

Ammer, Christine. Fruitcakes and Couch Potatoes and Other Delicious Expressions. New York: Plume, 1995

Coad, Brian W. and McAllister, Don E. Dictionary of Ichthyology. Online Edition

Dickson, Paul. The Dickson Baseball Dictionary. Third edition. New York: W.W. Norton and Company, 2009

Herbst, Phillip H. Wimmin, Wimps and Wallflowers: An Encyclopedic Dictionary of Gender and Sexual Orientation Bias in the United States. Boston: Intercultural Press, 2000

Morton, Mark. Cupboard Love: A Dictionary of Culinary Curiosities. Second revised edition. London, Ontario: Insomniac Press, 2000

Palmatier, Robert A. Food: A Dictionary of Literal and Non literal Terms. Westport, Connecticut: Greenwood Press, 2000

Rogers, James. The Dictionary of Clichés. New York: Wing Books, 1985

Room, Adrian. Dictionary of Confusable Words. Chicago: Fitzroy Dearborn Publishers, 2000

Index